NONE LIKE US

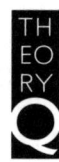

A series edited by Lauren Berlant and Lee Edelman

NONE LIKE US

| BLACKNESS, BELONGING, AESTHETIC LIFE |

Stephen Best

Duke University Press Durham and London 2018

© 2018 Duke University Press
All rights reserved
Printed in the United States of America on acid-free paper ∞
Designed by Courtney Leigh Baker
Typeset in Warnock Pro and Franklin Gothic by Copperline Books

Library of Congress Cataloging-in-Publication Data
Names: Best, Stephen Michael, [date] author.
Title: None like us : blackness, belonging, aesthetic life / Stephen Best.
Description: Durham : Duke University Press, 2018. | Series: Theory Q |
Includes bibliographical references and index.
Identifiers: LCCN 2018008212 (print)
LCCN 2018009463 (ebook)
ISBN 9781478002581 (ebook)
ISBN 9781478001157 (hardcover : alk. paper)
ISBN 9781478001508 (pbk. : alk. paper)
Subjects: LCSH: Blacks—Study and teaching. |
Aesthetics, Black. | Blacks—Race identity.
Classification: LCC CB235 (ebook) | LCC CB235 .B47 2018 (print) |
DDC 305.896/073—dc23
LC record available at https://lccn.loc.gov/2018008212

Cover art: Mark Bradford, *Crow*. Courtesy of the artist
and Hauser and Wirth, London.

For Paul

Having travelled over a considerable portion of these United States, and having, in the course of my travels, taken the most accurate observations of things as they exist—the result of my observations has warranted the full and unshaken conviction, that we, (coloured people of these United States,) are the most degraded, wretched, and abject set of beings that ever lived since the world began; and I pray God that none like us ever may live again until time shall be no more.

DAVID WALKER, *Appeal to the Coloured Citizens of the World* (1833)

CONTENTS

Introduction. Unfit for History 1

PART I | ON THINKING LIKE A WORK OF ART |

1. My Beautiful Elimination 29
2. On Failing to Make the Past Present 63

PART II | A HISTORY OF DISCONTINUITY |

Interstice. A Gossamer Writing 83

3. The History of People Who Did Not Exist 91
4. Rumor in the Archive 107

Acknowledgments 133

Notes 135

Bibliography 173

Index 193

| INTRODUCTION |

Unfit for History

A communitarian impulse runs deep within black studies. It announces itself in the assumption that in writing about the black past "we" discover "our" history; it is implied in the thesis that black identity is uniquely grounded in slavery and middle passage; it registers in the suggestion that what makes black people black is their continued navigation of an "afterlife of slavery," recursions of slavery and Jim Crow for which no one appears able to find the exit; it may even be detected in an allergy within the field to self-critique, a certain *politesse*, although I have no doubt that this last may be a bridge too far for some. My goal, at any rate, is to encourage a frank reappraisal of the critical assumptions that undergird many of these claims, not least and certainly most broadly the assumed conjuncture between belonging and a history of subjection, for as much as attempts to root blackness in the horror of slavery feel intuitively correct, they produce in me a feeling of unease, the feeling that I am being invited to long for the return of a sociality that I never had, one from which I suspect (had I ever shown up) I might have been excluded. Queer theorists have tended to bemoan the omnipresence of futurism in queer politics. I view black studies as burdened by a contrary malady: the omnipresence of history in our politics.¹ Disencumbering queer studies of its investments in the future, while not an easy task, at least retains a sense of the possible to the extent that it involves reassessing the optimistic hopes and visions of utopia to which queers find themselves attached.² Black studies, on the contrary, confronts the more difficult task of disarticulating itself, if it should so seek, after years of a quite different form of debate, from the historical accretions of slavery, race, and racism, or from a particular *commitment* to the idea that the slave past provides a ready prism for understanding and apprehending the black political present. In spite of the many truths that follow our acceptance of slavery as generative of blackness, as productive of the background conditions necessary to speak from the standpoint of blackness, *None Like Us* begins in the recognition that there is something impossible about blackness, that to be black is also to participate, of necessity, in a collective undoing, if not, on the occasion that that should either fail or seem unpalatable, a self-undoing.

I know that that last line reads a bit cryptically, so an example would seem to be in order. If I were to say to you, whoever you might be, that "I am not *your* Negro," it would have to be admitted, in spite of the disavowal, that I must be someone's—perhaps, meaningfully, only as I relate to myself.³ Not surprisingly, as that example and others to follow will suggest, James Baldwin inspires the difficult leap that a knowledge of belonging disarticulated from the collective requires.

> I was not . . . a Black Muslim,
> in the same way, though for different reasons,
> that I never became a Black Panther:
> because I did not believe that
> all white people were devils,
>
> . . . .
>
> I was not a member of any Christian congregation
> because I knew that they had not heard
> and did not live by the commandment
> "love one another as I love you,"
> and I was not a member of the NAACP
> because in the North, where I grew up,
> the NAACP was fatally entangled
> with black class distinctions,

or illusions of the same,
which repelled a shoe-shine boy like me.

I did not have to deal with
the criminal state of Mississippi,
hour by hour and day by day,
to say nothing of night after night.
I did not have to sweat cold sweat after decisions
involving hundreds of thousands of lives.
. . . .
I saw the sheriffs, the deputies, the storm troopers
more or less in passing.
I was never in town to stay.
This was sometimes hard on my morale,
but I had to accept, as time wore on,
that part of my responsibility—as a witness—
was to move as largely and as freely as possible,
to write the story, and to get it out.[4]

I find in Baldwin's formulations, tentative as they are, a model for thought and those difficult leaps of which I earlier spoke. This book seeks to break the hold on black studies that the oscillation between subjection and belonging has taken in the interest of the pleasures of a shared sense of alienation understood, in the first instance, as an unfitness for the world and history as it is. This introduction will, if nothing else, offer my reasons for advocating such a break.

I think it is important, for a start, to give an account of my first memory of where that break may lie. It would be more accurate, in truth, to say that it was felt rather than known, that feeling now hardwired into my critical nervous system, although the details remain sketchy.

I can remember how we were seated, but not where. The occasion was my last meal as an undergraduate, the night before my graduation. On my left sat my mother; to my right, my father; across from me, a favored political science professor, Grenada's former ambassador to the Organization of American States.[5] My motives for including her now feel expedient, short of beneficent. I had a sense that she might like them, and they her, liberating me to some degree from having to take full ownership of the evening. I feared the night would be celebratory for them, mournful for me. Perhaps their shared Caribbean origins would occasion a sense of mutual affinity. My parents might feel anchored, at long last, to my college experience, invited into that experience, though on the brink of its closure.

The conversation feels normal to me; at least, as I experienced normal at that time: across a chasm with my parents, and familiar in that regard; free-flowing and animated with my professor. My father excuses himself from the table, as if to lubricate the conversation by way of his absence, but after a time I am made uncomfortable by the fact that he is not here, like a splinter one might feel but not see. Eventually, we all feel it. Turning to my mother, her facial expression conveying a simple "I don't know," I turn back. I hear my professor: "The pride he feels for you, which he can't speak, can't say to you, is making him sick."

Her words are to this day far from easy to absorb. At first, they stirred in me an almost bitter confusion. In our black West Indian demimonde, carved here and there across suburban Connecticut, the message had always been that it was cool to be smart. This day was certainly one we had all contemplated and anticipated, and for which my father had prepared me: summer science and math courses, internships at the medical school, advanced placement courses; long drives to attend music and choir camps at elite New England private schools. And yet, by the time the day arrived, my father wasn't ready.

Whenever I mull over those words "pride" and "sick," I can feel all over again their mutual repulsion. They name so many dimensions of the relation between my father and me, not least our mutual alienation or, better, our mutual aversion. I think of that gathering as the moment that we slide into open retreat from our kinship—when a story begins to be told, a story in which my academic achievements feed the disaffiliation that keeps us in relation. The dinner, intended as a celebration, instead marks this aversiveness as our future condition, offers it not as a state to be overcome but as a condition of our moving on. (Even now, I hesitate to tell my father when I go on sabbatical, such perks sounding too much, to a man who worked for a wage, like getting paid not to go to work.) At the same time, the professor's words attune me to the strange gift that haunts my father's act of self-abnegation. It is as if the goal of reproducing the child is to *not* reproduce yourself.

I am reminded, though not entirely comfortably, of Baldwin's account of his own relationship to his father, as described in his essay "Notes of a Native Son." Baldwin is keen to show that his father, much like other blacks of his generation, bore an impossible duty: "how to prepare the child for the day when the child would be despised and how to create in the child . . . a stronger antidote to this poison than one had found for oneself."[6] Of course, from Baldwin's perspective, it doesn't appear that his father developed anything of the sort, having instead chosen to fight poison with poison: "In my mind's eye I could see him, sitting at the window, locked up in his terrors; hating and fearing every living soul including his children who had betrayed him, too, by reaching towards the world which had despised him."[7] Baldwin slides along an arc from inheritance to isolation to underscore his father's failure at the paternal function. The father, unable to pass on the defenses his children need, remains "locked up in his terrors"—paranoid, alienated, ashamed — his children abandoned to the world.

Baldwin wants us to focus on the pathos of this situation, marking it from the very first line of the essay as the disjuncture between death and life (father and child): "On the 29th of July, in 1943, my father died. On the same day, a few hours later, his last child was born." He doesn't shy from weaving this simultaneity throughout the essay: "The day of my father's funeral had also been my nineteenth birthday"; "Death . . . sat as purposefully at my father's bedside as life stirred within my mother's womb"; "When planning a birthday celebration one naturally does not expect that it will be up against competition from a funeral."[8] He makes little effort to muffle a sense that the simultaneity between black death and black life, which is also their mutual and aversive divergence and distinction, has about it a perfume of literary embellishment; every reader's task, however, is to figure out what it *means*.

I largely concur with Ismail Muhammad that Baldwin's figurations of his father challenge the idea of familial lineage and "the logic of perpetual trauma." Muhammad writes, "Baldwin's writing often looks askance at biological family ties, with language that figures generational bonds as a problem, laden as they are with oppressive histories. These bonds always threaten to become chains for Baldwin, and lineage seems coextensive with numbing repetition."[9] In Muhammad's reading of "My Dungeon Shook," Baldwin's letter to his nephew, which opens *The Fire Next Time*, "The paternal relationship means incessant repetition." One feels the force of repetition even in "Notes of a Native Son," an essay presumably intent on breaking it: "It seemed to me that God himself had devised, to mark my father's end, the most sustained and brutally dissonant of codas.

And it seemed to me, too, that the violence which rose all about us as my father left the world had been devised as a corrective for the pride of his eldest son."[10] That reference to God's "corrective" focuses our attention on Baldwin's efforts to distance himself from his father and interrupt the line of descent. Wanting to exit the paternal function and to supersede his father, Baldwin proposes in this essay, if I might hijack Muhammad's language, "a queered definition of reproduction."

Muhammad and I share the view that Baldwin's figurations of his father and the paternal relation, across his writings, represent as much a sustained working out of his relationship to history as a statement of personal biography. Baldwin resists "a traumatic model of black history" in which the present is merely an endless, Oedipal repetition of slavery and Jim Crow; a rigid relation to temporality or "narrative stiffness," in Eve Sedgwick's phrase, which feels like the generations marching in lockstep: "It happened to my father's father, it happened to my father, it is happening to me, it will happen to my son, and it will happen to my son's son."[11] Muhammad and I share, too, a sense of Baldwin's queer divergence from that inheritance, although we differ on its origin and locus. For Muhammad, Baldwin's letter to his nephew is itself "an interruption in [the] line of descent, a familial relation not premised on the paternal." For me, that queer exemption originates, paradoxically, in the father's disdain. In other words, the queerness isn't Baldwin's alone, isn't his either to own or to introduce. A sense of kinship shadowed by severance resides, in addition, in his father's orientation toward the world outside and his figuration as betrayal of his children's orientation toward that world.[12]

For me, to read Baldwin's "Notes" is to gaze into a mirror, though one in which everything has been reversed. The disdain for which he felt he was being prepared feels so removed from the support and privileges of my own world — the cruelty that his father directs at him ("his cruelty, to our bodies and our minds") a far cry from my father's wordless love. It is not the feelings here that have captured my interest, mind you; it is the structure—a structure of paternal self-exemption. The immediate question is this: why should Baldwin's father's disdain be so closely *structurally matched* with my father's pride?[13] From my understanding of this structure, in what I want to propose about it, the father inhabits the pathos of a necessary social condition, preparing his son for a social situation, a world, for which he all along knows himself to be unfit.

The anthropologist Elizabeth Povinelli celebrates Baldwin's ability to capture the pathos of a "subjective suicide" that is for her a condition of all progressive politics, or of any politics based on social rupture: "how bodies and minds can remain at once in the world and out of sequence with the world it is seeking to create or has successfully created."[14] Readers of Baldwin will recall that he often uses the word "apocalypse" to signal this simultaneity of creation and destruction, a language that reflects his earlier decision to leave the world of the church, as he once said, to preach the gospel. Povinelli prefers the term "extinguishment": "When I extinguish I am making a world in which I no longer make sense, and I am making it without the capacities that I am trying to bestow on the subsequent generation and without certain knowledge of the subsequent world."[15] Whatever the term of art, the father finds himself in the situation, in the existential condition, of seeking to create a world that will not have him.

In narratives of the closet, however, the specter of the breakup (the anticipation of severance) is assumed to be the child's alone. This affect haunted me throughout my adolescence: if I come out as gay, I will die in the eyes of my father, but I realize that a part of me is already gay and that he cannot not see that, so there must be a part of me that is already dead. I could choose to stay in the closet and pursue more socially sanctioned forms of achievement (I was no stranger to counterinvestment), but to become an intellectual is just another declension of becoming gay. We both know that; the affect is shared.[16]

My father was as much queered by the sting of disaffiliation as I was. Our familiarity (Lat., *familiaris*, of the family) threatened with rupture, it startles how easily queerness percolates out of the condition of blackness. Father and son find that they've arrived at a moment in which they *both* inhabit a queer time, their kinship shadowed, from both ends of the relation, by the specter of its obliteration and extinction, by its imminent severance. "Son looks at son, son at father, mother at daughter, and subsequent generations to antecedent ones with the same painful alienation."[17] The pathos may initially have belonged to my father, but in the end it becomes ours to share, as we are both living as insider outsiders, living outside the norm—father against the backdrop of the academy; son against the backdrop of family. Povinelli wonders why this pathos is so infrequently the focus of critical theory, and so do I, but with this one difference: I can see there are pleasures to be found in a shared sense of alienation, a shared queerness, emerging from a shared blackness that is still understood, in the first instance, as an unfitness for the world and history as it is.

It would be a misstep on my part to suggest that the mutual alienation between father and son is uniquely black, or specifically cultural or ethnic, even as my narration lends that alienation all the characteristics of an immigrant story. But it would be no less of an error to imply that blackness is not here. It is, but not as we might expect. I have chosen to begin in conversation with Baldwin, in an autobiographical meditation on fathers, sons, and the intimate kinship shadowed from both sides of the relation by its imminent severance, because I am seeking a way to understand the filial world of subjects and the ethics of subjectivity (etymologically, a "thrown-downness" [Lat., *subiectivitas*], the condition of being placed after something or someone else). In considering Baldwin's father's orientation toward the world outside as a betrayal of his children's orientation toward that world, and asking why Baldwin's father's infamous disdain for his son should be so structurally matched with my own father's pride in me, my intention is to chart a relay in the subject and in intersubjectivity between disdain and pride, shame and exaltation, cynicism and expectation, which the criticism of black art and the historiography of black life often seem unwilling to acknowledge even as black art and black life are so richly burdened with resources to illumine that relay.

Let me be blunt, at the risk of oversimplifying my claim. I want to force the question of whether there is something unique—or, rather, too tragically conventional and absorbed—about what surely must be understood as Baldwin's father's *antiblackness*.[18] In ways that should be obvious to anyone, and that I cannot ignore, that question is already present in the righteousness and vengeance of David Walker's *Appeal to the Coloured Citizens of the World* (1833), from which this book takes its title: "I pray God that none like us ever may live again until time shall be no more."[19]

Walker's "none like us" bears a set of alternatives that it also liquidates, in the manner of litotes, or "antenantiosis," implying a meaning by denying its semantic opposite. These alternatives constitute a "we" in the very moment of marking its apparent impossibility. I note three:

1. First, there is an impulse toward the *minor* in Walker's attempt to constitute the collective. Why not pray that none like them shall ever live again—"the most degraded, wretched, and abject set of beings"? What is it about "us" as we are right

now that prompts this prayer "that none like us ever may live again," a prayer that must also be understood as an invocation of an absolute right to life? Is there a situation in which we could consolidate self-extinction and the right to life, such perfectly contradictory impulses?

2   I sense, as well, an opposing drive toward the *universal* in Walker's turn of phrase. Perhaps the term "us" is not so easily interpreted as black people. Perhaps there is an assumed and impossible universality to Walker's "us." If that is so, the challenge of discerning the collective nominated by the term "us" presents a problem of interpretation all its own.

3   All the same, I feel the prick of a *personal* address every time I read the opening lines to Walker's *Appeal*. When I read his prayer that "none like us ever may live again," I find it impossible to avoid a sense that he is praying that one like me might never have lived at all. Can "our" disappearance from history preserve "me"? (Is that, as the phrase goes, my condition of possibility?) Or does that disappearance also constitute another continual advent given in the refusal rather than the achievement of the self?

These tensions bely resolution, yet the myriad concerns I wish to take up in this book converge in the grammatical complexities of Walker's prayer, in his fraught semantic attempt to constitute a collective first person: my concern for the ethics of history written against the consequences of slavery, the articulation of blackness and belonging, the involution of rhetoric and identity. Walker's "none like us" cannot be read as simple affirmation or negation, an expression of belonging or alienation. Rather, the very condition of possibility, the origin, of that "us" renders it impossible. In his grammar I hear the difficulty, pathos, desire, anguish, and frustration entailed in the effort to constitute the "we" of blackness. Black collective being finds itself acknowledged and refused in the same rhetorical act. What is more, in the very moment that Walker prays a black people—a "we"—into being, he leaves us in serious doubt as to whether that "we" can exist in history. The implication is not that black people have been excluded from history (although that will be a concern in what follows), rather their very blackness derives from bearing a negative relation to it. *None Like Us* finds purpose in sitting with this imponderable.[20]

In the longstanding debate over "the antisocial thesis"—particularly, say, Leo Bersani's view of sex as a "shattering" of the subject, as "the locus of the social's disarray"—the invitation to extend that negativity to include the black case has been met with something short of enthusiasm (largely on the grounds that a certain "shattering" experience, the object of political *resistance*, already defines the condition of being black).[21] Quite to the contrary, Robyn Weigman argues, race has been "the figure of a difference inscribed in, not against, the social."[22] Weigman asks, "Does race, conceptually speaking, 'belong' only to one side of queer theory's contentious distinction between the negativity of social differences that arise from histories of racial and gendered negation and the negativity that repels and annuls sociality as such?"[23] It will be my position that the answer to that question is a strenuous "no." In what follows then, I set about the task of drawing out the connections between a sense of impossible black sociality—the simultaneity of black exception and black exemption that Walker gives us to ponder—and strains of negativity that often have operated under the sign *queer*: on the one hand, what registers with and in me, concerning art and life, as the minority subject's sense of *unbelonging* (e.g., forms of negative sociability such as alienation, withdrawal, loneliness, broken intimacy, impossible connection, and failed affinity, situations of being unfit that it has been the great insight of queer theorists to recognize as a condition for living); on the other hand, my critical interest in what Valerie Traub has termed "unhistoricism," an animus toward teleology and periodization in queer studies of which she remains skeptical but that, in my view, appears rooted in the insight that we are all always outside of history, always inside the gap between that which can be eternally remembered and that for which the future will give account, inside "that divided site that must look both ways at once... between the writing of history as prediction and as retrospection," prolepsis and analepsis, if you will (more on that gap in the next chapter).[24]

Walker can stake a claim within this line of thought. His hope lacks hopefulness. His prayer reads like the hope of someone firm in the belief that black people will never have their moment in time; a peculiarly agonistic description of black life lived in proximity to its irrelevance, of black identity disarticulated from time, or, as I will be in the habit of saying, unfit for history. Walker gives us blackness as a condition of genealogical isolation.

Walker's prayer on behalf of the "coloured citizens of the world"; Baldwin's figuration of his father, and me of mine. I am certainly not blind to the fact that these men exist in three distinct social and economic situations. (It would offend to pretend otherwise.) But an anti-communitarian undertone vibrates within these examples, and only with effort can I resist hearing it. Walker's "none like us" accrues critical analogs over the course of this book: the sense of being held and rejected by a tradition, or what it means (will mean in these pages) to have a queer relation to it; the recognition that separation, fearful estrangement, is what makes relationship (makes relationships) possible; the challenge of calling an object into being without owning or being owned by the call of identity or identification, of recognition or acknowledgment. *None Like Us* makes use of that undertone, extracts from it a sense of both the joy and the pain in genealogical isolation. It stands at the ready, a tool to break the hold on black studies that the oscillation between subjection and belonging has taken.

The Scholar's Sacrifice

It seems right to inquire into when this oscillation may have gotten its start, as one of its effects has been the production of that "we" of black history, which effect continues to exert its hold on us. I would hazard that some of the first ripples were felt upon G. W. F. Hegel's assertion, in 1831, in *Philosophy of History*, that Africa "is no historical part of the world; it has no movement or development to exhibit. . . . What we properly understand by Africa, is the Unhistorical, Undeveloped Spirit . . . presented here only as on the threshold of the World's History."[25] Hegel's is arguably the most prominent in a long line of disavowals of black history and black culture, each of which, in its turn, has prompted a search for the black past.

If Hegel stands as the most prominent figure in the disavowal of the black past, as well he should, then the historian, law clerk, and bibliophile Arthur Schomburg can claim title to its signature rebuttal. His essay "The Negro Digs Up His Past," from 1925, captures the terms of what would become a century-long attempt to recover archival traces of black life. The opening paragraph reads:

> The American Negro must remake his past in order to make his future. Though it is orthodox to think of America as the one country where it is unnecessary to have a past, what is a luxury for the nation as a whole

becomes a prime social necessity for the Negro. For him, a group tradition must supply compensation for persecution, and pride of race the antidote for prejudice. History must restore what slavery took away, for it is the social damage of slavery that the present generations must repair and offset. So among the rising democratic millions we find the Negro thinking more collectively, more retrospectively than the rest, and apt out of the very pressure of the present to become the most enthusiastic antiquarian of them all.[26]

Credit Schomburg with outlining the practice of historical inquiry posthumously termed "the recovery imperative," a critical ethic that has prevailed in black studies since at least the publication of his essay.[27] Schomburg's essay bears the marks of this imperative—the idea that "history must restore what slavery took away," that recovered black traditions "repair" "the social damage of slavery" and "compensate[e] for persecution."

It is not hard to see in the recovery imperative a powerful and compelling theory of how history works—not simply the theory that the past persists in the present, or the proposition that the past has to be made relevant to the present, but the idea that history is at its core a fundamentally redemptive enterprise, the idea "that everything that has eluded [the subject] may be restored to him."[28] It is the promise, Michel Foucault once wrote, that "one day the subject—in the form of historical consciousness—will once again be able to appropriate, to bring back under his sway, all those things that are kept at a distance by difference, and find in them what might be called his abode."[29] This isn't simply a matter of history arrayed as teleology; it is, rather, the ethic of an empathetic historicism fundamentally recuperative in its orientation. It marks, in Foucault's words, "the founding function of the subject."[30]

Imperatives calling for the Negro to "dig up his past" were meant to found just such a subject, a collective subject, as is evident in Schomburg's talk of "the Negro thinking more collectively, more retrospectively" (far from a throwaway line). A collective is born of this inquiry into the past (what he calls "group credit" and "credible group achievement"), although the logic that connects the collective's formation to thinking about the past is simultaneously implied and obscured. Schomburg's recovery imperative is the manifestation of a command we have *all* obeyed since Hegel's regrettable move to exclude Africans from narratives of historical progress—to regard the recovery of archival evidence of black historical being, on the one hand, and recovery in "the ontological and political sense of reparation . . . recuperation, or the repossession of a full humanity and freedom, after its ultimate theft or obliteration," on the other, *as belonging the same order of thought*.[31]

Recovery has been the subject of considerable debate, particularly within the broad critical reorientation described as the "archival turn."[32] Some of the sharpest questions have emerged from the field of Atlantic slavery and freedom, particularly work focused on the crime of slavery, and the return to the scene of the crime—return not to its scenes of violence but, rather, to what is represented more often as the crime of "the archive." In this vision of the archive, everything from state archives (e.g., records of trial, orders of execution, coerced testimony, gallows confessions, provincial gazettes) to the records of commercial transactions (e.g., account books, planters' journals, ships' logs, colonial correspondence) "threaten to obscure the humanity of the people they describe."[33] The archival turn is thus born of a generative tension between recovery understood, on the one hand, as "an imperative that is fundamental to historical writing and research" and, on the other, as a project that is essentially impossible "when engaged with archives whose very assembly and organization occlude certain historical subjects."[34] Let me state as bluntly as I can the fundaments of my claim regarding the recovery imperative. I contend that, where the doubled imperative persists (in which recovery from the slave past rests on a recovery of it), it is not too difficult to see the search for lost or absent black culture as substituting for the recovery of a "we" at the point of our violent origin. That imperative has a way of persisting even in the case of the recent archival turn, where recovery itself has been viewed with the greatest skepticism.

Particularly eloquent statements in the archival turn include:

Death and Power. Vincent Brown—"It is thus less revealing to see the extravagant death rate in Jamaican society as an impediment to the formation of culture than it is to view it as the landscape of culture itself, the ground that produced Atlantic slavery's most meaningful idioms."[35]

"If people looked to the past to find the roots of contemporary forms of inequality, domination, and terror, rather than the origins of freedom, rights, and universal prosperity, they might see early colonial Jamaica as home to the people who made the New World what it became."[36]

Tradition and Modernity. Stephan Palmié— "Even though we may never physically recover the product of José Antonio Aponte's imagination and artistic creativity, we are left with the paradoxical record of an eloquent absence. Created and preserved by the same machinery of power and knowledge production that annihilated Aponte, the archival record has become the medium through which his ghostly voice—warped and distorted, to be sure, by the noise of multiple interferences—now speaks to us about a world of images that we will never see. . . . The remnants of the strange dialogue . . . may be taken as evidence of . . . the symbolic order on which the power of Aponte's executioners rested and that they reaffirmed by liquidating . . . him along with his book. Part of this gesture of affirmation by violence was the creation of a record that involves us— if we engage it at all—in an almost hallucinatory mission to recover a history that never was and whose creator was killed in the act of its enunciation. . . . Aponte speaks to us first and foremost as a self-appointed historian of a past that is, in the true sense of the word, a *vision*: a record of histories rendered impossible, unreal, fictitious, and fantastic by the obliterating agency of a regime of truth that, in a perverse but consistent gesture, preserved the excess of its own operation."[37]

Slavery and the Archive. Saidiya Hartman—"The stories that exist are not about them, but rather about the violence, excess, mendacity, and reason that seized hold of their lives, transformed them into commodities and corpses, and identified them with names tossed-off as insults and crass jokes. The archive is, in this case, a death sentence, a tomb, a display of the violated body, an inventory of property, a medical treatise on gonorrhea, a few lines about a whore's life, an asterisk in the grand narrative of history."[38]

Sexuality and the Colonial Archive. Anjali Arondekar—"The archival responsibility of this book, if you will, is to propose a different kind of archival romance, one that supplements the narrative of retrieval with a radically different script of historical continuation. . . . The critical challenge is to imagine a practice of archival reading that incites relationships between the seductions of recovery and the occlusions such retrieval mandates. . . . Through my readings, (lost and found) figurations of sexuality . . . are not objects that are lost and can be recovered, but subject effects sedimented through the enactments of disciplinary discourses."[39]

These responses to the conundrum of the archive share a figure of thought: an emphasis on discipline as the dynamic that produces historical knowledge, which is an idea with roots in the thinking of Foucault. It can be heard in Arondekar's talk of the archive's "sedimented . . . subject effects"; in Brown's focus on death as generative of "the landscape of culture," on terror as what made Jamaica "home to the people who made the New World what it became"; and in Palmié's "affirmation by violence," his vision of the archive as a site that "liquidat[es]," "obliterate[es]," and "preserve[s]." Foucauldian discipline has certainly sharpened perception of the epistemic violence transmitted via the archive in work on colonialism and Atlantic slavery.[40]

No one wants to be erased from history, of course. Obliterated. Snuffed out. And most scholars of slavery are drawn into the vortex of lives lost in the very moment in which they are found, quite in earnest, out of a longing to bear witness to violent extermination and in the hope that such witness may occasion compassionate resuscitation. Still, these repeated returns to the scene of the crime, a crime imagined as the archive itself, in practice have mirrored the orientation that Sigmund Freud called "melancholy," and these keen attunements to archival disfiguration within recent Americanist cultural criticism might then be filed under the term "melancholy historicism."[41] The turn toward melancholy has been propelled by the publication of a trove of important books in the field by Ian Baucom, Anne Cheng, Colin (Joan) Dayan, Paul Gilroy, Saidiya Hartman, David Kazanjian and David Eng, Stephanie Smallwood, and Michel-Rolph Trouillot, among others, and finds its identity in adherence to a particular structuring of the racial other, as Cheng describes it, "whereby his or her racial identity is imaginatively reinforced through the introjection of a lost, never-possible perfection, an inarticulable loss that comes to inform the individual's sense of his or her own subjectivity."[42] Frequently underwritten by traumas of slavery and middle passage that appear unknowable and irrecoverable and yet account for history's *longue durée*—the "root identity," in Édouard Glissant's phrase, "sanctified by the hidden violence of a filiation that strictly follows from [a] founding episode"—melancholy historicism provides for the view that history consists in the *taking possession* of such grievous experience and archival loss.[43] The massacre aboard the slave ship *Zong* and the Margaret Garner infanticide have proved the more memorable examples of this archival loss, although crimes of the archive at reduced scales of history have often also left their mark. Melancholy, whether in its Freudian or post-Freudian declensions, according to Baucom, "serves to preserve, safeguard, or protect the dead by offering them an unsurrenderable, interminable, commemorative lodging within the social, political, and psychical imagination of the living," but it does so in "profound mistrust of representation," aiming "to pass itself off not as a representation of the lost thing but as that lost thing itself."[44] Thus, the melancholy text tends to take on a "cryptic" quality and manifest a "paradoxical and anxious reiterativity" in its attempt "to reduce representation to the exclusive domain of the nominative, to the speaking, over and over again, of the secret name of the dead."[45] The vanished world of the black Atlantic comes into existence through loss and can be sustained only through more tales of its loss. To frame history in this way preserves faith in the lost object as a counterpoint to the past's irrecoverability. The injury of slavery engenders a loss that requires abundant recompense, which is never (can never *be*) achieved.[46]

Baucom's account of the occlusions that mark the circum-Atlantic archive is exhaustive, detailed, and compelling, as is his sense of the problems such occlusions present for both eighteenth-century abolition discourse and any cosmopolitanism that moves in its wake: "the problem of the unseen, the problem of nonappearance, the problem of blocked vision."[47] The task of any cosmopolitan politics, of any melancholy act of witnessing, is "to render the unseen visible, to bear witness to the truth of what has not been (and what cannot have been) witnessed"; a task that, as the language suggests, verges on the impossible. Melancholy weds "an inability to forget what cannot be remembered" to an "obligation to see what has not been seen." In short, melancholy's problem is the possibility (or, again, the impossibility) of obtaining a view for the interested observer understood as a problem of knowledge. Baucom continues: "The witness (and, by implication, humanity) . . . requires some theory of knowledge by which to render the invisible visible, some technology of displaced knowledge by which to make the work of witness possible, some way of authenticating the credibility of the melancholy facts it brings imaginatively into view."[48] One such technology, one answer to these problems of "nonappearance" and "blocked vision," has been a dark brood of "negative allegory" that melancholy repeatedly engenders, an obsession with "displacement, erasure, suppression, elision, overlooking, overwriting, omission, obscurantism, expunging, repudiation, exclusion, annihilation,

[and] denial"; an obsession, in essence, with the *failure* of something that was lost to history ever making an appearance.[49] The sustained focus on the irretrievable within the archive has been phenomenally intellectually generative, and the mutual attunement between archival disfiguration and melancholy affect strikes me as neither a problem nor a surprise.

Arondekar's search for a link between "the seductions of recovery" and "the occlusions such retrieval mandates," and Hartman's accent on "the archive [as] death sentence," suggest one source for these scruples regarding blocked vision, erasure, and annihilation in Foucault's essay "The Life of Infamous Men" (1977).[50] It would not stretch the truth to say that "The Life of Infamous Men" provides a template for how a current generation "digs up [its] past" on account of how frequently the essay has been cited.[51] More to the point, the essay sinks into questions of attunement, witnessing, and the complex entanglements of the archive with such unparalleled nuance, it figures so centrally in the way a number of scholars have seen themselves bound to their work and to the historical subjects about which they write, and it plays such a pivotal role in advancing the archive as a method of inquiry in queer and black studies, that we avoid exploring the terms of its influence at great peril.[52]

The introduction to a book he never wrote, "The Life of Infamous Men" was conceived as an unsystematic anthology ("a kind of herbarium") of the lives of obscure men he encountered in the prison archives of the Hôpital Général and the Bastille; individual lives that medical and juridical authorities sought to consign to oblivion through laconic statements which, in something of a paradox, preserved the very lives that would otherwise have vanished:

> All those lives destined to pass beneath any discourse and disappear without ever having been told were able to leave traces—brief, incisive, often enigmatic—only at the point of their instantaneous contact with power. So that it is doubtless impossible to ever grasp them again in themselves, as they might have been "in a free state." . . . Lives that are as though they hadn't been, that survive only from the clash with a power that wished only to annihilate them or at least to obliterate them. . . . The return of these lives to reality occurs in the very form in which they were driven out of the world. Useless to look for another face for them, or to suspect a different greatness in them; they are no longer anything but that which was meant to crush them—neither more nor less.[53]

In line with his thinking on disciplinary regimes of power, Foucault focuses attention on how lives that were putatively outside of history could be made to shine for a brief moment in their clash with the very power that would relegate them to oblivion—"lowly lives reduced to ashes in the few sentences that struck them down" as if "they had appeared in language only on the condition of remaining absolutely unexpressed in it."[54] By writing in a prose that mirrors these inverse movements of power in the archive, Foucault also gives us to know something of what it felt like to encounter these "flash existences"—"a knot of conflicted interdependence," as Catherine Gallagher and Stephen Greenblatt observe, between the paradox of the anecdote and the pathos of the anecdotalist, between a disciplinary power that allows these lives to "shine blindingly with a dark light" and the (counter) historian's attempt to clutch the life of the anecdote, which leads it to expire in his or her grasp.[55]

Foucault describes his somatic response to the archives as a "resonance" (*cette vibration*), conveying by that term a sense of the scholar's personal involvement in the lives of others. The language of resonance gathers many paraphrases throughout the essay, amplifying the sense of an affective continuum linking scholar and subject. *Seriatim*: "an emotion . . . *a certain dread or some other feeling* whose intensity I might have trouble justifying, now that the first moment of discovery has passed"; "it would be hard to say exactly *what I felt* when I read these fragments"; "one of *these impressions* that are called 'physical'"; "it was doubtless because of *the resonance* I still experience today when I happen to encounter these lowly lives"; "*I brooded* over the analysis alone"; "*the first intensities* that had motivated me remained excluded"; "it's a rule- and game-based book, the book of *a little obsession* that found its system"; "*the shock* of these words must give rise to a certain effect of beauty mixed with dread."[56] Foucault's talk of "dread" and "shock," his "brood[ing]" over fragments, far from a symptom of scholarly misadventure, models a sensorium for his readers in which scholar and subject coexist in a kind of archival "nervous system."[57]

It is not hard to see the appeal of these affective tremors to those who lack "some vantage on history, some view from the window by which to witness the melancholy facts of history."[58] Certainly, queer and slave historiographies appear to be on the same page with respect to what this nervous system affords. For Saidiya Hartman, the appeal of this language and method lay precisely in its suggestion of personal involvement—the sense of being empathetically connected to the lives of those about whom she wishes to write. One discerns this order of attachment when Hartman reflects that "this writing is personal because this history has engendered me, because 'the knowledge of the other marks me,' because of the pain experienced in my encounter with the scraps of the archive."[59] One detects it, too, when Heather Love describes the double-edged "cross-historical touch" she experiences in the archive, one caught between "the caress of a queer or marginal figure" and the "brutal touch of the law."[60] For Carolyn Dinshaw, this touch of the archive affords the sense of "desubjectified connectedness" necessary to the writing of queer history, a queer community "constituted by nothing more than the connectedness (even across time) of singular lives that unveil and contest normativity."[61]

Foucault has been accused of tending to overdramatize his situation, of protecting and projecting an "exaggerated sense of immediate moral brinkmanship" and "imagining [his] research to be implicated in the life-and-death struggles of . . . these unsung offenders."[62] These critics risk something of the same. Still, they draw our attention quite compellingly to the project of thinking through affective intimacy in the archive, specifically for queer theory, not because the archive's brutal energies "either transcend or disguise the coarser stuff of ordinary being, but because those energies are the stuff of ordinary being."[63] Hartman longs to extend a bit of what she feels to those locked in archival obscurity and (to quote Gallagher and Greenblatt on Foucault) "to bring something back to life that had been buried deep in oblivion." Love's subjects tend to recoil from our touch ("untouchability runs deep in queer experience"), but it is Dinshaw who gets closest to affirming the broader truth coursing through all of this work, the sense in which, in the energy running back and forth across this affective circuit, the mutual implication between scholar and subject is barely to be distinguished from the sense of community across time.[64]

The jolt of the archive (*cette vibration*) welds its figuration as scene of the crime to the scholar's implication in that figuration. And through these complex figures of entanglement, we have, in fact, made for the possibility of a "we" (whether queer or black), for the emergence of centripetal social bonds formed "at . . . the impact point of a collective disaster, one at which witnessing is mutually witnessed and so forms a momentary social encounter and joint world."[65] Witnessing promises mutuality, and that mutuality, in turn, a kind of intimate acknowledgment. The paradox is that, through the shock of the archive (the force with which these "few sentences . . . struck them down"), we experience "the joy of finding counterparts in the past."⁶⁶

That touch of the archive is no small matter, as it turns out, certainly not a simple matter of the scholar reaching out to touch a recalcitrant subject, certainly not innocent. But I wonder whether there are different stakes in that touch for queer and black studies. For Love, the sensation is negative ("as much a mauling as a caress"), a jolt that spurs recoil, one that is "queer" in the sense that it flags the ways the sexual past is nothing like the sexual present (again, see Traub on queer "unhistoricism"). For Hartman, it is a sign of life at the point of expiation, a symptom of what links lives prone to premature death across time and, arguably, as another scholar of the slave past suggests, a circuit in which "the continuum between past and present [is] made to be deeply felt."⁶⁷ I suppose that I am less ecumenical than Love, less hopeful and optimistic than Dinshaw, and more cynical than Hartman.

Sensitive of playing a hand in the expiation the archive effects, I am led to a more astringent take on affective history. Over the course of researching and writing this book, I have often felt undone by the archive, unable to find the subjects (the precursors) that I seek. Time and again, I would set out to recover something from the archive and fail in the attempt. But what seemed to be affirmed in each attempt was not the recalcitrance of the past but, rather, the extent to which I am drawn into being ecstatically dispossessed. Facing up to this fact, I am inspired to craft a historicism that is not melancholic but accepts the past's turning away as an ethical condition of my desire for it. I try to reframe the jolt of the archive—its refusal, its rebuff—as a call to sacrifice, seeing no reason not to put such failure to some use.

To sharpen the distinction I am attempting to draw, I find it helpful to rescript Foucault's "knot of conflicted interdependence" into two distinct types of scholarly sacrifice, torqued in each case by race and the ghost of slavery. Think of the first sacrifice (the melancholic) as a kind of debt: *As a scholar, you owe that other something by virtue of the fact that you exist and the other does not. This involution is what binds us, what ties our present to the past, our present to their past; but, on account of this involution, in writing about the past, we execute our debts not in living, but in reanimating the other.* Think of the alternative as more astringent, a version of Walker's "none like us": *I must acknowledge that were it not for the other's obliteration, I would not exist; the relation is self-eclipsing, but, by the same token, there is no alternative past that would still result in the production of me.*[68] This book makes every effort to predicate its thinking within the latter astringency.

I earlier spoke of "the scene of the crime" and *"return* to the scene of the crime," and now seems the right time to make explicit my reasons for stressing return. I mean to focus on an understanding of melancholy historicism as a kind of crime scene investigation in which a specifically *forensic imagination* is directed toward the archive. "Forensic" in my use of the term indicates not the police procedures of criminal law or the analysis of evidence and the examination of crime scenes, but (following the thinking of Michael Ralph) a political calculus, a power of translation.[69] I track the movements of this forensic imagination with the goal of drawing attention less to what searching finds (to what can or cannot be held, has or has not been retrieved from the archive) than to what searching itself brings about, what is born of the understanding of the archive as a scene of injury.

Now, between my interlocutors and me, in the pages to follow, the scene of the crime as a scene of origin is, in a sense, agreed upon. What remains in dispute is the question of what is born of that scene. Were I to reprise my earlier statements, this time with a bit of reverb, the nature of the dispute should become abundantly clear. Melancholy historicism is a kind of crime scene investigation in which the forensic imagination is directed *toward the recovery of a "we" at the point of "our" violent origin.* It participates in a broader intellectual matrix within black studies that assumes slavery as the point of origin of this we. Bryan Wagner writes,

> Perhaps the most important thing we have to remember about the black tradition is that Africa and its diaspora are older than blackness. Blackness does not come from Africa. Rather, Africa and its diaspora become black during a particular stage in their history. It sounds a little strange to put it this way, but the truth of this description is widely acknowledged. Blackness is an adjunct to racial slavery. . . . Blackness is an indelibly modern condition that cannot be conceptualized apart from the epochal changes . . . that were together made possible by the European systems of colonial slavery.[70]

The origin he calls forth generates a blackness that cannot and must not be understood as transcendent or as a positive negation of its origins in chattel slavery. Hartman's arguments on "dispossession" and those of Jared Sexton on "Afro-pessimism" yield further extraordinary leaps in our thinking on blackness and slavery, but the underlying assumptions in this matrix shore up a notion of black selfhood that is grounded in a kind of lost black sociality, in black sociality's groundedness in horror. We are given to understand slavery as the scene of the crime and that scene of the crime as a scene of origin. But it will be my intention to show, in *None Like Us*, across a range of materials and archival encounters, that there is and can be no "we" in or following from such a time and place, that what "we" share is the open secret of "our" impossibility. Walker's and Baldwin's prose, as I have already suggested, gestures toward this secret—and their turns of phrase offer a map, or sonar, in my search for a selfhood that occurs in disaffiliation rather than in solidarity. Whatever blackness or black culture is, it cannot be indexed to a "we"—or, if it is, that "we" can only be structured by and given in its own negation and refusal.

Aesthetic of the Intransmissible

In *None Like Us*, I set about drawing limits around the imperative toward melancholy in the historiography of slavery by building a new set of relations between contemporary criticism and the black past on the basis of aesthetic values and sensibilities that I espy in works of literature and art that, in my understanding of them, strive to forge critical possibilities by way of a kind of apocalypticism, or self-eclipse. The shimmering throwaway-aluminum constructions of the Ghanaian artist El Anatsui, the layered paper canvases of the Los Angeles artist Mark Bradford, Gwendolyn Brooks's free-verse poems, and (somewhat surprisingly) the recent novels of Toni Morrison: I have settled on these particular artworks, and foreground them in the first half of the book, not solely because that is what an "aesthetics of existence" calls for (Foucault: "We have to create ourselves as a work of art"), but because each appears to take on a self-consuming form in which the work itself strives to either close itself off or use itself up.[71] What is more, when taken as the manifest expression of an *aesthetics of the intransmissible* these works of art inspire me to the view that contemporary artists are in the process of enacting a kind of thought that literary critics are not yet willing to entertain, that they may be enacting a "style" of freedom: freedom from constraining conceptions of blackness as authenticity, tradition, and legitimacy; of history as inheritance, memory, and social reproduction; of diaspora as kinship, belonging, and dissemination.

Chapter 1, "My Beautiful Elimination," makes the case for a philosophical project of self-divestiture. It espies both an invitation to and a model for this project in the aesthetic tendencies at work in Anatsui and Bradford, which have been read by most critics of their work as moving toward the opposite goal of a kind of recognition, remembrance, and striving after cultural dignity and respect—a consolidation of diasporic identity. For example, in the case of Anatsui, the work is often taken as linking globalization to the ghost of slavery (Africa's liquor market merely extending the terms of the triangular trade). But in the case of Anatsui, it appears that a contrary sort of invitation is being issued in the form of a trompe l'oeil error (the mistaking of trash for gold) by which the work encourages the viewer unwittingly to take part in the perceptual effect of its own undoing. In the case of Bradford, this invitation typically arrives by way of the canvas provoking the viewer's curiosity as to what has been either erased from its once legible surface or immured within its stacked layers, a curiosity that the scholar, in any case, would be in the habit of satisfying by way of the recovery of meaning, context, or history, but that remains effectively foreclosed, an object of perpetual failure. In thus setting up the conditions for its final irrelevance, attributing its effects not to art but to a world without art (trash), or, alternatively, in creating the very object that must then go on to be destroyed, these artworks actively lose sight of their own forms. In Adorno's words, they "immolate themselves . . . , rushing toward their perdition" and conscript those who experience their effects in a similar and companionate act in which they lose sight of the coherence that goes by the name of the self.[72] Rather than accept critique as the adversarial inversion of terms of historical exclusion, these objects afford a view of critique as assimilation, appeasement, and leave-taking (the capacity to *"sich anschmiegen ans Andere,"* as Adorno phrased it in *Dialect of Enlightenment*: "to mold oneself to the other").[73] The more muted, contingent, and relativistic selfhood I seek is both held and conveyed in this array of disappearing artworks. Why should we think we can see anything else in a work of art besides the forms in which we see ourselves and see ourselves disappear?

In chapter 2, "On Failing to Make the Past Present," I argue that a similarly disintegrative impulse can be discerned in the recent writings of Toni Morrison (against the arguments of both boosters and detractors of the project of melancholy historicism that was inaugurated with the publication of her *Beloved*). The chapter questions whether the recovery imperative that motivates much critical melancholy offers the only way to either have or do slave history and ponders the possibility that the unforthcomingness of the past may be the fount of its deepest political (if not human) significance. The chapter makes the case for the writing of a history of discontinuity, the model for which is again provided by Morrison, in her novel *A Mercy*, which by way of its ungenial textual effects expresses its author's apparent turn away from the affective history project she earlier so capably inspired.

The third and fourth chapters offer examples of what this history of discontinuity might look like by exploring suicide and rumor in the eighteenth- and nineteenth-century archives of slavery as the kind of evidence often made to serve the goals of historicism, i.e., an idea of criticism as a redemptive project that continues, reanimates, or completes the political projects of those who were defeated by history. I argue for the need to shift from a historical to a rhetorical mode, from a mode of writing that keeps reintroducing the sense of loss that necessarily haunts any attempt at retrieval to one that, in the words of Michel de Certeau, "succeeds in failing," much like the tropes of metalepsis and litotes, which involve a negation or an awareness of moving "from a *can not say* . . . to a *can say* . . . by way of a *can say nothing*."[74]

Chapter 3, "The History of People Who Did Not Exist," presents another example of the kind of writing this shift toward rhetoric requires, taking up death as both the most persistent object of contemporary criticism and, in the form of slave suicide, an ideal object of metaleptic history. In the chapter I draw on slave suicide to fracture some of the presumed intimacies between our critical present and the historical past. In the struggles over slavery and the slave trade at the turn of the eighteenth century, nothing signaled what was at stake more than black death, and there was no more potent representation of those stakes than the image of slave suicide. Abolitionists often invoked the suicides of slaves as a barometer of the institution's horror while also glorifying such acts in their own romantic literature as forms of the "good death" (e.g., Aphra Behn's *Oroonoko*; Thomas Day's "Ode to a Dying Negro"). In the abolitionist cult of death, slave suicide was taken up as evidence of culture, as the sign that slaves possessed a code of honor that gave suicide meaning, and in nineteenth-century medical literature, slave suicide was often labelled "nostalgia."[75] In the recent rehabilitation of death and melancholy in the study of slavery, the imperative once again has been to make death in slavery mean (social death, civil death, necropolitics, necrocitizenship), which carries with it the demand that these acts be evidence of something—of a culture of resistance or of nihilism and social death. In this chapter, I argue that the slave's suicide is less to be interpreted than to be pondered as a problem for interpretation, drawing on the insight of historians such as Constantin Fasolt, who sees his discipline as uniquely challenged when it comes to writing about people who "consciously suppressed themselves in acts of self-immolation."[76] The chapter asks what it would mean to write about figures who resist our attempts to restore them to wholeness, who resist our projects of historical recovery—figures for whom our present does not (and cannot) represent the future they imagined. What they would require is certainly not history writing as we know it but a writing in full awareness of the negativity that labors to undo any historical project. This would be a writing predicated on knowing what withholds itself from the possibility of being known, one that sought to acknowledge without actually knowing. The chapter takes slave suicide as the theoretical object of this gossamer writing.

Chapter 4, "Rumor in the Archive," marks the intellectual origins of this project: the evidentiary problem of rumor in the archive and the tendency of Americanist/black studies critics to enshrine voice as the apotheosis of minor history. The chapter examines the first-person testimony of slaves recorded in the proceedings of various select committees that were appointed (as directed by the British House of Commons) "to inquire into the origin, causes, and progress of the late insurrection[s]" in the Caribbean.[77] These inquisitions were noteworthy for providing a subject where initially there was none, and retrieving an intention from language that could have none, with the effect that a voice comes to be engendered in its repression. (Historians of slavery will often make the error of taking these forms of utterance as the "voice" of their subjects.) My primary interest is in the attempt to preserve rumor as speech—or, to be more precise, to turn what functioned for all intents and purposes as a kind of "writing" into a "voice"; to turn everyday prattle (which circulates anonymously, as many commentators at the time noted, between dominator and dominated alike) into the confessional "voice" of conspirators. Focused in particular on the slaves' testimony that they believed the British monarch had freed them, I view their words neither as evidence irredeemably corrupted by the sovereign power that extracted them nor as verbatim speech through which we can recover subjects lost to history. These words are, rather, exactly what they appear to be: "impossible speech" that oscillates between loyalty and insurgency, speech and paraphrase, fact and prophesy, confession and coercion. In that sense, it reflects back to us the deeply felt uncertainty of the enslaved. Attention to the rumors on the surface of the archive challenges our conception of the latter as a repository of latent voices and "hidden transcripts" and requires that we reconsider whether the story of slavery can ever be narrated "from below" if our aim is to register what is inaccessible in the voice of the enslaved. Attuned to the component of meaning that is wanting in speech, the chapter performs what Brent Hayes Edwards has described as a "queer practice of the archive," or "an approach to the material preservation of the past that deliberately aims to retain what is elusive, what is hard to pin down, what can't quite be explained or filed away according to the usual categories"—a method that in practice involves, as he has shown, making multiple approaches toward one's object, never arriving at it.[78]

These essays will have their life. They are offered on the understanding that it is neither the recovery of an impossible community, nor the making of a utopia or dystopia that is at stake. They are offered out of a wish that, if some part of what I say here should catch, if any argument I make should find adherents, I may in that case have ended up creating a world that will no longer have me, as would be the point.

| PART I |

ON THINKING
LIKE A WORK OF ART

How strongly I have felt of pictures, that when you have seen one well, you must take your leave of it; you shall never see it again.

RALPH WALDO EMERSON, "Experience"

1

| MY BEAUTIFUL ELIMINATION |

On Thinking Like a Work of Art

In almost every respect, you and I had different experiences. You entered through a different door, into a different gallery, in a different museum, at a different time, or maybe simply from a different angle. Yet despite all, we report the same thing: that we have come across an object pieced together from a most precious metal, possibly gold (plate 1). "From a distance," you claim, it seems "to incorporate pristine materials . . . [to] look like a giant screen of gold and bronze."[1] As alive as it is radiant—an "immense sheet of undulant light," a surface "broken by shimmering swags and folds," you say.[2] It scintillates, phosphoresces, appears to give off more energy than went into its making. You are unsure whether to categorize it as sculpture, tapestry, mural, or installation. For a moment, you think it might be a rare piece of gilt cloth, "a vast cascading piece . . . in the Ghanaian kente style, glistening in red and gold."[3] You think you hear the sound of light (*Bling!*).[4]

You feel an impulse to approach the object, drawn in by its shimmer, and as you get closer you experience the frisson of thwarted expectations (plate 2).

"When I got up close, I saw that it was made of little strips of metal, 'sewn' together with copperwire."[5]

"Distance made a difference in understanding. When you moved closer you saw that the whole glinting thing was pieced together from countless tiny parts: pieces of colored metal pinched and twisted into strips, squares, circles and rosettes."[6]

Descriptions of the object don't appear to change, or to need to change, to accommodate the object itself, as you testify that others experience the same epiphany: "The woman sauntered up to the giant wall hanging . . . inspected its connecting pieces, then sat down on a nearby bench to get a more expansive view. Every five minutes or so, the pattern was the same. . . . Surprise. Inspection. Survey from afar."[7] What initially presents itself as precious metal appears upon inspection to be of the throwaway kind: cast-off aluminum screw tops and collars from liquor bottles—worthless bottle caps—cut and folded, hammered and stitched together with copper wire into swatches of color and texture. West African scrap metal resurrected as mural.[8] What was gold now reveals itself to be mere trash.

You feel the resplendence begin to fade upon the recognition that the work is built from these bits of trash. Yet you cannot avoid the thought that the artwork has instructed you to follow this precise perceptual itinerary; that the work itself has led you through this process. You feel that the work has guided you, and in a very controlled and particular way, into this encounter with its essence. You think, too, how curious it is that the work would subvert its own beauty—obliterate it, evaporate it—how the work contains the conditions of its own undoing. Why should the artwork issue such a powerful invitation to experience more intimately and intensely an effect it had every intention of subverting in the end? Why should an artwork be so corrosive of its own illusions, of the very illusion that it is art?

And once you see it for what it is, you can't quite unsee it, although you would like to. You want to wipe trash from your perception and capture once again the encounter with that initial shimmer. You make every effort to identify when the illusion fell apart. You ask yourself, At what point did I actually see it as trash, scrap, rubbish; as unformed matter, as shit? Had that moment not emerged in the wake of the shimmer, the materials not appearing to be trash until you looked past their beautiful, luminous sheen? And if to see this work as made up of trash you had to fast forward and look past its beauty, then what were these "countless tiny parts" before they were frozen into the structure of the artwork? Were they not trash before they were framed, as well? Why am I being invited to see trash as the before and after of the artwork? Why is trash its simultaneous origin and destination, point of emergence and disappearance, an analepsis and a prolepsis?

You aren't the first to observe these perceptual effects. Many art critics have also observed them while having surprisingly little to say about them, preferring to emphasize the work's historical and art-historical significance. Some see the work as exposing a web of symbolic links, past and current, between Africa and the Western world. El Anatsui has said as much himself, admitting that when he first spotted the bag of discarded bottle caps by the side of the road he immediately understood them as the "links" connecting Africa to Europe and the Americas. "Several thoughts went through my mind when I found the bag of bottle tops in the bush," he confesses. "I thought of the objects as links between my continent, Africa, and the rest of Europe. Objects such as these were introduced to Africa by Europeans when they came as traders. Alcohol was one of the commodities brought with them to exchange for goods in Africa. Eventually alcohol became one of the items used in the trans-Atlantic slave trade. They made rum in the West Indies, took it to Liverpool, and then it made its way back to Africa. I thought that the bottle caps had a strong reference to the history of Africa."[9] Here we have the direct testimony of the artist as to his inspiration; his assertion that the work is thoroughly committed to the revelation and representation of a web of symbolic links between Africa and the Western world.

Anatsui's talk of "links" has inspired a wide range of interpretations. Some commentators have taken the artist's emphasis on the "repurposed" nature of the materials to signal an attempt to recast these links within the frame of globalization, as part of a "symbolic economy of recuperation in relation to the spread of consumer goods and the pile up of waste in developing societies."[10] Anatsui, ever the perspicacious scavenger, alchemically transforms "the false gold of commercial packaging into a dazzling coin of artistic invention," with mordant connotations: a "doubling evocation of wealth and poverty" that lands a barbed riposte before any view of black Africans as a disposable people, or *négraille* (nigger trash), to invoke Yambo Ouologuem's infamous term.[11] For those critical of modernism's racial politics, the ripostes take aim at the devaluation not merely of African people but also of African art, talking back to early twentieth-century modernism's "primitivist" sequester and formal appropriation of African aesthetic form. Quite to the contrary, an Anatsui in this view produces shimmering effects on par with "the gold leaf squares that enliven the backgrounds of [Gustav] Klimt's paintings"; it bears a similarity to Donald Judd's "specific objects," so handily does it resist classification as either "painting" or "sculpture"; and its laterally expansive and intricate surface calls to mind Frank Stella's later experiments with textiles.[12] These links prove hugely generative of meaning in an Anatsui. In short, Anatsui's "links" produces an endless vortex of them, interpretations (each one something of an allegory for the others) that seem important to sustaining his instinctive sense of a "strong reference to the history of Africa" in the bottle caps.

I hope I may be forgiven, then, when I admit my indifference to the question of the "meaning" of an Anatsui, when I confess that meaning is not what I hope to find in it. It is not meaning that has kept this work in mind for me, which is why arguments that attempt to settle on a meaning (and Anatsui's own testimony) have not and will not figure prominently in what I have to say about the work. It cannot be terribly difficult to see why: such arguments seem crucially at an angle to the force of my direct encounter with the object. The direct and immediate experience of the movement from gold to trash, representation to matter, figuration to literality feels like a call to acknowledge what is simply there in front of me (rather than what ought to, wants to, or used to be there)—a call to acknowledge the force of the literal that issues from the bottle caps themselves.

It's gold. . . . No, it's trash. It's bottle caps. . . . No, it's artwork. We have seen effects like this before and called them gestalt. Jonathan Crary proposes that in gestalt ("the indeterminacy of an attentive perception") the capacity of our senses to generate forms leads us to attribute to artworks "qualities that are unrelated to the qualities of their individual sensory components."[13] The effects given off by an Anatsui can certainly be understood in terms of gestalt, the oscillation between aluminum debris and gold leaf generating an endless series of forms (Ghanaian kente cloth, *adinkra* funeral cloth, any "cloth" you might perceive).

It's gold. . . . No, it's trash. It's bottle caps. . . . No, it's artwork. Again, we could turn to gestalt to make sense of this oscillation, but there always seems to be an undertow, or gravitational pull, in one particular direction, an incessant drive toward the literal. The perpetual oscillation between *what the artwork is* and *what it is not* feels like a lingering, a detention. But why should the artwork linger here? Why should it want to detain me here—and me, you?

I have some explaining to do. My task is twofold. First, and obviously, I must explain what it means to begin here. Why begin with an artwork at all, especially one that has no representational content, makes no obvious or direct reference to history, and can be said to lead one back to slavery only by way of the most oblique and recondite path? The second task is to explore what kind of thought happens here. What sort of inquiry is the work itself attempting to instigate? What sort of thinking is it doing or inviting us to do? What thoughts are we inviting ourselves to have? Why choose to deepen one's critical attachment to a work that one knows is likely to lead (and leave) us here, in a vision of its own self-eclipsing denial? And why should I (why should anyone) long for this precise experience of denial, to seek out the arc of an experience that gathers waste, congeals it into a form (or identity) where the goal was always to occasion that form's dissolution? What sort of problem or challenge could such willingness to self-abnegate solve? Who gains from—what is gained by—the headlong tumble into such precarity?

Theodor Adorno proposed that artworks "immolate themselves" in the rush "toward their perdition." He writes in *Aesthetic Theory*, "They go over into their other, find continuance in it, want to be extinguished in it, and in their demise determine what follows them."[14] Anticipating the point somewhat earlier, with Max Horkheimer, he would specify that mimesis involved, not the artwork's imitation of the world, but its approximation of it (the capacity to *sich anschmiegen ans Andere* [to mold itself to the other].[15] *Sich anschmiegen*: Adorno effectively represses the demand of language that mimesis always be a mimesis *of* something, and embraces the idea that critique might express itself in a mimesis *onto* something (*an*, "onto" + *schmiegen*, "to nestle, snuggle up to"): mimesis as cuddling; mimesis as spooning.[16]

I seek a critical comportment that embraces these forms of mimesis, conspires with the world in this way, and in the process bases the case for a non-sovereign form of critical subjectivity on the idea that art thinks. By "art thinks" I do not mean that art contains propositional content; nor do I mean that it offers an analogy for what someone does when engaged in critical thought. Rather, following a line of argument set forth by Hubert Damisch, Ernst van Alphen, and Georges Didi-Huberman that "works of art appear to full advantage only if we deal with them as ways of thinking," I mean that artworks perform, in one way or another, an intellectual or philosophical project.[17] The artwork, in this theory of form, points reflexively to its own internal complexity. It can be considered a reflection, not in the passive sense of a mirror image, but in the active sense of an act of thought.

The works that command my attention in this chapter consist of surfaces that point reflexively to their own, internal complexities so that they can also be said to offer their own form of critical understanding and, in that sense, to be the very medium in which thought happens. These works are having thoughts regarding illusion and dissolution, failure and immurement, shattering and creativity. Each gives off perceptual effects that are fleeting, withheld, or marginal; each takes up a self-consuming form in which it strives to either close itself off or use itself up.

On thinking like a work of art: hold the phrase in tension with an idea of what it might mean to "think like a work of film" (to think and, more importantly, to feel our relation to history as an auratic thickness, a felt authenticity experienced as withheld or lost presence).[18] "Aura": the term is, as we know, Walter Benjamin's and refers to the "spiritual deposit" that every handmade artifact receives from its maker, which mass-produced objects lack, and yet it is *a deposit that in many ways becomes cognizable to Benjamin only at the moment of its disappearance or loss*.[19] No cinema, no aura. No reproduction, no deposit. As he writes in "The Work of Art in the Age of Its Technological Reproducibility":

> In even the most perfect reproduction, *one* thing is lacking: the here and now of the work of art—its unique existence in a particular place. It is this unique existence—and nothing else—that bears the mark of the history to which the work has been subject....
>
> [Various circumstances of technological reproduction] may leave the artwork's other properties untouched, but they certainly devalue the here and now of the artwork.... [In] the work of art this process touches on a highly sensitive core, more vulnerable than that of any natural object. That core is its authenticity. The authenticity of a thing is the quintessence of all that is transmissible in it from its origin on, ranging from its physical duration to the historical testimony relating to it....
>
> One might focus these aspects of the artwork in the concept of the

> aura, and go on to say: what withers in the age of the technological reproducibility of the work of art is the latter's aura.... The social significance of film ... is inconceivable without its destructive, cathartic side: the liquidation of the value of tradition in the cultural heritage....
>
> What, then, is aura? A strange tissue of space and time: the unique apparition of a distance, however near it may be.[20]

What, then, is aura? As I phrased it, it is a felt authenticity experienced as withheld or lost presence.

I will have more to say in the following chapter about the formative influence of Benjaminian historical formulae on recent melancholic work on race and slavery. For now, I want only to avail myself of a stratum of symmetry between the filmic and the historical in Benjamin's thought—that is, between his logic of auratic emergence (as demonstrated earlier) and his understanding of history as a "pile of debris" (in the ninth of his "Theses on the Philosophy of History"). "Benjamin's 'pile of debris,'" Alan Liu writes, "precisely disintegrates the 'aura' he theorized in 'The Work of Art in the Age of Mechanical Reproduction.'"[21] I would substitute the verb "declines" or "conjugates" for "disintegrates."

Paul Klee's watercolor *Angelus Novus* (1920) inspires Benjamin's ninth thesis:

> A Klee painting named "Angelus Novus" shows an angel looking as though he is about to move away from something he is fixedly contemplating. His eyes are staring, his mouth is open, his wings are spread. This is how one pictures the angel of history. His face is turned toward the past. Where we perceive a chain of events, he sees one single catastrophe which keeps piling wreckage upon wreckage and hurls it in front of his feet. The angel would like to stay, awaken the dead, and make whole what has been smashed. But a storm is blowing from Paradise; it has got caught in his wings with such violence that the angel can no longer close them. This storm irresistibly propels him into the future to which his back is turned, while the pile of debris before him grows skyward. This storm is what we call progress.

How does this "pile of debris" inflect or parse "aura"? How has it come that for Benjamin this painting essentially conjugates ideas that were originally cinematic? Much rests on the transformation effected by the thesis itself.

The thesis narrates a substitution, an insertion—the insertion of history into the space that yawns before the angel, at "his feet" or, in the place where we stand, as it happens, when facing the picture. The watercolor occasions, on further reflection, a series of glances, a precise set of geometric bearings from which Benjamin's theory of history is taken to emerge. "He is about to move away from something he is fixedly contemplating." "His face is turned toward the past." "He sees one single catastrophe." Benjamin gazes upon Klee's *Angelus Novus* and imagines that he is looking at the Angel of History; the Angel of History looks back at him (Benjamin) only to *see* "wreckage upon wreckage" accumulate in a "pile of debris . . . in front of his feet," bearing witness to the horrors of history; we, the viewers, gazing upon Klee's angel, readily accept its transformation into the Angel of History and, consequently, our own turn as heirs to Benjamin's melancholy critique. In the thinking of Alan Liu, it is now time for us to immerse ourselves in history's "pile of debris" (and note the filmic vocabulary): "The task of cultural criticism today is to take some of the burden off the individual Benjaminian angel by revolving our observer's camera angle hemispherically around so that we view his stance from the back, framed against—in the act of confronting—history."[22] Wherever we stand, history holds the place of an absence, whether it is the absence projected in the thesis's fabulation of the painting's content or, accepting that fabulation, our view onto history's "pile of debris," which is necessarily blocked by the angel's back. It is all a matter of shifting camera angles: "Benjamin's 'pile of debris' precisely disintegrates [conjugates, parses] the 'aura' he theorized."[23]

On thinking like a work of art: a phrase born of a desire to move *beyond* the project of "complicating" and "immersing" ourselves in history:

> The strenuous (rather than facile) act of *freeing* ourselves from the complicated history we are immersed in or, phrased another way, of choosing ethically to be emancipated from historical context through the very act of allowing ourselves to be so fully and deeply absorbed in that context that we discern the alternative pathways between past and future emergent from its complexity. . . . At this core level . . . *the only thing that registers is a break in the tight, clenched little history of our selves*; and the most accurate statement of that break is a method (like a grammar or a syntax we would ourselves not naturally speak) that enacts a certain alienation or remove from ourselves.[24]

This coveted alienation would entail a gesture best parsed as a kind of doubled movement: away from the "clenched little history of our selves" and into a language we would not naturally speak.

My beautiful elimination: a two-way verbal pun in which that movement is experienced as a subservience before the artwork, in which that transformation is worked out as self-dissolution; an attempt to enact that undoing as a kind of reading of the artwork, not an interpretation or contextualization of it, but a description that allows one to inhabit it.[25] Detained and distracted by a number of artworks, I want to explore what it means simply to allow for this visitation by contemporary art, making the case for the value of a criticism that is watchful of its own self-importance by exploring what it means to think "like" a work of art (what it means for a critical project to nestle up to and assimilate the aesthetic values and sensibilities one espies in a work of art—what it means to think of critique as accommodation). On this account, I shall turn repeatedly to works of art that, in my understanding of them, strive to forge critical possibilities by way of a kind of apocalypticism, or self-eclipse, appearing to take on a self-consuming form by attempting to either close themselves off or use themselves up. The works call us to practice a kind of self-dismissal or *black ascesis*: "The work that one performs on oneself," as Foucault put it, "in order to transform oneself or make the self appear which, happily, one never attains," significance falling on that anticipation of failure, of a self that never appears.[26] (I have more to say about that failure in a moment.) These artworks are having thoughts that cultural critics ought now to be having but seem reluctant to embrace.

We must begin to think like artworks.

Our Loss

The heart of the wise is in the house of mourning.

ECCLESIASTES 7:4

There is little denying the extent to which critical inquiry into slavery and black culture has assumed a melancholy cast of late, or the extent to which, for as long as the melancholy affective history project has prevailed in cultural criticism, many have questioned its validity as a ground for politics and called for its supersession. As early as 1972, Orlando Patterson admonished in "Toward a Future That Has No Past" that "the

Blacks of the Americas . . . must abandon their search for a past, . . . [must] transcend the confines and grip of a cultural heritage, . . . becom[ing] the most truly modern of all peoples—a people who feel no need for a nation, a past, or a particularistic culture, but whose style of life will be a rational and continually changing adaptation to the exigencies of survival, at the highest possible level of existence." Later, in *Poetics of Relation*, Édouard Glissant called for "the right to opacity for everyone" and for a cultural criticism willing to moderate its epistemological ambitions, because, as he understood the relation between ethics and epistemology, "to feel in solidarity with [the other] or to build with him or to like what he does, it is not necessary for me to grasp him." And more insistently, Wendy Brown warned in *States of Injury* that our "present past . . . of insistently unredeemable injury," where the habit is to frame that injury as epistemologically necessary and ontologically grounding (as in some way "ours"), this present past comes into conflict with the very urgent need "to give up these investments"—to divest from our "wounded attachments"—if we are ever to pursue an emancipatory democratic project. The limits of the historiographical project rooted in affective attachment to past suffering have been evident for some time.[27]

In my own prior attempt to establish the authority of the slave past in contemporary black life, the goal was "to interrogate rigorously the kinds of political claims that can be mobilized on behalf of the slave (the stateless, the socially dead, and the disposable) in the political present."[28] What is the time of slavery? Is it the time of the present? What is the story about the slave that we ought to tell out of the present we ourselves inhabit? These are some of the questions I (and my co-author, Saidiya Hartman) sought to address. In taking up these questions, we were concerned to elaborate neither "what happened then" nor "what is owed because of what happened then" but, rather, the particular character of slavery's violence that appears to be ongoing and constitutive of the unfinished project of freedom.[29] I have felt the urge of late to dissent from my own, earlier investments in this approach and to question the epistemological frame this view of history compels on me, not least a tort historicism that views slavery as a site of wrongful injury.

A way to construe injury under common law, tort derives a sense of the proper value of an individual by identifying "an incident that interrupts the value" that person would have had "in the most plausible projection of his future as a direct extension of his past."[30] Tort's restoration of the

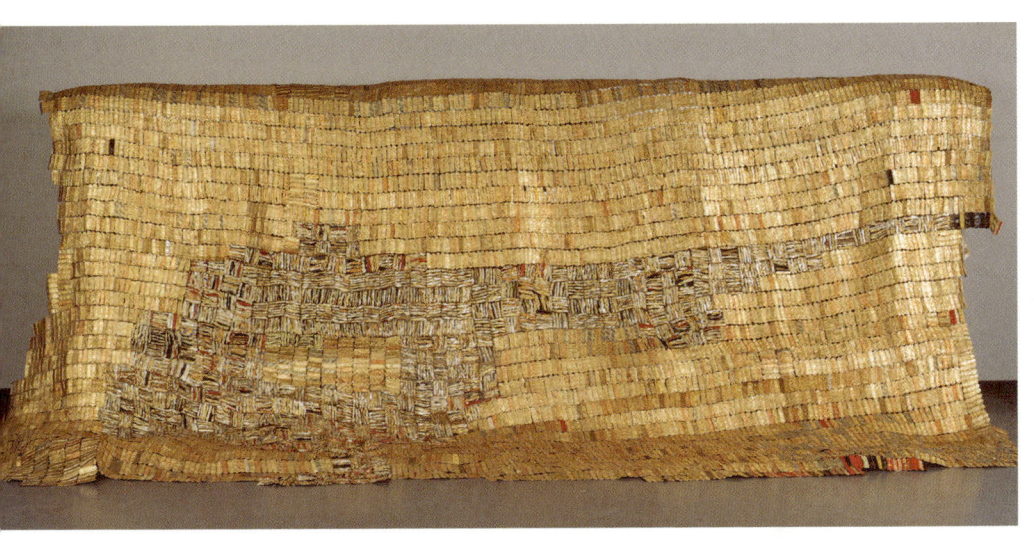

PLATE 1. El Anatsui, *Hovor II* (2004). Woven aluminum bottle caps, copper wire. 120 × 144 in. Fine Arts Museums of San Francisco. Museum purchase, James J. and Eileen D. Ludwig Endowment Fund, Virginia Patterson Fund, Charles Frankel Philanthropic Fund, and various tribute funds. Image courtesy of the Fine Arts Museums of San Francisco.

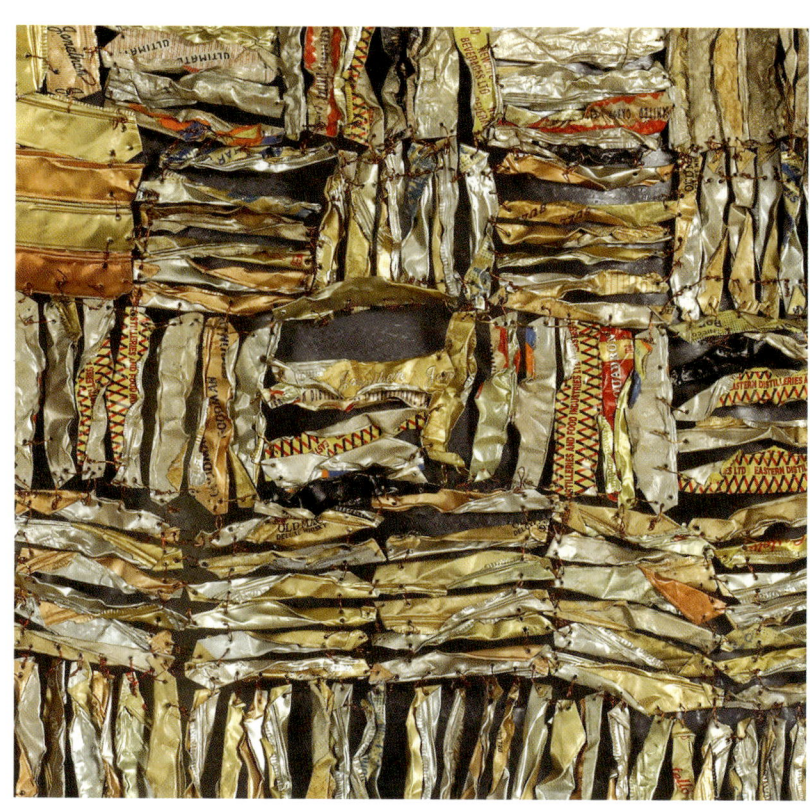

PLATE 2. El Anatsui, *Hovor II* (2004), detail.

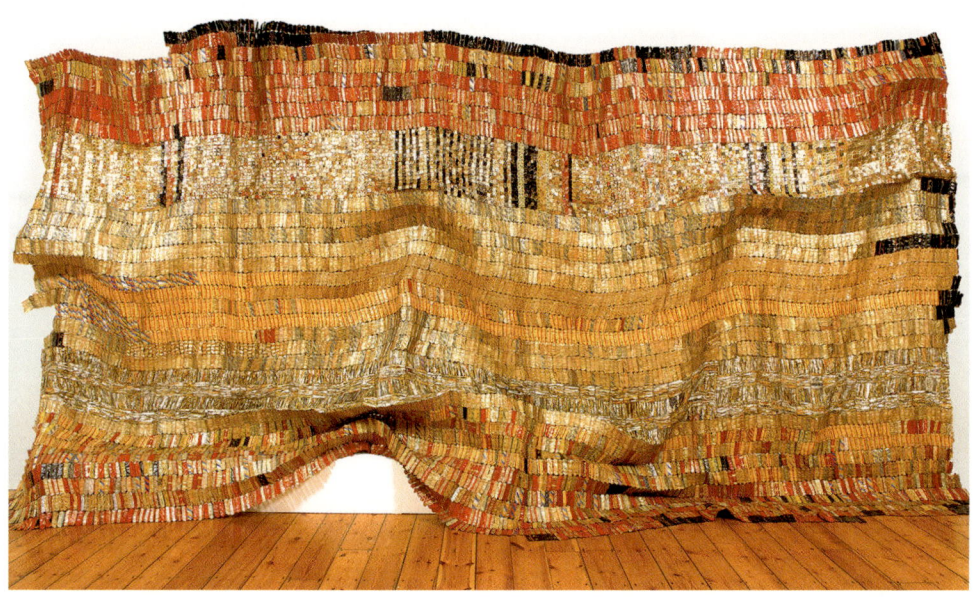

PLATE 3. El Anatsui, *Fading Cloth* (2005). Woven aluminum bottle caps, copper wire. 126 × 256 in. Courtesy of the artist and the October Gallery, London.

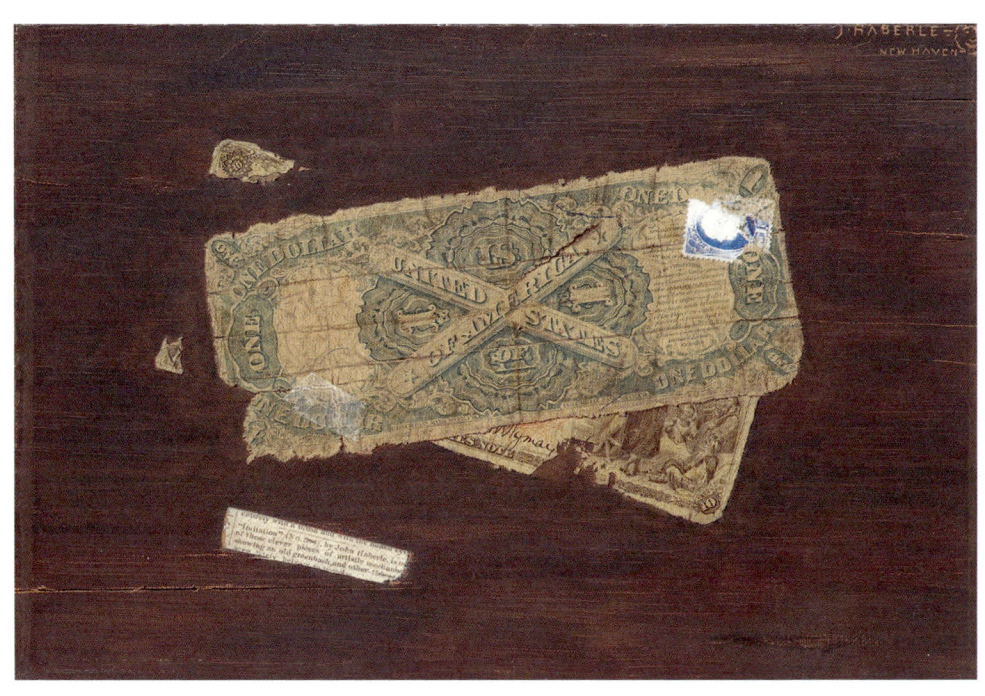

PLATE 4. John Haberle, *U.S.A.* (1889). Oil on canvas. 8.5 × 12 in. Indianapolis Museum of Art. Gift of Paul and Ruth Buchanan.

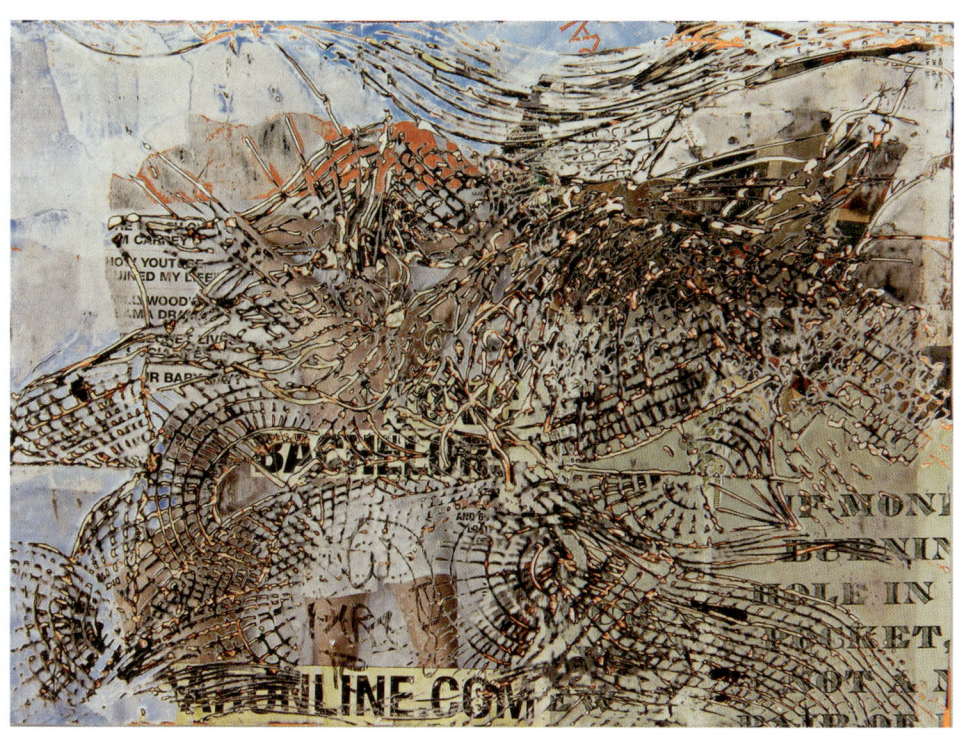

PLATE 5. Mark Bradford, *PARATE* (2008). Mixed-media collage on canvas. 36 × 48 in. Courtesy of the artist and Hauser and Wirth, London.

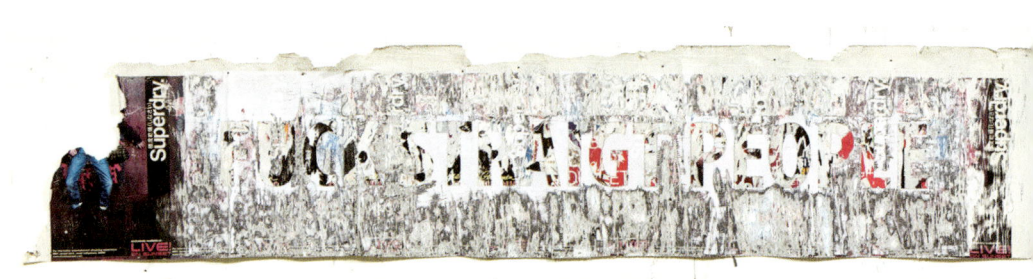

PLATE 6. Mark Bradford, *Paris Is Burning* (2010). Billboard paper, photomechanical reproductions, acrylic gel medium, and additional mixed media. 42 × 200 in. Courtesy of the artist and Hauser and Wirth, London.

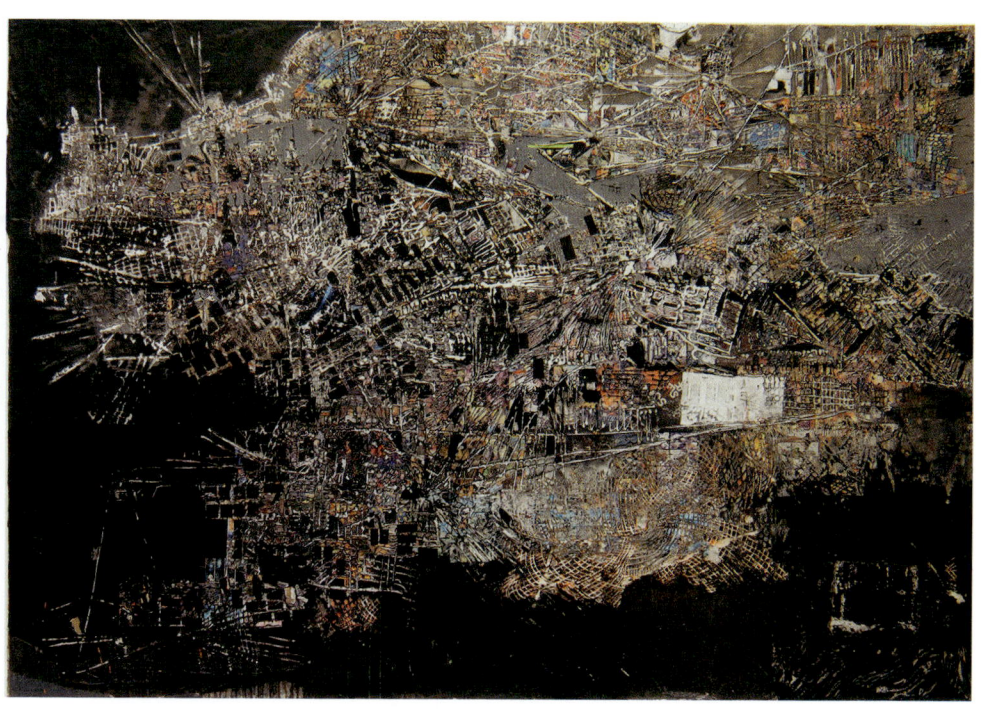

PLATE 7. Mark Bradford, *A Truly Rich Man Is One Whose Children Run into His Arms Even When His Hands Are Empty* (2008). Photomechanical reproductions, acrylic gel medium, comic-book paper, carbon paper, acrylic paint, caulking, and additional mixed media on canvas. 102 × 144 in. Courtesy of the artist and Hauser and Wirth, London.

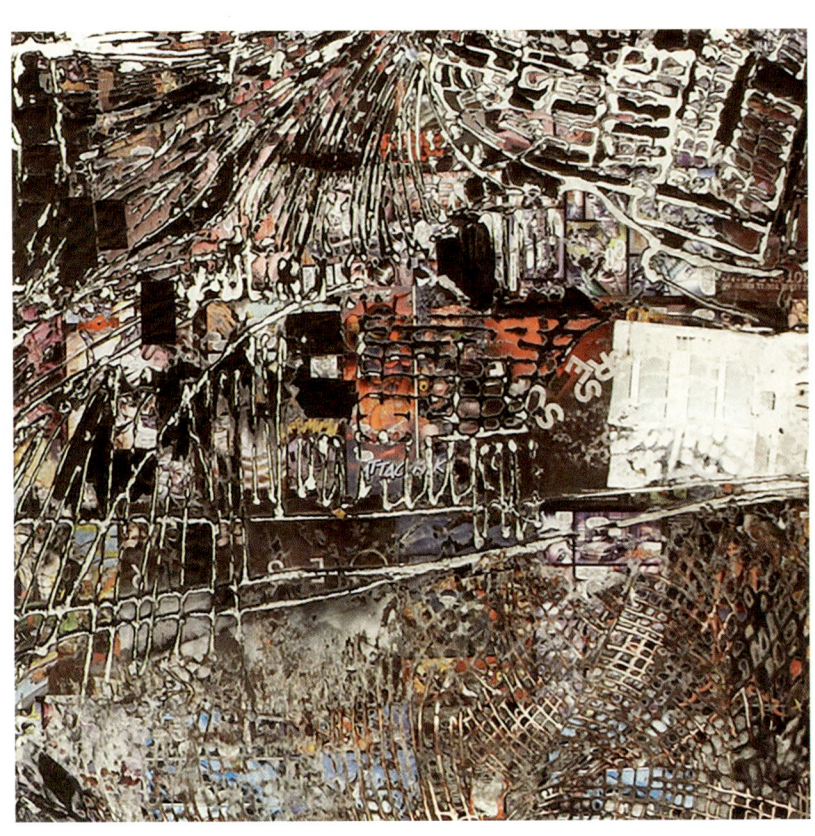

PLATE 8. Mark Bradford, *A Truly Rich Man Is One Whose Children Run into His Arms Even When His Hands Are Empty* (2008), detail.

subject assigns value to the person by assigning property to her, both in all things that are obviously property and in extrapolations from that property (potential earnings, psychological distress, reputation, and so on). In a tort claim, Frances Ferguson writes, "The notion of value is converted into a version of property, so that past possession seems the crucial means of asserting a claim to value. Tort law, for all its attentiveness to the significance of omission as well as to positive action, fails to provide a sense of potential value apart from a perceived past."[31] Tort binds us to two principles: (1) the idea that claims for the future must be based in history and the past; and (2) the requirement that one go back and look for the injury that interrupted the subject's march toward his or her future and try to recover the subject who existed *before* the injury. When it is made the basis for a traumatic model of history, this epistemology holds that our birth into relation, our admittance to the social order, is the result of an injury from which we have yet to recover; that the social is "historical" in the sense of being structured by a present past of suffering and injury so that, for me to understand myself today, I must necessarily believe that I was someone else (or potentially someone else) in the past; that the person I was before my wounding can in fact be known, and the scholar's recovery of that knowledge paves the royal road to a kind of tolerance or repair of damaged life. These sorts of historical and political investments (the acquisitive urges, strong claims making, perfective activity) have been hard-baked into the structure of agonistic critique.

I am most keen to find a way around the dark brood of "negative allegory" that has typified the melancholic turn, an obsession with "displacement, erasure, suppression, elision, overlooking, overwriting, omission, obscurantism, expunging, repudiation, exclusion, annihilation, [and] denial."[32] I am interested in the way such figures sustain an effort to determine political goals according to a model of representation. In this regard, melancholy historicism feels to be navigating an impasse for which (once again) we have Hegel largely to thank. It is Hegel who, in *The Philosophy of History*, taints Africa as unfit for history, as the repository of an "Unhistorical, Undeveloped Spirit" motivated by frenzy rather than ideas and thus inaccessible to thought.[33] Yet it is Hegel who, in a precisely contrary spirit in *Philosophy of Spirit* (and elsewhere), by way of his famous accounts of the "struggle for recognition" and the "dialectic of master and slave," enshrines the struggle for recognition as the only dynamic that makes the social world intelligible, for it is through a dependence on the other that one comes to "be."³⁴ Patchen Markell argues in *Bound by Recognition* that the pursuit of recognition expresses an aspiration to *sovereignty*; the politics of recognition involves us in efforts to escape the condition of non-sovereignty.³⁵ These efforts have more likely been thwarted than advanced by the recent turn to melancholy, for melancholy, by engendering an illusion of sovereignty in the acknowledgment of sovereignty's negation, in this way "celebrates our capacity for mastery by locating it *where it was not*."³⁶ In similar manner, Anita Sokolsky maintains that in melancholy, "The only audience who counts—the one whose loss has precipitated the melancholy—cannot or will not hear the protest that without it is not worth mounting," and this appeal to representation has the odd effect of transforming melancholy into an affect that "claims the prestige of an affliction which cannot be meliorated."³⁷

The struggle for recognition, the making of an appeal, the longing to have one's protest be heard: a long-standing effort to wed politics to appearance is captured in these phrases. The black tradition has not always been about these concerns with appearance—or, better, not every corner of the black tradition has been concerned with appearance in this way, committed to an ideal of the social structured around a sense of mutual acknowledgment. That numerous incidents of loss in the history of the African diaspora don't appear to harbor such ideals warrants our interest. These exceptions have often been classed under the rubric of *the black radical tradition*.

Chapter 7 of Cedric Robinson's *Black Marxism: The Making of the Black Radical Tradition* is, at a mere five pages, the shortest but, I believe, most important chapter of that book, for it is there that he provides the dispersed origins of that tradition. These origins suggest that it may not always serve us to conceptualize the social as ideally structured around a sense of mutual acknowledgment.³⁸ Loss in the black radical tradition simply does not serve these conceptions of appearance and recognition.

Origins of the black radical tradition include:

1. The moment in 1856 when the Xhosa prophetess Nongquawuse convinced her followers that the ancestral spirits told her that the Xhosa should slaughter all their cattle and destroy their crops (the repository of all of their wealth), in return for which the spirits would banish their British occupiers into the sea. Her millennialist prophesy would result in a cattle killing of

such apocalyptic proportions that three-quarters of the Xhosa nation would die of the resulting famine.[39]
2. The states established by the enslaved Africans, mulattoes, and poor whites who throughout much of the seventeenth century escaped into the Palmares, a region of steep and precipitous mountains on the coast of Brazil, where they established settlements, a republic consisting of smaller *quilombos*, and a king with the power to negotiate treaties with the colonial governor of the State of Pernambuco. Fully aware that a forensics was being deployed to follow them, *palmaristas* would abandon and burn their settlements to the ground every time the Portuguese approached, melting away into the surrounding forest—their state reclaimed by wilderness; their society leaving no perceptible trace of itself.[40]
3. The moment in 1915 when rebels in the British colony of Nyasaland struck valiantly, though futilely, against their colonial overlords when they heard the following entreaty from their leader, John Chilembwe, a millenarian Christian minister: "We have determined to strike a first and a last blow and then we will all die by the heavy storm of the whiteman's army."[41]

These are a few of the roots from which the black radical tradition emerges, and each resists being understood in terms of a desire to bring about positive social change, resists translation into the terms of class conflict or individual resistance most common to Western rationality—that is, "The individualistic and often spontaneous motives that energized the runaway, the arsonist, the poisoner." These origins provide evidence, on the contrary, of a "very different and shared order of things," of a tradition founded on a "very different historical role for consciousness than was anticipated in Western radicalism."[42]

With violence "turned inward" rather than directed at their oppressors, these rebels, Robinson explains, "lived on their terms, they died on their terms, they obtained their freedom on their terms," and they "defined the terms of their destruction."[43] What lends this tradition its "radical" accent is as much the inwardness of the violence as the violence itself, the tradition's actualization through self-abnegation rather than against it. But as a politics (if politics is what we want to call it), such communities sought not to achieve a positive set of social outcomes (e.g., the attenuation of the objective power of the enemy, the overthrow of slavery, the actualization a new world). Instead, they prioritized "the renunciation of actual being for historical being," the community's successful mobilization "against its material aspect."[44]

Evidence of the black radical tradition seems to have been recondite, more felt than seen, its presence more intuited than witnessed, its actualization more paradoxically present than empirically given. In the black radical tradition, Robinson asserts, activity was focused on "the structures of the mind," where defeat or victory were largely "internal affair[s]"—it was a tradition that "more easily sustained suicide than assault."[45] The people stake their claim on and as community in the moment of its dissolution—an ethics (a far more accurate term, in my view) committed to "the integral totality of the people" against their material aspect. In Robinson's summation, this ethics involved a "shared sense of obligation to preserve the collective being, the ontological totality."[46]

What kind of tradition is this?[47] By what logic does it become possible for acts of self-destruction, self-renunciation, inwardness, and collective disappearance to "preserve" the collective being? What is that?

Some observers, knowing the level of violence the situation warranted, and knowing too who ought to have been its proper recipient, dismissed those who chose the route of self-immolation as an "outlandish people." Although this description was intended to disparage and dismiss, it seems in fact to be the most accurate.[48] Robin D. G. Kelley sees the change inspired by the black radical imagination as having affinities with the surreal and surrealism, and I would accept his invitation to view an aesthetic as crucial here.[49] Victory and freedom make their appearance in disappearance, the tradition sustaining a kind of negative capability. There is an essential opacity to the black radical tradition, an "imagination" amenable to neither the *utopianism* of a revolutionary consciousness nor the pure *negativity* of a black nihilism.

The black radical imagination inspires the urge to find other ways to articulate loss. This project requires a return to questions of appearance and belonging, but not from the side of slavery and the violence of the archive but, rather, from a desire to puzzle out why we attach so fervently to objects that are beneath the threshold of appearance. Toward this end, I have found Stanley Cavell's queries into the psychological dimensions of skepticism supremely helpful, and following a line of argument in *The*

Claim of Reason, I would observe that the agon of wrestling with the failure, resistance, or impossibility of something that was lost to history making an *appearance* often carries with it fears and desires about social *acknowledgment*.[50]

I mention Cavell because no one has been more committed than him to exploring how the problem of appearance gets infused with the need for acknowledgment, which line of thought can help us to think a bit more clearly and critically about the habit of positing a return to appearance from archival oblivion as a salve for damaged life. Rei Terada summarizes Cavell's project on "the skeptic" (described by Terada as one "who seems to care inordinately about appearance and reality"), writing, "Interpreting the mutually irritable conversation between the skeptic and her or his—almost always, his—interlocutors, Cavell explains that the skeptic is perceived as wanting something fundamentally unreasonable, something more than conditions on our planet can provide. Cavell interprets the skeptic's language as a request for social acknowledgment in the guise of a failed epistemic statement. In his account, skeptical scruples about appearance and reality transmit fears and desires about interpersonal understanding: 'acceptance in relation to objects' corresponds to 'acknowledgment in relation to others.'"[51]

"'Acceptance in relation to objects' corresponds to "acknowledgment in relation to others.'" Cavell, by his own admission, connects this failure to accept the given with an inability to acknowledge or accept the human condition.[52] I view the Cavellian formulation otherwise, taking the correlation between appearance and acknowledgment as axiomatic—that is, assuming he means their relation not to be causal but, rather, to specify two poles of a philosophical entailment. The formula in this regard is more of a heuristic: it provides a way to understand how our attachment to objects that are beneath the threshold of appearance bears the weight of various modes of belonging. I propose that the correlation has something to teach us about a concern with appearance that persists in work on race and slavery.

Both Terada and Cavell mean by "acceptance" that moment when the skeptic no longer disputes the givens of the phenomenal world, a moment that, forever foreclosed from arrival on account of his dissatisfaction, nevertheless carries both his hope and his fear of acknowledgment in the final instance, of the end to his "antagonism toward a world that prevents [him] from joining [his] own being."⁵³ As is the case when the melancholic looks upon the world, this moment of acceptance never arrives for the skeptic.

The best one can do, Terada argues, is to take "vacations" from the coercive demand for one's acceptance by cultivating what she calls "phenomenophilia," or a practice of looking away—"looking away at the colored shadow on the wall, or keeping the head turned to the angle at which the sunspot stays in view."⁵⁴ The phenomenophile feels particularly drawn to perceptions that seem marginal to normal appearance because they seem, in Terada's words, "to figure the possibility of fleeting relief from the pressure to endorse . . . the world 'as is.'"⁵⁵ We become attached to "transient perceptual objects" that fall beneath the threshold of normal appearance, Terada observes, "because only they seem capable of noncoercive relation."⁵⁶ My own readerly impulses are phenomenophilic, in that regard, as evident in the works that I have assembled here, all of which involve fleeting and withheld perceptions and thus clear a path toward the "vacations" from a demand for acceptance that Terada inspires in a way that invites us to think differently about loss, and, as it happens, race and relation.⁵⁷

We return to Anatsui.

Epiphanic Shimmer: El Anatsui

> What is it about the trompe l'oeil of appearance and reality
> that gets this job of tacit world-criticism done so well?
>
> REI TERADA, *Looking Away*

It's gold. . . . No, it's trash. It's bottle caps. . . . No, it's artwork. I described this oscillation as a movement between what the artwork simply is and what it is not, which is another way to say that an Anatsui is a work of trompe l'oeil.

The most fundamental claim that one can make about trompe l'oeil painting is that it predicates a mistake. Trompe l'oeil, in the words of Walter Benn Michaels, "[reproduces] in the perception of representations the physiology of perceiving the objects they represent."⁵⁸ John Haberle's *U.S.A.* makes that clear (plate 4). Mistake is trompe l'oeil's categorical imperative and persists in the experience of any Anatsui, but arguably not in the way that the tradition of trompe l'oeil painting has prepared us to understand. *Fading Cloth* (plate 3), as a work of trompe l'oeil, reproduces the mistake general to the form but solidly *inverts* the terms of that mistake, for where trompe l'oeil wants you to mistake it for an object in the world, and not to see it as art, an Anatsui, inversely, wants you to mistake it for art and not see it as an object in the world. Or to put the matter in the affirmative, trompe l'oeil painting looks like an object in the world, although it turns out just to be art, while an Anatsui looks like a work of art, though it turns out just to be another object in the world.[59]

It matters that the conundrum be phrased just so—that an Anatsui "looks like" a work of art rather than that is simply "is" one—for stating the matter in this way draws out two consequences to Anatsui's trompe l'oeil. First, it recognizes that, while the work invites us to linger between its two objects of attention, between trash and gold, it cannot itself be reduced to one or the other—what it is (bottle caps) or what it is not (gold). Instead, the artwork must be perceived in terms of the *form* that it takes—that is, as matter striving to "look like" a work of art.[60] Second consequence: if to perceive this object as simultaneously and irreducibly both what it is and what it is not we have to see it as striving to take on another *form*, as gesturing to be a "work of art" as such, we are forced to grapple with the way an Anatsui complicates what we mean when we say that a work of art is something around which we have *put a frame*. The curious thing is that an Anatsui both has a frame (has to have a frame) and doesn't have a frame.[61] The bottle caps confront you with the force of their literalization and in that way conduct you past their frame.

I have spoken of the artwork's trompe l'oeil effects, of a "literality" that circumvents the work's frame, with the express goal of addressing two concerns. I wish first to address a strain of critique that accepts the frame as dispositive of the artwork's politics; and second, to argue with a particular end to which this understanding of the frame as a politics has been put—that is, the critique of what Michaels, in *The Beauty of a Social Problem*, labels "the appeal of the literal."[62] First the acceptation, then the appeal.

Writing in the shadow of Immanuel Kant's Third Critique, critical theorists seem curiously burdened by the obligation to assert (and reassert) the artwork's frame as "decisive for aesthetics":[63]

> Jonathan Culler: "The frame is what gives us an object that can have an intrinsic content or structure ... [and] makes possible the distinctions

of the analytic of the beautiful, between formal and material, pure and impure, intrinsic and extrinsic."[64]

Stanley Fish: "Literature is language . . . but it is language around which we have drawn a frame, a frame that indicates a decision to regard with a particular self-consciousness the resources language had always possessed."[65]

Leo Bersani and Ulysse Dutoit: "Before they even begin to work, [painters] have already made their most confident gesture: the choice of a canvas that will contain their art, that will define their work *as* art by the distinctness of the frontiers between it and the untreated, unaestheticized world beyond it. . . . To make a frame is perhaps a way of announcing a belief in the possibility of a subject: in this privileged space, with its carefully drawn boundaries, something will take place."[66]

Walter Benn Michaels: "The opposition between what can be framed and what can only be experienced is foundational. The removal of the frame means that in Minimalism there is nothing within the beholder's field of vision that 'declares its irrelevance to the situation, and therefore to the experience, in question . . . Everything counts—not as part of the object but as part of the situation.' . . . The point here is not that art cannot succeed in being as oceanic as the quarry; the point is rather that it's the act of containment that produces the concept of art. It is the 'container' (the frame) that makes the art because it is the frame that renders much of the experience of the beholder (his experience of everything outside the frame) and thus his experience as such irrelevant."[67]

These critics accept the givenness of the frame as an "act" that transfigures matter into form, an "act of containment" necessary for matter or the world to be engendered with a significance, a meaning. A founding gesture of the artist. An act of sovereign assertion. The frame, in this sense, is decisive not only for aesthetics but for politics.

Frame is processual. Frame indicates a decision. Frame constitutes a politics. It represents a "force" subversive of what Michaels calls "the appeal of the literal," an appeal that has long concerned him (about which more in a moment) and one that is experiencing a bit of a resurgence across a range of aesthetic and theoretical projects, from Tom McCarthy's enthusiasm for "sheer materiality"—a materiality observed in the breach in his novel *Remainder* by way of its narrator's misguided financial and psychic investment in "reenactments" (Michaels writes, "They turn the world from a place where people are who they are and do what they do into a place where who they are and what they do has 'significance'")—to proposals by Sharon Marcus and me respecting "surface reading," where our impatience for allegorical reading is accompanied by a call for criticism to take up the project of description, stopping short of delving more deeply in pursuit of meaning (a claim Michaels takes to be correct but in only a limited way).[68]

This literalist turn is fueled by an enthusiasm for what McCarthy (after Simon Critchley) calls letting "matter matter" and echoes an earlier turn in the visual arts away from modernism toward minimalism, a turn toward "literalism" that Michaels and Michael Fried have been interested in since Fried's seminal "Art and Objecthood." As Fried writes on that turn:

> To the literalists [Donald Judd, Robert Morris, Tony Smith, and Carl Andre], what mattered or ought to matter were not the relationships within a work of art, as in modernist painting and sculpture, but the relationship between the literalist work and the beholder, as the beholder was invited to activate (and in effect to produce) that relationship over time by entering the space of exhibition, approaching or moving away from the work (or, in the case of Carl Andre's floor pieces, literally walking on them), comparing changing views of the work with an intellectual comprehension of its basic form, and so on.[69]

What matters in the case of literalist art is the encounter with "an object in a situation—one that, virtually by definition, *includes the beholder*."[70] Literalist art tries to occupy a position in which artwork and beholder are no longer separated by a frame. Literalism always involves "the removal of the frame" and partakes of a desire "that nothing should be framed," and these are the mistakes it shares with trompe l'oeil.[71] Such are the grounds of the literalist espousal of objecthood, and thus, for Michaels, here is the rub: *letting "matter matter" is not possible with any artwork, for with anything that is framed and not part of the infinity that is the natural world, one has to grapple with meaning.*[72] To the extent that we want the literal, then, in the view of Michaels and Fried, we can have the *punctum* ("a kind of ontological guarantee" of antitheatricality).[73] "The *punctum*," Michaels writes, "turns the photograph from a representation—something made by someone to produce a certain effect—into an object—something that may produce any number of effects, or none at all, depending on the beholder."[74]

The echoes here are to Roland Barthes's *Camera Lucida*, of course, where he distinguishes between a photograph's *studium* and its punctum. The studium refers to what the photographer tries to get you to see through the act of framing, the social and political legibility of all aspects of *what* has happened or is portrayed. Barthes writes, "I invest the field of the *studium* with my sovereign consciousness."[75] The punctum, for its turn, refers to the wounding detail that, only upon having been framed, establishes a direct relationship between the viewer and the object photographed. Punctum "rises from the scene, shoots out of it like an arrow, and pierces me," Barthes writes. "A photographer's *punctum* is that accident which pricks me (but also bruises me, is poignant to me)."[76] The punctum's "attraction consists precisely in its being by definition something that is in the photograph, despite the fact that the photographer has not himself meant to put it there."[77] It is unintentional and thus (in the phrase made famous by Fried) antitheatrical, for reasons it should not be hard to see: "If you don't (consciously or unconsciously) mean to be doing something, you can't possibly be doing it *for someone*."[78] The punctum's presence depends on the frame, on the act of framing, but it spills over the edge of that frame to the extent that it exists in excess of the photographer's intention or meaning. Piercing, pricking, bruising: the punctum is that which within the work speaks precisely to the presence of the *non*-worked, the accidental or non-intentional that interrupts the work's discursive and historical unity.[79] Piercing, pricking, bruising: Barthes's vocabulary gives us to understand the punctum as a precondition of non-sovereignty.

I said that the curious thing is that an Anatsui both has a frame (has to have a frame) and doesn't have a frame. Let's restate that. The curious thing about a work such as *Fading Cloth* is that its punctum (the prick or wound of thwarted expectations) precedes Anatsui's act of framing—or, better, the punctum is internal to the bottle caps themselves, their striving to "look like" a work of art in some ways precedes their being part of one. Abandoned by the side of the road, the bottle caps await someone's encounter with them, and Anatsui, encountering their punctum, oddly fails to mention it as one of the things that, to quote his own words, "went through my mind when I found the bag of bottle tops in the bush." The bottle caps announce their own difference from themselves by way of their shine. Framing is part of the internal structure of the trash itself, a sort of systole and diastole whereby the fragments both remove themselves from the flow of the material world and dissolve themselves back into it. It startles to consider the similarities between Anatsui's roadside encounter and Jacques Lacan's anecdote of the sardine can.[80]

You were right to hear a bit of the elegiac in my description of the trompe l'oeil mistake: *trash is the before and after of the artwork*. This way to describe the mistake gives us to understand that what is of value here, what may be of irreducible significance, is a process whereby the work *denies its own representational aspect*—where it gathers waste, congeals it into a form (or an identity), when the goal all along was to bring about that form's dissolution. This isn't merely clever. It isn't a move in the game of modernism. It's much more than that. It's a way of finding beauty, losing it, and, rather than getting attached to the loss, attaching instead to the movement from gold to trash. (Because of their self-consuming frame, the bottle caps, in their relation to the artwork, exhibit the qualities of "termite art"—of art that "goes always forward eating its own boundaries.")[81]

Through its perpetual metamorphosis, *Fading Cloth* fakes its own beauty, walks you *back* from form to matter as a way to walk you *through* the work itself. Confronting you with intensity and shimmer, the work would appear to want to affirm its beauty, but the perceptual drift back to trash that it affords presents another possibility entirely. Confounding the relation of before and after, cause and effect, the work wants you to see that there is beauty in the world, that that beauty has been there all along, and that we are able to see that beauty inherent in the fragments of the material world on account of their being taken out of it and placed in the proper frame. But to the degree to which the work succeeds in getting you to see that its beauty is ubiquitous, that it is actually *un*framed and part of the infinity that is the material world, the irony is (and this is why this work is the real thing) that it sets the conditions for its own obsolescence, for its ultimate irrelevance. It is beauty itself that, in the final instance, "eats away" at the boundaries of the work and smooths the path toward its disintegration. Beauty is a force for erasure.

In the split second when you recognize that your perception has been a mistake, when time dilates just enough to open up a bit of space between what you thought was gold and what you now recognize as trash, the form of the artwork disappears, and the bottle caps (for a brief moment escaping that form) return themselves to the world. In that trompe l'oeil blink of an eye, the artwork ceases to exist; it forces you to lose sight of its form, and what have disappeared along with this form are all of the symbolic "links" it was said to sustain. The connection to Africa. Gone. The slave trade. Gone. Liquor. Gone. The West Indies. Gone. Liverpool. Gone. What remains is one's presentness before a matter that quivers, flickers, and shimmers without you, without being pushed.[82] Frayed, fragile, denied the privilege of not being in the world because always already dented by the world. A world in which *Fading Cloth* has achieved what its name suggests—and faded away—is the very world that the work itself invites you to imagine. To see the beauty to which this work of art directs your gaze, in short, one would actually need a world without art.

Immurement: Mark Bradford

But they crossed, they survived. There is the epical splendor.
Multiply the rain's lances, multiply their ruin,
the grace born from subtraction as the hold's iron door
rolled over their eyes like pots left out in the rain,
and the bolt rammed home its echo, the way that thunder-
claps perpetuate their reverberation.

So there went the Ashanti one way, the Mandingo another,
the Ibo another, the Guinea. Now each man was a nation
in himself, without mother, father, brother.

DEREK WALCOTT, *Omeros* (XXVIII: 25–33)

I would describe the works that draw my interest as queer objects—queer in the sense that they feel inadequate to sustain the representational claims made on their behalf, queer in the sense that the work sets itself up to fail and, in producing its own failure, proves adequate to the appearance-in-disappearance that is the crux of the black radical tradition.[83] In my effort to understand how an artwork might afford such a form of de-realized social relation, how it may be the only means of making those relations apprehensible, I have found Leo Bersani—specifically, his essay "Sociality and Sexuality"—supremely helpful.[84] Bersani observes that contemporary criticism frequently works on the assumption that relations are grounded "in antagonism and misapprehension," which gives rise to a reactive politics focused on the past where the best one can hope for is the "transgressive reversal" or "antithetical reformulation" of social hierarchies.[85] For Bersani, this is the critical habit of psychoanalysis; it applies, as well, to habits of conceiving racial relation in the style of thought I have been calling "melancholy historicism." Homosexuality, on the contrary, Bersani associates with "new relational modes" that are for the most part "unforeseen" (following the thinking of Michel Foucault). Positioned "slantwise" in the social fabric, the homosexual introduces an always "improbable" set of relational possibilities: "The diagonal lines he can lay out in the social fabric allow these virtualities to come to light."[86] Such relations can be arrived at not adaptively nor transgressively but only by taking a foundational approach to relationality—that is, by way of a search for beginnings. Yet this birth of relation is not historical and cannot be said ever to have existed ("There was never any moment when we were not already in relation"); it therefore cannot be recovered. A "genealogy of the relational . . . a certain threshold of entry into the relational": this "moment" is so purely hypothetical that it can be arrived at only through the *performance* of antirelationality.[87]

To Bersani's way of thinking, abstraction in art makes this performance happen. The nearly "unpunctuated whiteness" of a Turner canvas, the uniform darkness of a Rothko: a will to abstraction epitomizes the erasure of figurality that the entry into relation demands. It is as if "the lines of movement in space that art represents could, as it were, be ontologically illuminated as they almost disappear within a representation of their emergence from nothing." Bersani continues: "Origination is designated by figures of its perhaps not taking place; the coming-to-be of relationality, which is our birth into being, can only be retroactively enacted, and it is enacted largely as a *rubbing out of formal relations*. . . . If art celebrates an originating extensibility of all objects and creatures into space—and therefore our connectedness to the universe—it does so by also inscribing within connectedness the possibility of its not happening. Relationality is itself related to its own absence."[88]

Bersani requires a figure of non-relationality to project the "still improbable" forms of connection that homosexuality augurs. A figure of non-relationality describes the form of the improbable that interests me here—the negative sociability spawned by the black radical tradition—for it is this appearance-in-disappearance that contemporary black art's "rubbing out" of formal relations seems intent on making possible.

In the canvases of Mark Bradford one can find an invitation to this project of self-divestiture, one embedded in the surface's actively working out of a crux, a critical thought happening in its very form.

In a Bradford work such as *PARATE* (plate 5) much of the critical activity is given over to textual fragments drawn from the accumulated detritus of the artist's South Central Los Angeles neighborhood. The fragment in Bradford triggers a dialectical process. On the one hand, it introduces a logic of part and whole that encourages a recovery of the fragment's past, but on the other hand, it defies and resists this desired historical recovery by reminding us that the putative "more" to which it points can never be recovered or fully experienced. Fragment corresponds not to a dynamic of part and whole, but to notions of disturbance, interruption, performance—it is "a question of function, a philosophical concept, a manifestation of a theory . . . a self-labeled 'thought.'"[89] Fragment frustrates, deranges, and disrupts the project of historical reconstruction. A Bradford canvas can thus be understood to have taken on its history in the form of the fragments it has had embedded, encrusted, and enfolded within its surface, and that surface, by ensuring our failure to get either outside of or beneath it, by demoting to inconsequence anything that is not it, forecloses the possibility of its being conceptualized as a surface that hides a depth accessible to thought. To phrase this in the language of formal relation, a Bradford canvas, often consisting of a great deal of text, attempts to forestall any further textualization of its surface, inhibiting its appropriation by those projects that would "ad[d] an explanation" to it or "pu[t] it into a frame" as a way to wrap up its meaning.[90] The work strives to close itself off, in short, and this is how it fails.

To fully appreciate the fragment's performativity, we must see the artist's material practice as an expression of it. Bradford builds his canvases by first gathering up various kinds of found paper, such as advertisements from the underground black economy, comic book pages, concert announcements, wheat-paste posters, advertising copy, album covers, and the like. He soaks this paper in water and other agents, rendering the rigid materials pliant. Finally, he adds further bleaching agents, caulking, plastic mesh, mason's string, polyester cord, packing cord, and other materials to generate effects of relief within the surface itself. Once the surface hardens, acquiring its bulk and solidity, Bradford then power sands the result to reveal the hidden strata underneath.[91] Let me add this: there is no appreciating a Bradford canvas independent of this violence against the semiotic order, no mere looking at the work outside the struggle to perceive how its effects have been made to come about: scraping, sanding, purging, and erasure as painterly performance. The work commands you to see and experience its effects in light of the forms of obliteration that have caused them to appear: a "grace born from subtraction," to recall the words of Walcott.

In *Paris Is Burning* (plate 6), the artist has taken a series of cardboard advertisements for Superdry jeans, lined them up horizontally, and attacked them with a belt sander to reveal the stenciled (and misspelled) phrase "FUCK STRAIGT PEOPLE." The ghostly traces of the original advertisements suggest a palimpsest, but in something of a visual paradox, the stenciled letters appear both to be on the same surface plane as the sheets of Superdry ad copy and to be the negative space created where a different type of print copy has been allowed to come through an overlying surface. There is a layer of found paper sandwiched between the layer that is closest to the viewer and the one on which everything else hangs, and this inner layer provides the negative relief that the eye needs to read the stenciled message ("FUCK STRAIGT PEOPLE"). But whatever writing that paper may have had imprinted on its surface, as language it is now obscured and indecipherable, forever lost to us.

There is a metaphor struggling to assert itself here, one central to recent critical theory, which it will be my intention to suppress. With a deconstructive genealogy in Jacques Derrida's writing "sous rature" and a psychoanalytic one in Sigmund Freud's "Mystic Writing Pad," the metaphor of text as palimpsest (L. *palimpsestos*, "scraped clean or used again") has come to mean that "the authority of the text is provisional, the origin is a trace" and the idea that a wax slab imprinting itself on the layer of paper signifies that "no consciousness is possible without the unconscious reaching out to the receptive apparatus."[92] The metaphor has its roots in the image of writing on parchment, "writing material or manuscript on which the original writing has been effaced to make room for a second writing," the previous writing bumping into and shaping the reading of the next layer of writing, though these figurations of surface and depth have done their part to muddle conceptual thought.[93]

On the observation that Bradford's surfaces consist less of multiple layers of writing than of multiple layers of paper, I would propose that we see these surfaces less as palimpsests than as structured according to a logic of immurement (*immure*: L. *mūrāre* 'to wall'; to shut up or enclose within walls; to imprison; to confine as in a prison or fortress). *What if we saw the surfaces themselves as part of a process of building a history, of archiving fragments from our everyday world and then walling them up, sealing them off, imprisoning them, and entombing them within layers of paper?* How does the politics of the artwork shift if, rather than a palimpsest, we thought we were looking at a deliberate act of immurement?

In *A Truly Rich Man Is One Whose Children Run into His Arms Even When His Hands Are Empty* (plate 7), one begins to see what is made available by a structure of immurement. As the belt sander clears away the various layers of the painting, we recover not so much an underwriting as an under*painting*—or, rather, not paint per se but a writing that has been turned into paint through the very act of erasure.[94] What was originally "print" finds itself transformed into "paint"; what was once a language has been drained of its semantic content. In this manner, in this movement back through the surface via erasure and obliteration, the work is not so much recovering a history, repairing a sense of damaged relation, or reconstructing writing and syntax, as it would if it were a palimpsest. Rather, it is drawing forth new relations, ones signaled by the image's transformation into something that resembles a map or a bird's-eye view of a city, in neither case corresponding to any territory currently in existence and thus unnavigable for sure. The canvas maps, in a way, Foucault's "improbable . . . new social relations"—itineraries never before seen that the eye now has occasion to follow.

Once sandpapered, the surface will occasionally reveal orphaned bits of writing, words that appear to have been part of some proposition or advertisement or sentence: broken syntax, orphaned phonemes, solitary syllables (plate 8). To understand the fragment's performance, we might take our cue from Mieke Bal: "As we look—teased by the representational illusion of the bits of glossy magazine—and try to hold the object each of them carries as its past before it was torn up, and as we try to surround it with a projected narrative that gives it meaning, *we fail*."[95] There is every hint that these fragments may find completion in what exists just beneath the surface, but everything that suggests the possibility of more depth is cut off from you, and as soon as you attempt to supplement for missing depth by attempting to link the fragments to a missing context, *you have left the work and therefore failed*: failed in the sense that it is quite impossible to "hold the object" on a scale larger than the object itself without that entailing a venture at reading far past the edges of the fragment, and thus past the limits of the work. The whole purpose of the work, it seems, again, is to help you to fail.

Accept Bradford's canvases as structures of immurement rather than palimpsests and it becomes hard to understand their purpose as one of returning to the plane of appearance something that has been lost. Rather, the accent seems to be on what is occasioned by loss, by disappearance, for when I stand before one of these canvases, dazzled by this resurrection of print into paint, I feel enjoined to imagine a relation to the written word that would not involve signification or the working out of meanings. I feel invited to rethink my relation to the written *world*—to rethink relationality as such—a thought experiment that feels "improbable" because it is so fundamental.

A Bradford canvas instigates and directs an inquiry into what it is saying by "holding in reserve the power to defy, resist, and derange the very process of discovery it engenders."[96] These are its conditions of aesthetic immersion. But even if I were able to resist the work's power to derange, even if I were able to restore all these fragments to their myriad historical contexts in a way that told a narrative of the origin of the work of art, and in a way that made that repressed and forgotten history "appear," the ineluctable demand spawned by the sheer beauty of its surface would still seem to be, Why should any of that matter?

Shattering: Gwendolyn Brooks

I said earlier that this book has its genesis in the encounter with a resistance within the dominant strain of Americanist literary criticism on race to calls to renounce the critical attachment to suffering and grievance that figures such as Édouard Glissant, Wendy Brown, and others have urged on the field. The resistance arises from fears that the admonition sound painfully close to a Nietzschean call for black Americans to simply "forget" the past, or a sense that it just seems impertinent to counsel expiation when a certain "shattering" experience defines the condition of being black. In Gwendolyn Brooks's "Boy Breaking Glass," shattering is precisely the point:

BOY BREAKING GLASS
To Marc Crawford
from whom the commission

Whose broken window is a cry of art
(success, that winks aware
as elegance, as a treasonable faith)
is raw: is sonic: is old-eyed première.
Our beautiful flaw and terrible ornament.
Our barbarous and metal little man

"I shall create! If not a note, a hole.
If not an overture, a desecration."

Full of pepper and light
and Salt and night and cargoes.

"Don't go down the plank
if you see there's no extension,
Each to his grief, each to
his loneliness and fidgety revenge.
Nobody knew where I was and now I am no longer there."

The only sanity is a cup of tea.
The music is in minors.

Each one other
is having different weather.

"It was you, it was you who threw away my name!
And this is everything I have for me."

Who has not Congress, lobster, love, luau,
the Regency Room, the Statue of Liberty,
runs. A sloppy amalgamation.
A mistake.
A cliff.
A hymn, a snare, and an exceeding sun.[97]

Two speakers: the boy of the title and a narrator. *Two voices:* one somber and dispassionate; the other ecstatic, intense, hortative. *Two moments in time:* a present of social inequality, beyond the pale of Congress, Hawaiian vacations, the Statue of Liberty, and a slave past invoked by way of the "cargoes" that dangles at the end of the third stanza and "the plank" whose edge threatens at the start of the next. *Two objects:* poem and glass. *Two acts:* the writing of poetry and the breaking of glass.

The poem, by opening up these gaps and fissures, raises the question of relation, of separation as a condition of relation. What are the relations between the positions that the poem establishes between past and present, boy and narrator, poem and broken glass? What form of relation is adequate to bridge these gaps?

Marc Crawford, a writer and editor of the literary journal *Time Capsule* and the person to whom the poem is dedicated, invited Brooks to write a poem about inner-city blacks surviving "inequity and white power."[98] Brooks wrote "Boy Breaking Glass" against the historical backdrop of the riots that rocked major American cities during the late 1960s—specifically, the events of the long, hot summer of 1967. Some of Brooks's most sensitive critics, finding the force of this history hard to ignore, read the poem not only as a record of violence against personal sovereignty, but as an attempt to repair that violence. R. Baxter Miller writes, "The sensitive narrator loves the Black boy because his art suits his socialization.... His aesthetic, a paradox, is both revolutionary and reactionary, since it *resurrects* for the future that humanism *lost in the past.*"[99] By this reading, the poem's agenda is reparative: the move to aestheticize the countless glass storefronts destroyed during that turbulent summer bridges the many social and temporal gaps represented in the poem itself.

But on return to those gaps, I am surprised by how stubbornly they resist reparative suture. I might imagine the poem as a *conversation*, in light of its two distinct voices, but nothing feels particularly dialogic about what unfolds, as the speakers appear to talk past rather than to each other. There is some suggestion in the fourth stanza's reference to "grief" and "loneliness" that a *shared melancholy* might serve as adequate ground for their relation, but even here the boy strikes a note that sounds more like a critique than a defense of melancholy: "Nobody knew where I was and now I am no longer there." *I am no longer there.* This feels like a very pointed and barbed riposte, an effort to point out the folly of locating mastery "where it was not" or where we can't have it, or of staging an appeal for one who, "no longer there," either "cannot or will not hear the protest."[100] Do me this one favor, the poem seems to ask: do not base your relation to me or to my boy on a sense of recognition, on some assumption

My Beautiful Elimination 57

that our pain is shared. "Each to his own grief, each to / his loneliness and fidgety revenge." There feels to me to be one last possibility, the *pedagogic*, with the narrator redirecting puerile and misguided energy toward more productive arenas and pursuits (out of "a sloppy amalgamation" and toward the "sanity" of "a cup of tea"). If anything, the poem fails to repair the world, and its energy flows in the opposite direction, from shattered glass back into the poem itself.

Allan Grossman's thoughts on what he calls "virtual poetry" and "the bitter logic of the poetic principle" provide an aid to thought here.[101] A poem is virtual, in Grossman's argument, because there is an unbridgeable gap between what the poet wants the poem to do and what it can actually do, and it is structurally foredoomed, or "bitter," because of this virtuality. "The lyric poet is moved to make a poem because she is dissatisfied with the human world, the world of representation. But the stuff of poetry, language, invariably reproduces the structures it aspires to replace."[102] The poet's wish is to get beyond the finitude of the given, of history, but that song of the infinite is always compromised by the finitude of its terms. "*Bitter* is the sentiment of undecidable conflict," then, "between the will to (re)build the human world, and the resistance to alternative (heterocosmic) making inherent in the materials of which any world must be composed."[103] A poem is thus "always a record of failure because you can't actualize the impulse that gave rise to it without betraying it."[104] Terminally prone to such failure, a poem can do what it does only *to itself.*

Brooks's "broken window" looks to be doing precisely this sort of work.[105] Certainly, the broken window serves as the poem's foundational "cry of art"; it is what has inspired the wish to rebuild the human world (the first line of the poem says as much). But the shattering it precipitates moves *through* the poem like a stain or a metabolic enzyme, fracturing the chains in the poem's syntax along the way. I will have much more to say about that amalgam of stuff in the poem's closing lines, but first I must address what brings that heap about: the movement of the broken window's shattering, or again, specifically, its metabolic undertone as enzyme.

If one accepts syntax as the circulatory system of the verbal artifact, a precondition for the fluidity of sound and sense, it is hard not to see those colons in the first stanza producing a particular effect:

Whose broken window is a cry of art
(success, that winks aware
as elegance, as a treasonable faith)
is raw: is sonic: is old-eyed première.

There is something conspicuous about these colons, a failure to mask that they've stepped in for the commas that ought to reside in their place, and colons substituted for commas do a more forceful job of regulating (just short of arresting) the flow of sound and sense, slowing them down, breaking them up. The movement is peristaltic (colons are colonic). Moving on to the third stanza, one has a sense that the hendiadys of "salt and pepper" has had its spine broken; what was a unity has had its parts strewn across the surface of the stanza by a proliferating series of "ands." The assonance between "night" and "light" finds those sonic effects dispersed, as well, as if "night" has been instructed to find another place to reside in the poem—or again, in the fifth stanza ("Each one other / is having different weather"), where the first line makes syntactic promises the second line can't keep, to form a kind of syllepsis. A note and a hole.

"I shall create! If not a note, a hole / If not an overture, a desecration." The boy announces a creative aesthetic that reads like some long-undiscovered black law of thermodynamics—a vision of art as neither more nor less than energy transformed. Creation and destruction, making and unmaking differ in degree rather than kind, and thus neither classification nor definition is an appropriate tool of assessment. Rather, what matters are the shifts in degree that represent perspective. Brooks's poem commands attention within the current argument on two accounts. First, it invokes slavery, but without melancholy, insistent in its refusal of connection and empathy, classification and judgment. Second, the poem is unbiased in its insistence on broken glass as art *and* trash, "note" *and* "hole," and the insistence on the irreducibility of broken glass suggests the refusal of black culture to resolve itself into any particular sense ("overture" or "desecration"). This is not classification and definition but perspective, hovering, adjacency.

I espy in Brooks's poem an attempt to abide the overdetermination of the object by first conjuring that object *in the only way that a poem can*—a broken glass whose every aspect, from its objectness to its brokenness, it is alone the *poem's* to conjure—and then, by a curious twist, failing to remain sovereign over that object. Perhaps even more curiously, the poem not only conjures an object to effect its own undoing. It plays out that undoing (that non-sovereignty) in submission to an object that can barely be said to exist. The poem conjures a "broken window" that is an object only to the extent that it has been converted into a "syntactical substance," one that is most material when it is deranging the poem itself.[106] More an imaginary object than a real one, the broken window has strongest affinities with the "mistake" (if one were to choose from the elements of the amalgam to which it gives rise), sharing with it the insolidity of an abstract noun that has no reference in the real and, in that way, like a mistake, forming at best a sort of theoretical or hypothetical object. A note and a hole. It is hard for me not to think that the poem's work is to imagine an object and then, subjecting itself to that object's shattering effects, relish in the plethora of aesthetic possibilities to which that act (disintegrating in the extreme) gives rise—a mistake, a cliff, a hymn, a snare, an exceeding sun. "A sloppy amalgamation." The poem seeks to get you attached not to the loss in fact, but to the movement, to divestiture or what it announces as the "runs"—the movement from monumentality to amalgam, the enzymatic movement of broken glass through the poem itself, a *metabolic* movement that makes and unmakes the poem. The poem issues an invitation to want *all* of the aesthetic possibilities opened up by its shattering form and asks of me, the critical me, only if I can bear to have a method that honors the overdetermination of the object—all of the possibilities afforded once the fragments of its "broken window" embed in that "exceeding sun" (the poem able to preserve and transform that energy by observing its own internal law of thermodynamics).

I would wager that Brooks settles on the adjective "sloppy" not in judgment of the boy and his act of creation, but out of a desire to suggest mere adjacency, as if to promise a proximity arrived at without any critical intervention or aesthetic judgment. Either would produce orderings that, if not sloppy, would at least have their own discernible logic, as if to suggest that running indiscriminately between these objects is life's dessert, a movement adequate to the goal of surviving "inequity and white power." The "success" of this "cry of art," in other words, is to leave us in that space of adjacency, where "broken glass" has replaced itself with "a sloppy amalgamation"; an object has replaced itself with a plurality of objects. The question that should present itself most urgently at this juncture is why the maximalism of hortative rhetoric and heroic gestures should resolve in what feels like a relatively humble laying out of objects. In short, *how can we explain such minimalism?*

From Watts to Ferguson, the cliché of black rage often has been, "They're only hurting themselves."[107] The poem "Boy Breaking Glass" operationalizes this claim and shifts it to a different register. The aesthetic turn here is not, however, a mere empty formalism; it is, rather, an affective reworking, an immanence, transforming reading into an ascetic practice of self-emptying.

You may sense where this is heading.

It is my view that "Boy Breaking Glass" anticipates—from within the very crucible of a political ferment that would nurture a contrary set of historiographical and political impulses—what some, in reference to recent literary critical trends, have called "the incrementalist turn," a critical turn toward minimal variations, fleeting perceptual experiences, and small nonevents "below or marginal to normal appearance" that figure the possibility of "fleeting relief from the pressure to endorse what [Immanuel] Kant calls the world 'as is.'"[108] This attunement is in fact a reattunement, as the critics annexed to this turn, who generally are allergic to the immodest and melodramatic claims of agonistic critique, intend to reverse "the maximalist claims of transnational and transchronological turns, which seem at times to assume the literalism of a direct political, or emancipatory, impact on the world or even past worlds" (or, at the very least, to run on the belief, as I put it elsewhere, "that to study [the] past is somehow to intervene in it").[109] Ripe for inclusion in this critical moment are the "exercises in minimal affirmatives" that make an appearance in the late work of Roland Barthes and Eve Kosofsky Sedgwick—"vindications of a right to demand little," in the words of Anne-Lise François, which one discerns in Barthes's emphasis on the noncommittal ("of leaving one's force in place, without directing or finalizing it") in *Le Neutre*, and Sedgwick's "laying out" or enhancing of the range of critical responses to aesthetic objects (beyond received styles of perfection, demystification, or transgressive reversal) in *Touching Feeling*.[110]

Perhaps nothing better illustrates what we might gain in embracing Brooks's "sloppy" adjacency than Sedgwick's turn, in *Touching Feeling*, toward planar relations that are *beside* rather than behind, beneath, or beyond. Sedgwick sensed late in her career how the prevailing style of ideology critique would frequently project a topos of depth followed by a drama of exposure. A successful reading exposed either the "residual forms of essentialism lurking *behind* apparently nonessentialist forms of analysis" or the latent and "oppressive historical forces hiding *beneath* or *beyond*" manifest aesthetic content.[111] Behind, beneath, beyond. Such spatializations of thought have tended to underwrite a dualistic thinking it has been hard for critique to shake: cause and effect, subject and object, presence and absence, manifest versus latent, surface versus depth, and so on. The term "beside," Sedgwick argues, offers a way out of this critical cul-de-sac, because "a number of elements may lie alongside one another, though not an infinity of them."[112] "Beside" presents a fund of resources, "compris[ing] a wide range of desiring, identifying, representing, repelling, paralleling, differentiating, rivaling, leaning, twisting, mimicking, withdrawing, attracting, aggressing, warping, and other relations."[113] The additive and accretive prevail in the open-source program of "beside"—its goal is "to assemble and confer plenitude on an object that will then have resources to offer to an inchoate self."[114] These exercises intend alternatives to the well-trodden paths of agonistic critique: its acquisitive urges, perfective ambitions, and imperatives (under the banner of suspicion) to expose concealed truths. Sedgwick presents "besideness" as critical comportment: as one of her more sympathetic and astute observers notes, it is a critical posture that wishes to occupy neither "a position of superior vantage, looking down at art; nor [one] of inferior vantage, looking up to art."[115] It is a comportment that is "not *about* art" at all, but "*inside* art"—a comportment that involves thinking *like* a work of art.[116]

2

| ON FAILING TO MAKE THE PAST PRESENT |

No resurrection can be anything other than a prelude to ultimate erasure.

ALAIN CORBIN, *The Life of an Unknown*

Currently, it passes for an unassailable truth that the slave past provides a ready prism for apprehending the black political present. It can be hard to acknowledge that that past was not always thought to explain the present.[1] Under the sway of habit, many scholars have staked their own critical agency on a recovery of the political agency of the enslaved, making the slaves' "hidden history" a vital dimension of the effort to define black political goals in terms of a model of representation. The slave past has thus come to assume a primacy in black critical thought that it did not necessarily have previously, entailing a particular black intellectual conception of politics—but slavery's political perspicacity should not be taken to imply universal applicability.

In fact, why has the slave past had such enormous weight for an entire generation of thinkers? Why must we predicate having an ethical relation to the past on an assumed continuity between that past and our present and on the implicit consequence that to study that past is somehow to intervene in it? Through what process has it become possible to claim the lives and efforts of history's defeated as ours either to redeem or redress? If we take slavery's dispossessions to live on into the twenty-first century, divesting history of movement and change, then what form can effective political agency take? Why must our relation to the past be ethical in the first place—and is it possible to have a relation to the past that is not predicated on ethics? It is time to ask these questions again, though I am far from having answers to them.

The idea of continuity between the slave past and our present provides a framework for conceptions of black collectivity and community across time. This idea, a proxy for race, nests within it a significant thesis: the present most African Americans experience was forged at some historical nexus when slavery and race conjoined, and in the coupling of European colonial slavery and racial blackness, a history both inevitable and determined proved the result. Nonetheless, with terms of coalition and political solidarity increasingly difficult to articulate, a sense of racial belonging rooted in the historical dispossession of slavery seems unstable ground on which to base a politics. My goal is merely to clear some space for a black politics that is not animated by a sense of collective condition or solidarity.[2]

The project of rethinking racial belonging might well begin with forms of unbelonging, negative sociability, abandonment, and other disruptions that thwart historical recovery. These premise a kind of social connectedness on what anthropologists term "social abandonment," the idea that the social destinies of the unwanted "are ordered."[3] The traces of abandonment frustrate historical recovery (or the attempt to solicit the past for present purpose) to the extent that they signal "an insistent *previousness* evading each and every natal occasion," especially when the names proposed for that natality are either "race" or "blackness."[4] One critical origin for these ideas comes from queer theory—specifically, the ethics of what Leo Bersani calls an "anticommunal mode of connectedness," or, in Daniel Tiffany's phrase, "a sociological sublime magnetized by abjection."[5] These strains of thought not only acknowledge the radical alterity of the past but announce that "it may be necessary to check the impulse to turn . . . representations [of the past] to good use in order to see them at all."[6] This chapter invites contemplation of the gains to be derived from extending the queer acknowledgment of non-relationality between the past and the present to the racial case.

An understanding of slavery in relation to the politics of abandonment (as articulated especially in queer critique) responds to the calls of David Scott and David Lloyd to invigorate discussions of the usable past with the idea of failed futures. Extending the insights of Reinhart Koselleck's *Futures Past*, Scott argues that the political projects begun by earlier revolutionaries and historical predecessors can be neither continued nor completed. It is futile to attempt to redeem the past, as formerly dominant cognitive and political categories can no longer "have the same usefulness, the same salience, the same critical purchase, when the historical conjuncture that originally gave [them] point and purchase has passed." Any revisionary practice of historical criticism in the present must unfold against the backdrop of "the dead end of the hopes that defined the futures of the anticolonial and ... postcolonial projects."[7] Faced with such foreclosed possibilities, we have only our present conjuncture, only our current predicament. Writing in much the same spirit, Lloyd argues that the figures in the past with whom we crave a connection possess their own "specific and unreproducible orientation to the future," and our present, rather than representing the fulfillment of that projection, is more likely "the future imposed on the dead by past violence." The restlessness of the dead, Lloyd proposes, "stems from the lack of a future fit for them."[8] To be historical in our work, we might thus have to resist the impulse to redeem the past and instead rest content with the fact that our orientation toward it remains forever perverse, queer, askew.

With its goal of replacing holding with letting go, clutching with disavowal, this chapter runs against the grain of work advanced under the banners of "recovery" and "melancholy." The goal is to specify some of the limits to these modes of critique and to propose other ways to think about loss than have been offered by the melancholic turn in recent African-Americanist and African-diasporic cultural criticism.

A Thesis on the Philosophy of History

As for when slavery emerged as the constituent object and metaphor in African American studies, I would nominate 1988 as an important turning point. In the advent of that year, significant works had appeared that placed the slave's narrative and habitus at the center of the symbolic order that Hortense Spillers would name "the American grammar book": Houston Baker's *Blues, Ideology, and Afro-American Literature*; Hazel Carby's *Reconstructing Womanhood*; Henry Louis Gates's *The Signifying Monkey*; Valerie Smith's *Self-Discovery and Authority*; and Spillers's own "Mama's Baby, Papa's Maybe."[9] The paragon literary text of this moment was, of course, Toni Morrison's *Beloved*, which won the Pulitzer Prize in that year—around the time the Schomburg Library of Nineteenth-Century Black Women Writers also began to appear. Soon after, Paul Gilroy's *The Black Atlantic* (1993) promoted slavery to a unified field theory, which anchored the black experience of modernity in "a continued proximity to the unspeakable terrors of the slave experience."[10] Gilroy's compelling claim for the connection between "living memory and the slave sublime" served many of the same critical ambitions as the Morrisonian proposal that "all of it is now, it is always now."[11]

Gilroy's "black Atlantic" provided Atlantic studies with a solid academic brief, inspiring the shift toward a historiography that was recursive and generally athwart the established practice of writing history as a rational, developmental national narrative. One successor has been Ian Baucom's *Specters of the Atlantic* (2005), about which I will have more to say. In another, *The Reaper's Garden* (2008), Vincent Brown offers a powerful revision of the view (rooted largely in Enlightenment ideals of revolutionary overcoming) that the threat of death in slavery presents the signature face of a one-dimensional and top-down exercise of power. Instead, Brown argues, slaves and their antagonists struggled over the meaning of death and out of that process forged a society from a human catastrophe—they spun "hope from fear and community from chaos."[12] In *Lose Your Mother* (2007), Saidiya Hartman compellingly substitutes the affect of her own encounters with traces of the slave past for the dispassionate analysis that prevails in most histories of slavery. Her embrace of slavery's dispossession as the generative condition of African Americans ("We may have forgotten our country, but we haven't forgotten our dispossession") corrects for a vindicationist strain in several generations of work in social history that has tended to find only resistance to slavery's oppression worthy of historical recovery.[13] Add to these books Alexander Byrd's *Captives and Voyagers* (2008), Peter Linebaugh and Marcus Rediker's *The Many-Headed Hydra* (2000), Cassandra Pybus's *Epic Journeys of Freedom* (2006), Rediker's *The Slave Ship* (2007), Joseph Roach's *Cities of the Dead* (1996), James Sidbury's *Becoming African in America* (2007), and Stephanie Smallwood's *Saltwater Slavery* (2007) and one gets a picture of how incredibly rich this critical moment has been.[14] Collectively this work has enabled the traumatic events of slavery and middle passage to suffuse the vastness of the Atlantic itself as a general historical framework and condition.

As a model for a "counter-culture of modernity," black Atlantic history substitutes recession, vanishing, and dispersal for the expansionist conceits of Enlightenment-inspired histories. As Elisa Tamarkin summarizes this shift, "Atlantic history is a fantasy of relation that is not transmitted across time so much as embraced through the imagined origins of material from a vanished world."[15] Within the predominant modes of Atlanticism, the data of historical experience are connected by the geography that disperses them—or, to phrase the matter in an affective way, the history of the black Atlantic comes into existence only through loss and, in turn, can be sustained only through more tales of its loss.

Displaced and subordinated in this moment were traditions of thought that took "the legacy of slavery" to be at best a psychological inheritance that needed to be rejected and at worst a reactionary explanation of black character. "There is no a priori necessity," wrote Orlando Patterson in an essay I quoted earlier, that "because a people has experienced slavery, they will all share a legacy of slavery." Instead he proposed that the next great cultural advance of mankind will involve the rejection of tradition and of particularism:

> The Blacks in the Americas now face a historic choice. To survive they must abandon their search for a past, must indeed recognize that they lack all claims to a distinctive cultural heritage, and that the path ahead lies not in myth making and in historical reconstruction, which are always doomed to failure, but in accepting the epic challenge of their reality. Black Americans can be the first group in the history of mankind who transcend the confines and grip of a cultural heritage, and in so doing, they can become the most truly modern of all people—a people who feel no need for a nation, a past, or a particularistic culture, but whose style of life will be a rational and continually changing adaptation to the exigencies of survival, at the highest possible level of existence. . . . Should blacks succeed in doing this, they will indeed make themselves unique. In a world where every group still strives to be unique, to preserve its past, and to hold sacred the principle of continu-

> ity, a group which discards uniqueness and spurns tradition will by that very fact become unique in a truly revolutionary way.[16]

Morrison no doubt played a major hand in smothering Patterson's vision, directing attention within black studies straight toward the slave past and diaspora. It would not be going too far to add that her winning of the Nobel Prize in Literature in 1993 positioned *Beloved* to go on to shape the way an entire generation of scholars conceived its ethical relationship to the past. For a distinctive, if not singular, moment in the history of the interpretive disciplines, a novel managed to set the terms of the political and historiographical agenda. The rise of *Beloved* moved the entire field of literary studies to a central place within African American studies, and this move redressed what Eric Slauter describes as literary criticism's "trade deficit" with the discipline of history.[17] With Morrisonian poetics as a guide, the black Atlantic provided a way to make history for those who had lost it and thus secured the recent rehabilitation of melancholy in cultural criticism.

Whereas mourning, in Sigmund Freud's account, represents the successful acceptance of loss, affiliated with "the repetitive divestment of what has passed,"[18] and with a capacity for dawning or awakening, melancholy marks a refusal of such detachment and a persistent identification with the lost object.[19] The melancholic historicism that is currently resurgent celebrates the commitment to remain "faithful to the lost object" and to "refus[e] to renounce [the critic's] attachment to it."[20] Morrison has given countless descriptions and reminders of what we have at stake in melancholy. As she proffers in one of her many interviews,

> Well, that's the carnage. It can't be abstract. The loss of that man [Halle, in *Beloved*] to his mother, to his wife, to his children, to his friends, is a serious loss and the reader has to feel it, you can't feel it if he's in there. He has to *not* be there. . . . The notion of the devastation of those families is real, and you can't communicate how serious it is without indicating that at some point the system will stop you. . . . Usually it's an abstract concept—but I and the reader have to yearn for their company, for the people who are gone, to know what slavery did.[21]

To "know what slavery did," to make it not simply an object of experience or epistemology but the grounds of memory, Morrison resists a view of loss as the property of an immediate circle of kin and encourages us to claim that loss for ourselves. These are the historical ethics that underwrite "rememory," Sethe's idea that the slave past is "never going away," for "the picture is still there and what's more, if you go there—you who never was there—if you go there and stand in the place where it was, it will happen again; it will be there for you, waiting for you."[22] This formation of history as memory, as well as the compelling critiques of it, should be familiar to most readers.

A good deal of recent scholarship on slavery has readily accepted a literary model of historiography, with *Beloved* as the paradigm. Literariness is key here, for narrative and the act of reading together sustain the feeling of loss. It is a feeling that literature produces, not history, because literary texts, as intentional objects, possess silences and ellipses that are structural, whereas silence in nonliterary discourse is not always the sign of an intention. Consider the sentence that structures the last chapter of the novel: "This is not a story to pass on."[23] Morrison adopts a trope of negation—paralepsis, or *occultatio*—that is common to a poetics of revelation, one that recalls God's promise to Moses of a shielded revelation in the book of Exodus:

> And he [the Lord] said [to Moses], I will make all my goodness pass before thee....
> And he said, Thou canst not see my face: for there shall no man see me, and live.
> And the LORD said, Behold, there is a place by me, and thou shalt stand upon a rock:
> And it shall come to pass, while my glory passeth by, that I will put thee in a cleft of the rock, and will cover thee with my hand while I pass by:
> And I will take away mine hand, and thou shalt see my back parts: but my face shall not be seen. (Exodus 33:18–23)[24]

God denies the full presence of his divine glory as a response to Moses's limited ability to withstand the fullness of divine presence. In *Beloved*, paralepsis is called on to gentle the reader's experience of the terror of slavery, and, as in the Bible, the novel's koan-like phrase ("This is not a story to pass on") emphasizes the recovered story by appearing to pass over it. Yet such tropes of negation become adequate to the project of history writing only on the turning of the past into an object—"an object of cathexis . . . something that might be lost or found, defended or surrendered"—that is, on the hypostatization of the absence of evidence as the evidence of absence.[25]

"The past is never dead. It's not even past."[26] This famous quip by a famous character in one of William Faulkner's less than famous novels has settled in as a commonplace in contemporary criticism. Of the recent work in slavery studies, Baucom's *Specters of the Atlantic* represents perhaps the most tenaciously committed statement of this axiom. Baucom argues that our traumatically hyper-financialized contemporary moment repeats a capitalist moment from the past, rather than embodying a final stage in the historical unfolding of capitalism (as it might be scripted in a progressive Marxist narrative). The signature of that earlier moment was the incident that occurred aboard the slave ship *Zong* in 1781, when Captain Luke Collingwood threw 132 sick, dying, and healthy slaves overboard to recover their value under the terms of the vessel's insurance bond. What made the *Zong* incident signature was an act of vanishing achieved, not in the moment in which the captain exercised his homicidal intent, but in a prior moment in which finance asserted its power to transform the slaves "from bearers of personhood to bearers of an abstract quantum of value."[27] Baucom argues that risk capitalism's predication of loss value as a condition of value as such continues to the present era, which "inherits its nonimmediate past by intensifying it, by 'perfecting' its capital protocols, 'practicalizing' its epistemology, realizing its phenomenology as the cultural logic 'of the entire social-material world.'"[28] Quoting Walter Benjamin's *The Arcades Project*, Baucom concludes, "It is not that what is past casts its light on what is present, or what is present its light on what is past; rather . . . what has been comes together with the now to form a constellation."[29]

There is an accepted truth at the basis of all this—not the idea that the past is made available only through the present, or David Scott's injunction that "morally and politically what ought to be at stake in historical inquiry is a critical appraisal of the present itself," but, rather, the notion that the past simply is our present.[30] In this view, history aims not to come to terms with the past *"wie es eigentlich gewesen"* (as it really was) but to discern structural inequalities that are repeated in the present.[31] The idea that the persisting past reduces the present to its mere repetition captures the essence of Benjamin's "Theses on the Philosophy of History," particularly his statements of the *Jetztzeit*. Historical materialism consists in continuing, reanimating, and completing the political projects begun in the past: "Only that historian will have the gift of fanning the spark of hope in the past who is firmly convinced that even the dead will not be safe from the enemy if he wins. And this enemy has not ceased to be victorious" (Thesis 6).[32] Fanning the flames of hope, however metaphorical, transforms the historian from a subject who provides an account of the past into a historical figure in it, "thereby casting the present-day historian in the role of potential hero, or even freedom fighter."[33]

This critical tendency can be felt even in work that does not march behind the banner of Benjamin's "Theses." For Colin (Joan) Dayan, to see the past as autonomous and knowable is to conspire with a legal sorcery that has engendered and exploited slaves and criminals, the oppressed and the outlawed, as exemplars of a negative personhood that the liberal state requires. A past that is periodizable is also, paradoxically, unhistorical; it ignores, for example, "that the shame that is Guantánamo has a history." To recover "a perplexing legal history too often lost in linearity," Dayan seeks "to make readers complicit in a world without demarcations such as those between the past and present. . . . For those who adhere to a myth of progress or faith in reason, the continuum between past and present must be made to be deeply felt."[34] For Dayan, critique involves seeing ourselves in league with the victors of history and thus motivated to disavow that identification. Hartman has similarly proposed (in an erstwhile formulation) that historical empathy ought properly to attach to the vanquished. The "time of slavery" is neither to be resigned to nor confused with the past, for "the distinction between the past and the present founders on the interminable grief engendered by slavery and its aftermath."[35] In this largely affective conception of history, "the injury of slavery and the long history of defeat" can be regarded as events that have "yet to end."[36] ("Can one mourn what has [not] yet ceased happening?" she asks.[37]) She solicits empathy with history's defeated through assertions that time has shown no movement: "then and now coexist; we are coeval with the dead."[38] I have no quarrel with the ethical imperatives and political commitments that motivate much of this work, but I do want to interrogate what seems a pretty consistent tendency here: the promotion of a feeling to an axiom. Morrison's ethic ("the reader has to feel it, you can't feel it if he's in there") has been transformed into a critical method (e.g., "the continuum . . . must be made to be deeply felt"; "the distinction . . . founders on . . . interminable grief").

As in Baucom's *Specters of the Atlantic*, Benjamin's Angel of History may be taken as the spirit motivating this enterprise, the angel who, with face "turned toward the past" and bearing witness to history's "piling wreckage upon wreckage," longs "to stay, awaken the dead, and make whole what has been smashed" (Thesis 9).[39] These words, called on often to represent the theater of the historical situation, inspire in historians the hope that, through various means, they may linger as Benjamin's angel had wished, as well as a faith that the power of redemptive historiography need never come at the price of severing the present's relation to the past.[40] To repeat my earlier questions: why must we predicate having an ethical relation to the past on the idea that there is continuity between that past and our present? What kind of history would permit one not only "to stay" with the dead but to rouse them from their sleep?

Bersani might answer, "a history that has forgotten how much it shares with theology," for a good deal of criticism written in the redemptive vein starts from a conception of modernity as postlapsarian. Following Benjamin's division of the world into "something inauthentic and familiar" and "something authentic but lost," the melancholic privileges, as he does, whatever has been resigned to the category of loss.[41] Here the office of art is to afford a kind of repetition that "repairs inherently damaged or valueless experience."[42] In taking on Benjamin's theologically tinged vision of a "lost wholeness" or "fallen being" as a spur to critique's will to redemption, critics who write in the Benjaminian vein have enshrined an authentic origin as something not merely to be regretted but to be resituated as the telos of all historicist thought: "It is a mode of being toward which we can aspire, which can be 'restored' (or perhaps even realized for the first time). The conceptual visibility of this ontological preference depends on its *presentation* in historical metaphors, its translation into a temporal priority."[43] In short, Bersani assesses, the commitment to the idea that art has a redemptive function depends "on a devaluation of historical experience and of art."[44] In line with his view that redemptive criticism is a refusal or inability to reckon with the true alterity of the past, an apt reckoning with historical experience ought to require a failure or short-circuiting of the redemptive function.

If in what I have said to this point it has felt as if I were writing the epitaph to the *Beloved* moment, then your instincts have been admirably astute. Indeed, Morrison herself has set the conditions for this elegy, for her novel *A Mercy* (2008) opens the door to an appreciation of the slave past as it falls away, as that which falls away—a separateness resistant to being either held or read in melancholic terms.[45] The form of *A Mercy* thus undoes a crucial aspect of the historical ethics that *Beloved* played such a pivotal role in bringing about. The critical question remains whether the undoing of the affective history project is something Morrison intended—that is, whether it is something done by rather than to her. The answer to this question rests on an assessment of Morrison's relation to the thesis that our present was forged when slavery and race conjoined to create a history that was both inevitable and determined. All epitaphs aside, if it feels at times as if all we can do is think through Morrison, then so be it.

Morrison's Undoing

It was hard to figure out how to die.

TONI MORRISON, *A Mercy*

Beloved issues from a call for an accounting: a daughter's death at the hands of her mother compels a universal demand for judgment. That call may be universal, touching those who knew or knew of Margaret Garner, who know or know of Sethe, but it solicits a judgment that most people cannot satisfy. Morrison would admit as much, proffering the book as a necessary prop for the only person who could: "I got to a point where in asking myself who could judge Sethe adequately, since I couldn't, and nobody else that knew her could, really, I felt the only person who could judge her would be the daughter she killed."[46] Governed by this need to account for death, *Beloved* secures the idea (figured in its ghost) that we may strive to restore meaning to death as an epistemological goal. In this regard, *Beloved* reads as the paradigm of a critical moment, of the general drive in critical theory to make death an aspect of knowledge, to "recover" it for knowledge, as a means of articulating how the past structures our present: for instance, social death, civil death, "necro-citizenship," necropolitics, *homo sacer*.[47]

A Mercy shares with *Beloved* a concern with the destruction of slavery, the production of slavery, and the mother-daughter bond. A wound in that bond inaugurates both plots, constituting, for Morrison, a mythic gesture from which all others flow. Morrison makes separation and fearful estrangement a condition of relation, so kinship appears not a given in the world but something forged. But in *A Mercy*, rather than kill the child,

Morrison hands her off, and this decision, by leaving much else intact, seems deliberately to negate the infanticide in *Beloved*. In the abandonment of death Morrison has made abandonment itself a primary concern.

That concern is with the fate of Florens, a sixteen-year-old slave girl who had been adopted eight years earlier, at her mother's urgent prodding, by a homesteader, Jacob Vaark, in partial settlement for a debt owed him by a Portuguese slave trader, Senhor D'Ortega. It is 1690, and Vaark takes Florens from Chesapeake Bay to "Mary's Land where [he] does business," and to his seat in that unstructured land, Milton.[48] There Florens joins a group of women who orbit around Vaark, or "Sir," as she calls him: his wife, Rebekka, or "Mistress" to all the servants; a Native American named Messalina, who had her name "shortened to Lina to signal a sliver of hope" (47); and Sorrow, a young woman who survived a shipwreck and was raised by the sawyers who discovered her before she joined the Vaark sodality. A "united front of dismay" (53), the women form a society of orphans when Vaark succumbs to smallpox, with Rebekka the widow at their center. "Belonging to no one," they "became wild game for anyone" (58). The Vaark community also includes the white indentured servants Scully and Willard, lovers to each other; "the blacksmith," a free black man and Florens's sometime lover, whom she is sent to retrieve in the hope that he might cure Rebekka when she contracts smallpox; and Florens's mother, referred to only as *minha mãe* (Portuguese for "my mother") and most palpably present in a dispatch addressed to her estranged daughter that closes the novel.

Florens's abandonment by both mother and lover, and the women's abandonment before the world generally, though critical themes in the novel, appear also to be something of a symptom *of* it, a trope for the standoffishness of the novel itself. Morrison's prose has often isolated readers by depriving them of the usual coordinates in time and space. *A Mercy* intensifies that aesthetic: the chapters oscillate, confusingly at first, between Florens's first-person narration and a third-person omniscience, with the apparent goal of isolating the book itself, leaving it, too, with no place in the world. The novel reads like an archive of dead letters. What distinguishes these dispatches, however, is that their failure to arrive comes from having never been sent. The chapters written in the first person are letters in the figurative sense—that is, they read like autonomous documents that, taken together, make up a weave of failed attempts by the characters to address one another (Florens to the blacksmith, the minha mãe to Florens). Thus, a novel about the late seventeenth-century rise of racial slavery appears to resuscitate the literary genre that arose at that time: the epistolary novel.

Failed scenes of address pervade the novel. For instance, Florens's narrative, written on the walls and floor of a room in the unfinished mansion that Vaark started before his untimely death, resembles a note that one might leave a roommate or a lover, which stubbornly waits for an addressee to come to it: "You will have to bend down to read my telling, crawl perhaps in a few places" (158). No one is likely to do so, of course, as the house stands not simply incomplete but empty, Rebekka having prohibited all from entering her husband's "profane monument to himself" (44). The failure of this address is perfectly complete, incapable of being undone, because the blacksmith cannot read it ("You read the world but not the letters of talk" [160]), and the minha mãe will not ("All this time I cannot know what my mother is telling me. Nor can she know what I am wanting to tell her" [161]).

Moreover, failed address is signaled as often by a dispatch's form as by its fate. The novel's first sentence ("Don't be afraid") sounds as if it is addressed to the reader, but it is not: it is addressed to the blacksmith. It is some time before Florens is revealed as the speaker, long after she has further confounded any possibility of sending or receiving the right message by endlessly musing about her narrative's proper genre. "You can think what I tell you a confession, if you like" (3), she invites, only to undercut that solicitation with the observation that "confession we tell not write as I am doing now" (6). Confession or not, the chapter certainly anticipates the irresolution of those to follow. Clarity ostensibly emerges at the end of the narrative, when mother explains to daughter the motives behind her abandonment, but here, too, confusion seems to be the order of the day, for although the last chapter reads like a self-exculpatory epistle, it is unanchored, without identification of source or recipient, which leaves the reader wondering where this bit of writing *is*. Reading *A Mercy* requires an attentiveness to who is speaking, and to whom, and through which medium, and in which genre, but then the novel evades capture by resetting all of these conditions of utterance with every turn of the page.

Curious to know how readers orient themselves in this environment, I have asked a number of friends, colleagues, and students what they think *A Mercy* is all about. The responses fall largely into two intriguingly contradictory camps. One set of readers notes a world in which racial distinctions have not yet formed and much is up for grabs. "1682 and Virginia was still a mess" (11), the omniscient narrator observes early on, a perspective confirmed on the ground by many of the characters. Vaark sees himself as "making a place out of no place" (12), and Scully takes himself to have stepped into a world unformed, one "before Creation . . . [with] dark matter out there, thick, unknowable, aching to be made into a world" (156). And while the indentured whites languish unpaid for their labor, a free black such as the blacksmith does not: "[He] had rights . . . and privileges, like Sir. He could marry, own things, travel, sell his own labor" (45). The other camp of readers registers characters motivated by a desire to escape a world where racial formation already exerts a determinative force. "Barbados" was the name of this force, for as Florens's mother confesses, "It was there I learned how I was not a person from my country, nor from my families. I was negrita" (165). But in abandoning Florens to a new world in which "there is no protection but there is difference," mother unwittingly enmeshes daughter in the very tangle of forces she hoped to escape (166). Florens's Virginia is choked with "new laws . . . eliminating manumission, gatherings, travel and bearing arms for black people only; . . . granting license to any white to kill any black for any reason; [and] compensating owners for a slave's maiming or death." These laws have their intended effect in that "they separated and protected all whites from all others forever" (10). As John Updike observes, in affirmation of this second view, *A Mercy* "circles around a vision, both turgid and static, of a new world turning old."[49]

Race, then, is also something of an orphan: present but precarious, unburdened, ungrounded, not yet operating to its maximum potential. Or, better, the racial scripts and beliefs that are said today to make up slavery's legacy have yet to settle into a lexicon. Jostling nominatives describe what the characters think they are perceiving—"all whites," "the Europes" (54), "the 'Black Man'" (109), "children of Ham" (92), "negrita," "Afric" (111). Likewise, race has not yet congealed into protocols of ownership and dominion. Sorrow was "accepted, not bought, by Sir" (51), though she is African; Lina, was "bought . . . from the Presbyterians" (52), though she is Native American; Scully was "leased to the Synod" (153), and Willard was "sold for seven years to a Virginia planter" (198), and each in turn was "exchange[d] for land under lease from Sir" (7), although both are white. One can even hear race's impotence in Florens's rotten English:

> These thoughts are sad in me, so I make me think of you [the blacksmith] instead. How you say your work in the world is strong and beautiful. I think you are also. No holy spirits are my need. No communion or prayer. You are my protection. Only you. You can be it because you say you are a free man from New Amsterdam and always are that. Not like Will or Scully but like Sir. I don't know the feeling of or what it means, free and not free. But I have a memory. When Sir's gate is done and you are away so long, I walk sometimes to search you. (69)

Defiant of grammatical rule, Florens's speech confounds temporality and agency. It appears intended to disorient readers. And lacking the signatures of both black grammar and idiom, it sounds like no currently recognizable Bajan dialect, slave cant, or Southern seaboard creole. Like so much else in this novel, it is of its own world.

Morrison has produced a text of marked ungeniality, even by the measure of *Beloved*. In that comparison, *A Mercy* appears less invested in either unmasking or bearing witness to historical trauma than in securing what Stanley Cavell calls a kind of "reproachfulness" by building a set of "defenses against being read," seeking no given assembly of hearers or readers and repelling every approach.[50] In that regard, perhaps nothing could better figure the novel's standoffishness than what Florens describes as her "talking on stone" (6). But why should a novel about a denial of filial claim work so hard to make it hard for us to claim it? For us to get a handle on it or feel directly addressed by it?

Now might be an ideal moment to return to the ripple that sets the plot moving—Florens's abandonment by her mother—and to consider it in the light of failed futures and recovered pasts. It is almost a commonplace that the filial bond between parents and children protects a future of mutual belonging, with abandonment irreducibly figured in *A Mercy* as both betrayal and denial of that future. Florens's mother takes pains in her chapter to explain that the abandonment was always in the name of something, if not better, at the very least other—that "a mercy" was specifically intended to serve the end (if it could serve only one) of "difference." The future—ascetic and reduced to such compressed aperture—feels like "no future" at all.[51] In this it comes to resemble Scott's "failed future," whose lack of specifiable or retrievable content is precisely as it was meant to be, without redemption or redress, completion or authentication. This rigorously attenuated future serves to concentrate the abandonment's force and consequence ("the insistence, the pulsive *force*, of negativity"),⁵² and we can begin to perceive the effect of that force on the novel's narrative synopsis: a character, in giving up a future with her child, abandons not only that child but also any attachment to the idea of a future with her. The *child*, the *future*, and *kinship* are all claimed by the gesture of abandonment and promote that gesture to the status of narrative cause. Morrison arguably wants to add *novel* to this array, to the extent that she insinuates abandonment within the textual capillaries of *A Mercy*. But why leave the reader stranded along with the characters?

A Mercy's ungeniality implicates the reader in the novel's internal structure of foreclosed claims. It secures a set of "counter-transferences to its desired and feared 'readers,'" a set of resistances to "their (fantasied) transferences to it."⁵³ What end does the ghost of *Beloved* serve, if not that of making possible the text's investment in the reader's transferences? For what else does the ghost's ontology function, if not to form a bridge between the book's characters and its readers and thus make the act of reading an act of judgment in (and of) the historical past? But where *Beloved* calls us back to witness in the mode of melancholic historicism, *A Mercy* abandons us to a more baffled, cut off, foreclosed position with regard to the slave past. And where *Beloved* requires transference from readers to characters to construct an ethical relation to the past, *A Mercy*'s transposition of abandonment from character to author (from minha mãe to Morrison) raises a bulwark or countertransference against that very possibility. If I reconsidered my narrative synopsis in light of what I am calling Morrison's "transposition," it might read this way: a character gives up a future with her child, and this abandonment, through its transposition from character to author, allows the novelist better to represent the past as the particularity and crisp actuality of a thing or relation that used to exist. We are meant to harbor that relation without looking at it too closely, to see it as something other than a haunting. If *Beloved* incites melancholy, *A Mercy* incites mourning—the very kind of mourning, as I have suggested, that affiliates with a waking or dawning rooted in repetitive divestment. By representing history as a recalcitrant orphanhood, the novel awakens us to the past in its concretion.

A Mercy conjures up a moment of pure possibility, before a decision has been made and history has begun to rumble down the path that leads to us. To get here, Morrison settles on a moment not when things come together, but when things fall apart. But how can the effort to get back to another beginning amount to a reversal of the melancholy attachment to beginnings as such? With the ambiguous genitive of this section's title—"Morrison's Undoing"—I am implying that there are at least two plausible accounts of the relation between *A Mercy* and *Beloved*. One assumes continuity between the texts (and takes the undoing to be something done to Morrison); the other assumes discontinuity (and takes the undoing to be something done by her). In the first case, the argument is that *Beloved* preserves the view that, once slavery couples with race, a history both inevitable and determined results, and all the pathos in *A Mercy* derives from the novel's recognition that history could have been otherwise. Those predisposed to accept that the effect of an author's oeuvre is cumulative might also be inclined to accept this view. But this is not my inclination. I believe that there is a deliberate disjunction between the texts and that Morrison here demonstrates the limits and ultimate impossibility of the affective history project she so capably inspired. In *A Mercy*, Morrison touches down at the moment before slavery acquired its "legacy"—that is, its power to claim us. By doing so, she arrives counterintuitively at a moment before the origin, at a moment before slavery coupled with race with determined results. By embracing precariousness and indeterminacy, Morrison has espoused Nathaniel Mackey's concern, in *Bedouin Hornbook*, with an "insistent *previousness* evading each and every natal occasion" and made this her concern, as well.[54] In *A Mercy*, unlike in *Beloved*, once the filial bond is broken, its affiliative form (i.e., racial kinship) appears no more ready-to-hand as a substitute. We seem less held together by race here and more held together in our abandonment.

Returning to meditate on race and slavery, by refusing to make the slave past the progenitor of the existential condition of black people, or of black people alone, Morrison throws into question the idea that the slave past provides a ready prism for understanding and apprehending the black political present. Morrison invites us to think about what it means to be held by the grip of slavery but not race. The past is here to be appreciated as a falling away—slavery to be appreciated in the failure to make its racial legacy present.

Is it possible to imagine, then, that Morrison's effort to articulate the formative moments of blackness, slavery, and racial identity is simply the flip side of their death (the falling away of their conjuncture) in our historical present? Are we being invited to ponder how thoroughly we cannot conceptualize the order in which we are living—to see that we have arrived in a world of "no protection but . . . difference"?

| PART II |

A HISTORY OF DISCONTINUITY

Is alcoholism today the same social object that it was, say, under the Nineteenth Amendment and prohibition?

For what length of time are cruising patterns among male homosexuals along the various social margins of the city likely to remain invariant?

What sort of institution is suicide, and how has that institution changed in the United States between the early 1930s and the late 1990s? . . .

What lets us consider such questions—today—as falling under a certain concept of history?

    SAMUEL DELANY, "Historifying Marginal Practices"

| INTERSTICE |

A Gossamer Writing

The coming chapters respond to a scholarly proclivity that has never felt quite right to me: the tendency for those who trawl through the archive of slavery to perceive it as either wonderfully capacious or utterly bereft and to apprehend the voice of the enslaved as either startlingly eloquent or disturbingly mute. Toni Morrison once remarked, on the topic of African American slave culture, that "no slave society in the history of the world ever wrote more—or more thoughtfully—about its own enslavement."[1] Yet on the evidence of the archive, no scholar who attends to slavery in the broader Atlantic context seems willing to extend this claim of fabled abundance. What is the ontology, then, of this thing we're calling "the archive"? Jacques Derrida spurred this question when he observed in *Archive Fever* that if we find nothing, we will find nothing in a place. It might be worth it to recall, on a similar note, Jacques Lacan's claim that the perception of lack or surplus is an effect produced within the symbolic.[2] What, then, is the symbolic order (or the order of history) served by the production of these perceptions of surplus and lack? Does it continue to make sense to think of the project of accounting for slave culture in terms of this systole and diastole of surfeit and scarcity?

At least since the publication of John Blassingame's *The Slave Community* in 1972, the historiography of slavery has been structured around a logic and ethic of recovery.[3] Some scholars have sought to uncover sources of strength and evidence of self-organization on the part of the enslaved, while others have been motivated to discover how African slaves participated in a broader "hidden history" of the revolutionary Atlantic.[4] Following George Lefebvre's model of "history from below," most have taken the evidence of hidden history to be "abundant"—in the literature of the fugitive slave, in the musical form of the spirituals, in the material artifacts of everyday life, even in testimonies delivered long after the institution's demise.[5] The challenges for the field arise less from a sense that this evidence never existed than from the fact that it had been overlooked and ignored by a previous generation of scholars. The archive is taken to be a rich repository of material from which one may recover and reanimate the lives of the enslaved. Nell Painter encourages us to continue this work, to "look beneath the gorgeous surface" that defenders of the institution presented to the world and "pursue the hidden truths of slavery."[6] Her topography of hiddenness, while it sounds purely metaphorical, in fact distills a core methodological assumption of the field: that the "hidden history" of slavery exists in a "beyond" that has been interrupted by representation. The fiction of the archive is one of plenitude.

This assumption extends even to the work of those who see recovery as impossible. Ian Baucom, Saidiya Hartman, Stephan Palmié, and others are vexed *by* the problem of recovery, for the archive serves as much to impede as to enable our access to the enslaved. The enslaved are so entangled with the institutions that denied their humanity and with the machinery that annihilated their being as to be nearly impossible to approach with anything like the required rigors of historical recovery. Hartman asks, "How does one recuperate lives entangled with and impossible to differentiate from the terrible utterances that condemned them to death, the account books that identified them as units of value, the invoices that claimed them as property, and the banal chronicles that stripped them of human features?"[7] This fiction of the archive is one not of hidden richness but of poverty.

Decades of thinking within the parameters of "the recovery imperative" have predisposed us to read the archive in terms of quantifiable loss, where the imperative consistently has been to give "voice to the voiceless," to write the "hidden history" of resistance, or to "demystify" structures of inequality. These perceptions have only intensified of late with the resurgence of melancholy in cultural criticism. But I would be remiss if I failed to observe that the scholarly yield on both sides of the recovery imperative has been nothing short of astounding.

It warrants observing, however, that both the recovery imperative and its melancholic counterpoint appear to share a presumption that we can know in advance what will be the reward of pursuing them as methods: the redemption of the dead, the returning to the dead of all that has been denied by history. But here is where we encounter the problem I seek to address: it has been too easy to equate the recovery of the past with a recovery from it, to take our methods as indistinguishable from our ethics. Recovery floats, Lisa Lowe writes, between "a sense of the retrieval of archival evidence and the restoration of historical presence," on the one hand, and "the ontological and political sense of reparation . . . the possibility of recuperation, or the repossession of a full humanity and freedom, after its ultimate theft or obliteration," on the other.[8]

With regards to ethics, I wonder whether, having gone to such lengths to stake the fate of the past on the present, we haven't placed too rigid a set of constraints on the ethical relations we can have with the past, forcing ourselves to hold on to the belief that there is something better, something brighter—for figures in the past, that would be us; for us, that would be a future beyond present melancholy. I want to put into question the consonance between our critical predicament and the condition of the enslaved on which so much of this work depends, for I believe that we have reached a point at which it has become difficult to distinguish the conditions of our own critical agency from the political agency of the enslaved. This gets me to the question of method.

From Buried Essence to Metalepsis

Wittgenstein invited us to consider the possibility that philosophy inherited from science a biased understanding of logical thinking as a looking past the surface in search of explanation; a search "to the bottom of things" founded on an ideal of hiddenness.[9] Toril Moi has argued that when Wittgenstein declares that in fact "nothing is hidden" (Wittgenstein, *Philosophical Investigations*, no. 435) or that meaning is in plain view, he "doesn't mean that everything is obvious, in the sense of easily grasped, self-evident or banal." What he means is that we shouldn't go around thinking that "language itself—our sentences, our utterances—hides something just because it *is* language."[10] Moi means to extend this insight to the practice of literary criticism, whereas for me it inspires thoughts on the forensic imagination as relates to the archive.

We create ideals of hiddenness against which we then aggress "in order . . . to dwell on concerns about how the subject can become more expressive and more 'authentic.'"[11] These ideas of the hidden motivate my concern for one of the recovery imperative's implicit maxims: the notion *that what is hidden is more authentic than what is visible for all to see*; that the most significant truths are not immediately apprehensible and may be veiled or invisible. It is not hard (or even wrong) to feel the encroachment of this "buried essence" model of authenticity in discussions of slavery, where it has come to mean, at base, that slave culture is cunning, always shrouded in a cloak of secrecy, because open, "disinterested" knowledge was impossible "in a society with an extreme imbalance of power."[12] And while this may be true in the firsthand experience of the enslaved, the presumption of hiddenness forces me as a scholar to hold the same suspicious relation to slave knowledge as did the inquisitors, planters, and colonial administrators who left most of the evidence of it—a kind of historical "transference," as Dominick LaCapra has termed it, in which we reproduce in our own work the dynamics about which we write.[13] One need only consider here Vincent Carretta's work on Olaudah Equiano, which asks the same question as contemporaries of the man who believed him to be a fraud: Who are you?[14]

An idea of the hidden lies at the core of the reading practice in slave historiography. This practice is in fact two—practices that are at variance with each other and at times conflated. I refer to the two types of "deep reading" much in dispute within the recent "reading debates." In the first kind of deep reading, the point of critique is to demystify, and its goal is forensic, to peel back obfuscating layers of representation with the aim of revealing structures of inequality (its genealogy points to Paul Ricoeur's "hermeneutics of suspicion"). In the second kind of deep reading, critique struggles to conspire with, and be complicit with, the object. Here the goal is to offer procedures whose effect will be to conjure what was lost (its genealogy points to Ricoeur's "hermeneutics of recollection").[15] In the debate over "structure" and "agency" in the constitution of the lifeworld of the enslaved, the description of structure is aided by a "hermeneutics of suspicion," and the recovery of agency is aided by a "hermeneutics of recollection." The tension between these hermeneutic alternatives is, of course, a part of all interpretive practice, but blindness to what distinguishes them leaves us at risk of mistaking the *recovery* of the past for its *redemption*, and when that happens, it isn't long before one hears claims for our politics that sound immodest and celebrations of our critical agency that ring melodramatic.

As it can be hard to check the impulse to redeem the past, to relinquish the desire to set it right, I want to explore what it feels like to write about figures who resist our attempts to restore them to wholeness, who resist our projects of historical recovery—figures for whom our present does not (and cannot) represent the future they imagined. In terms of ready modes of accounting for such people in the historical record, what they would require is certainly not history writing as we know it but a writing in full awareness of the negativity that labors to undo any historical—or descriptive—project. Rather than think of the archive as a serendipitous or immutable repository of texts and objects (what simply happens to come in, or, in the phrase of Carolyn Steedman, "that which will not go away"[16]), I shall make the case for a conceptualization of the archive as process—attending principally to archivization as a process whose goal is both to preserve some record of black culture and to deform it in the process. My goal is to account for the culture of the enslaved in a way that does not inspire hope of recovery—the very hope that stands behind efforts to write "history from below" and to restore documents to their proper "context." I will want to suggest that what in fact makes black culture in the archive historical is less its power to "reference" the past than the simultaneity of excess and emptiness that it affords. These shifts will serve to advance my larger thesis: *that it is a foundational paradox of the archive to shape black culture as indispensable to and yet hopelessly beyond the reach of cultural preservation and historiographical recovery*. It is my intention to show that our challenge isn't to successfully recover the past so much as it is the more modest task of simply *describing* something that appears to be vanishing.

The structure of this book serves this end. It is presented as two halves in analogical relation, in which the first half addresses a disturbed object and the second extends that thought to a disturbed archive. The instability and apocalypticism of El Anatsui, Mark Bradford, and Gwendolyn Brooks returns, in this respect, modeling the self-dissolution of the subject. The problem of the archive is less a question of the ontology of the object of the past than the ontological *disturbance* the archive produces, less a concern with having or losing one's object (with the presence or absence of the thing slavery and supremacist culture are alleged to have caused me to lose) than a recognition that the objects of black culture are, to coin a term, "anarchival."

To account for this ontological disturbance, I propose a shift from a historical to a rhetorical mode, from a mode of writing that keeps reintroducing a sense of loss in the hope of retrieval to one predicated on "knowing what withholds itself from the possibility of being known," much like the tropes of metalepsis, paralepsis, irony, and litotes, which involve a negation or an awareness of not saying something.[17]

In a metalepsis, a "word is substituted metonymically for a word in a previous trope, so that a metalepsis can be called, maddeningly but accurately, a metonymy of a metonomy."[18] A present effect attributed to a remote cause, metalepsis has staunch adherents in the precincts of minor history. Advocates for metalepsis as analytical tool see it as embodying the spirit of queer analysis because of "its willful perversion of temporal propriety and the reproductive order of things."[19] It is precisely on this score that others have given it a bad rap. In "The New Unhistoricism in Queer Studies," Valerie Traub delivers a searing indictment of metalepsis in queer theory on the grounds that it supports a tendency toward "analogical argumentation."[20] A "compressed chain of metaphorical reasoning" that "links A to D but only by eliding B and C," metalepsis allows scholars in search of a queer historical analytic to slide from one conceptual domain to another—among psychic, social, temporal, formal, and historiographic registers that ought to remain discrete.[21] As one advocate defends the practice, "Metalepsis telescopes time so that the far appears near, and vice versa."[22] None of this adds up to a cogent defense of metalepsis as a mode of queer argument, according to Traub; rather, it reads like magical thinking. Under this rhetorical sleight of hand, "the ground of critique . . . keep[s] shifting."[23]

One might well accept Traub's view that queer unhistoricism seeks to capture "a range of relations that do not aspire to any intelligible identity," her claim that "readings . . . are not the same thing as history," and a good deal of her critique of queer uses of rhetoric and still find analytical purchase in the trope of metalepsis. It remains my sense that the work of unhistoricism could be more fruitfully pursued with a slight but important tweak in the conception of metalepsis, forsaking its emphasis on time and causation to stress the agency of the letter. When Gerard Genette gives us to understand metalepsis as a "taking hold of (telling) by changing level," he helps us to achieve just that.[24] Metalepsis, in this respect, is the narrative situation in which a narrator or character outside the diegetic universe intrudes "into a frame in which they do not belong," a transition or change of level "achieved only by the narrating"—for example, when the author brings about the effects he celebrates; when the author entreats the intervention of the reader; when "characters escap[e] from a painting, a book, a press clipping, a photograph, a dream, a memory, a fantasy," and other extraordinary effects.[25] "All these games," Genette concludes, "by the intensity of their effects, demonstrate the importance of the boundary they tax their ingenuity to overstep, in defiance of verisimilitude—a boundary *that is precisely the narrating (or the performance) itself:* a shifting but sacred frontier between two worlds, the world in which one tells, the world of which one tells."[26] Metalepsis is, in this sense, a "troubling" play with boundaries; its inversions precipitate in us a sense of "uneasiness," though for Genette they may also produce "an effect of strangeness that is either comical . . . or fantastic."[27]

In the final chapters of this book I will not be concerned with sustaining a rigorously formal understanding of metalepsis. Rather, it is my wish to follow this trope only into insights it may afford regarding the linguistic traces of the enslaved in the archive. We discover in Genette's metalepses "shifting" ground that we might celebrate rather than decry, a framework in which to hold the *disturbances* in the archive to which I will be calling your attention: anecdotes set down in the archive of Africans who, beyond all rational explanation, blew themselves up in the midst of negotiations with European traders; rumors in the archive of slaves who whispered of a "black woman" who was queen of England and of slaves who believed that their "friend," the "King of England," had given them their freedom, a wish his underlings refused to execute. Did slaves actually say such things? Were these words put in their mouths—and, if so, were they put there *before* the slaves decided to rebel or after, once their masters sought evidence of their conspiracy? What would it look like to "get to the bottom" of these questions, to ascertain their truth? Flush with errors, the anecdotes in the coming chapters will strike you as odd or misplaced and, therefore, from my vantage, uniquely amenable to the frame of metalepsis understood as rhetorical matter out of place. My hope is that these anecdotes will also strike you as comic, fantastic, otherworldly, and that you will persist in feeling the strangeness and intensity of their effect—their semantic *failure*—choosing not to abandon that strangeness for the sake of discerning their meaning. In the hope of retaining this sense of the infelicitous, of the nonsensical, my design for a metaleptic history will take the form of a writing that, as Michel de Certeau once phrased it, "succeeds in failing" by moving "from a *can not say* . . . to a *can say* . . . by way of a *can say nothing*."[28] I want to avow our ability to say nothing and will offer suicide and rumor as signatures of this gossamer writing, drawing on evidence from the slave archive that presents as tropological—that is, people and utterances that appear to be not available for recovery, but metaleptic, the figure of a figure.

3

| THE HISTORY OF PEOPLE WHO DID NOT EXIST |

I have no desire for death
no suicide ever had

watch me vanish
watch me

                                          vanish

watch me

watch me

                                          watch

SARAH KANE, *4.48 Psychosis*

A Suicide Bombing in 1659

Tasked by his bosses at the Dutch West India Company to account for his many years of service to them, Willem Bosman asserts that they would be nowhere without him. In his *New and Accurate Description of the Coast of Guinea* (1703), we are given to understand that in the decades preceding his arrival on the Gold Coast in 1688, the Dutch were failing on all fronts to secure their interest in the burgeoning gold trade. Every trick had been used to beat back foreign powers and other interlopers, and every effort had been deployed to establish (as Bosman framed the matter) "absolute Dominion over the *Blacks*."[1] The erection of Fort Ruychaver in 1654 went a considerable way toward the achievement of the first goal, for the decision to build the fortification farther up the Ankobra River than other European traders had yet managed to reach provided the Dutch with a real chance both to stay ahead of the competition and to circumvent the ubiquitous African middlemen. As to the goal of "absolute Dominion" over their African partners, the Dutch, Bosman laments, "never could yet accomplish their End" (8), and one particularly curious incident, involving the fort in question, exemplifies the "very Tragical manner" by which the Dutch completely "lost [their] Footing" (12) in the region's gold trade.

According to the first English edition of Bosman's text,[2] that demise would come at the hands of the "Commander in Chief of the *Negroes*," who had long been "closely Besieged by our Men" (12). When this commander was finally ready to "Trade with the Beseigers," he summoned them to his location, "hinting" of his intentions "by Signs" (12) that no one was likely to ignore, though most would have found them bewildering. In a gesture to rival the call of the Sirens, the commander began to shoot at his assailants "with Gold instead of Bullets" (12). Soon after, the Dutch and the Africans ceased their aggression and sat down to negotiate the proper way to deal with "the Afflux of Gold" (12) that was then making its way through the delta. Each negotiator discourses in the company of his slaves. However, in the middle of the negotiations, Bosman reports, the commander "blew up himself and all his Enemies at once . . . putting an end to our Siege and his life" (12). Only one slave lived to bear witness. He belonged to factors of the Dutch West India Company and told a tale of conspiracy sealed in death. The African chief, by his account, had "encouraged [his] Slave . . . to stand ready with a lighted Match, with which he was to touch the Powder when he saw [his master] stamp his Foot"

(12). This single directive, Bosman recollects, "the silly Wretch but too punctually perform'd" (12).

The African chief's act of self-destruction potentially means a wide variety of things to us, from nihilism to resistance, all of which depend on how we understand the matter to have been framed in Bosman's first draft of history, and how deeply we believe our histories to be enjoined by that original framing. To my understanding, that initial framing can at best be described as irresolute.

From one perspective, the suicide appears generative, history making in the flesh. Bosman analogizes the unanticipated act to "*Sampson* revenging his Death upon his Enemies" (12), calling to mind the most memorable example in the Old Testament of suicide as a creative act. Samson, you recall, once brought within the temple's walls by his persecutors, the Philistines, asks God for the strength and permission to avenge what they had done to him—and with that permission granted, he brings about the temple's implosion, killing himself, the Philistines, and a number of innocents besides: "So the dead whom he slew at his death were more than those whom he had slain during his life" (Judges 16:30). I find Talal Asad helpful in pondering the creative dimensions of this act. Through the act of religious suicide, Samson redeems not only himself but also his people's freedom; through this act, Asad writes, "A new political world is initiated," and "a new collective beginning" is inaugurated.[3] When Bosman admits that such crimes "hath very perniciously weakened the Power of all the *Europeans* on this Coast, and filled them with apprehensions not altogether groundless" (10), one senses the emergence of this new political order. But here is where the other frame emerges, the frame that suggests that the act cannot be analogized to anything at all and is thus not creative in the least.

For "Samson" substitute "Antigone" or "Sethe" and one begins to sense that what provoked the Europeans' apprehension was the absolute singularity of the act, the completely unverifiable motive behind it, the utter isolation of the person who committed it. Could even biblical analogy have been enough to assuage the traders' "fear and trembling" here? It was Kierkegaard, after all, who proposed that "all true ethico-religious acts ... cannot be justified by any appeal to pre-existing standards," cannot be analogized in the interest of arriving at a meaning or used as a basis for further extrapolation.[4] Such acts are solicitations of thought that insist on where thinking must stop. To the mind of a seventeenth-century chronicler, a suicide bombing appears absolutely unprecedented in the way it deranges colonial power. It was, if anything, a riddle—as beguiling to the rational mind as the prospect of trading gold with someone who appears to believe that it has greater value as ammunition. It produces a crime without a criminal, a tear in the fabric of time through which the offender who brought it about disappears. It is outlandish, out of this world. Bosman's words were foreboding on crimes such as this one. "If this Bloody Fact escaped unpunished," he writes, "no Body is here secure of Life" (10).

Could the bombing at Fort Ruychaver, therefore, have been an "instance" of anything, knowable in that regard? Or might Bosman have heard reports of Africans doing similar things that, though befuddling to the imagination, nevertheless spoke of an incipient collective consciousness? Reports of slaves who would eat enough clay to induce serious vomiting and weakness, and through this self-inflicted pain liberate themselves from proceeding farther along the coffle's slow march toward the sea? Of slaves' hanging themselves, or starving themselves, or drowning themselves to end their living apocalypse; of holding their breath or swallowing their tongue in attempts at self-strangulation? Could Bosman make something of the bombing in light of all this?[5] Or was it, rather, the ultimate sign of what was to remain uncoded, withheld, cryptic?[6]

Colonial incursion, slavery, suicide bombing: does the act of self-wounding bear an antagonistic relationship to the logic of the system, or is it an *expression* of that logic? Was it an eloquent act of martyrdom or a nihilistic act of self-immolation?

These are not the questions I want to ask. These are the questions I want to question. I want to probe a certain habit of mind that is triggered when we deal with issues of slavery and death—a tendency to toggle between positions of martyrdom and nihilism, agency and dispossession. I want to entertain a different type of question: to ask whether self-immolation presents a problem for history *writing*; whether a suicide bombing can even be made available to historical consciousness. In this, I am following the lead of historians who see their discipline as uniquely challenged when it comes to writing about people who "consciously suppressed themselves in acts of self-immolation."[7] Is the narration of self-abnegation, the attempt to give it meaning, such a challenge for history as to define its very limit? Could suicide represent a singular principle of negativity at the center of the order of history?

I believe that the answer to these questions is "yes"; that we have always known this but have pretended otherwise. Or, rather, in our attempt to make death in slavery "mean," we perhaps have been too insistent in our demand that these acts be evidence of *something*—of either a culture of resistance or a culture of nihilism and social death. To my mind, however, unaccountable events are being conscripted to ends for which they cannot give account. I thus have to wonder whether, in our fervent search for historical precursors who feel in line with our aspirational hopes, we are failing in our effort to "recover" the very subjects who, we claim, compel our interest.

My proposal would be to stop short of interpreting the suicide at Fort Ruychaver and pause to consider the sorts of problems it poses *for* interpretation. But even if I were to convince you of why this might be a compelling desire, that would still leave open the issue of what is left for us to do as readers of texts. In other projects ("surface reading," most centrally), I have been trying to figure out frameworks for reading that postpone interpretation, that defer saying what the bewildering acts we stumble upon in the archive mean and leave the gnawing dissatisfactions alone to see whether they might be fluid and continuous with other social experience:

— With the recognition that most people leave this world without explaining their motives;
— The recognition that most people leave no written record of their lives, and thus the lives of unlettered slaves, far from anathema to most experience, actually appears to exemplify it;
— The recognition that we are alone; that our severance from one another and our resistance to being made present to one another can in fact be a condition of our humanity (the precondition of a sense that you are not me, that you are not a projection of me); and, finally,
— The recognition that separation, fearful estrangement, is what makes relationship (makes relationships) possible.

My intention is to preserve a sense of latency in my objects; to hold in abeyance the impulse to demystify them. In this I take my inspiration from a single sentence in Friedrich Nietzsche's *On the Use and Disadvantages of History for Life*, in which he cautions that "a historical phenomenon, known clearly and completely and resolved into a phenomenon of knowledge, is, for him who has perceived it, dead."[8] Nietzsche's project is to unburden history writing of both presentism and teleology, to free it from the assumption that the past was what it was in any given moment for the sake of our being what we are now, and to show how human life requires us to adopt both a "historical" and an "ahistorical" perspective on ourselves.⁹ To take up his call to untimeliness, I have had to ask myself, as a historically minded literary critic, what specific orientation toward the past allows it to remain still alive to my critical senses? What orientation forestalls the moment in which a "historical phenomenon" resolves into a "phenomenon of knowledge"? These are the questions that motivate my desire to write "the history of people who did not exist"—not the history of people who line up with our hopes and frustrations, but the history of people we have the hardest time not rushing to imagine as our predecessors; a history of people with whom we fail to identify, who appear stuck in the past beyond the reach of our historical categories; a history of people whose minds we can acknowledge but cannot know; a history, in short, of those who are unfit for history.

Unfit for History

> If "impersonal intimacy asks of us what is the most inconceivable thing: to believe in the future without needing to personalize it," the belief becomes at least somewhat conceivable if we can believe, to begin with, in an impersonal past.
>
> LEO BERSANI AND ADAM PHILLIPS, *Intimacies*

Vincent Brown's *The Reaper's Garden* has enriched our vocabulary for talking about death and power and our sense of the role of the dead in any attempt to write about slavery. I find the idea at the heart of that book as indisputably powerful as it is persuasive—that slaves and their antagonists forged a society from a human catastrophe, that death itself was not ruinous but generative, a fount for the human creativity necessary to spin "hope from fear and community from chaos."¹⁰ Death was not the face of a one-dimensional and top-down exercise of power. Rather, Brown espies, death occasioned a dynamic in which catastrophe gave birth to creativity.

During the final minutes of an evening panel on the social death thesis at a conference on the historiography of slavery, Brown shared with the audience the primary sources of inspiration for his argument. The book was forged, he explained, in the crucible of the early years of the AIDS crisis, when Brown witnessed gay men in particular suffering beneath the barrage of an indiscriminate virus, on the one hand, and an indifferent (though more often downright hostile) polity, on the other. In this atmosphere of crisis, gay men and their allies created institutions of self-care and sustenance such as the Gay Men's Health Crisis, forged impromptu and tactical forms of political action into the organizations ACT-UP and Queer Nation, and, generally, created communities of support and survival in the face of catastrophe.[11] I admit that I was struck by this historical analogy, in part because it illuminated for me why I found *The Reaper's Garden* both so moving and so politically articulate. The creativity thesis at the heart of this analogy resonated as true from the perspective of my own recollections of early adulthood.

All the same, while it may echo both sonorously and compellingly across the span of centuries, Brown's historical analogy remains disturbingly mute to my ears. I have found it hard to expel from my consciousness the broad spectrum of responses to the onslaught of AIDS that don't appear "creative" in the terms set forth in *The Reaper's Garden*—that appear, in retrospect, to be the very social embodiment of a principle of negativity (against a politics of hope and futurity and at variance with any project of redemption, restoration, or reclamation). Crystal meth, special k (ketamine), and various designer drugs were used to amplify feelings of emotional euphoria at a high price to self-care but provided one way to get over the hump of catastrophe. Although tales of life on the "down low" could titillate when they percolated to the surface of our national consciousness, the complex psychology and possible social costs of lives lived so thoroughly in denial were what deserved (and so rarely received) our attention. And, at the time, the turn toward "barebacking" was perhaps indicative of what Tim Dean calls "impersonal intimacy"—that is, some gay men actively pursued the HIV virus on the understanding that actively sharing the virus was a way to forge connection and kinship.[12] Here was life lived entirely outside parameters set by public health authorities and actuarial assessments of risk. It would be all too easy to reduce these responses to the singularity of mere "pathology" and in that gesture make them both legible and readily available to the historical gaze as objects of scrutiny.

I propose that they cannot be so made available. I would underwrite that proposal with the even stronger claim that the purpose of self-abnegation, self-immolation, and self-mutilation, if they serve a purpose in the project of writing history, is to make that enterprise more acutely aware of the poverty of its methods. Understand what it is that I am asserting: I am not claiming that Brown has missed something in the present (as a historian, that is not his job). Rather, I am saying that the way he has seen the past has helped me to see something else entirely; it has opened my eyes to the possibility that there is something we might not be able to see about the past if we look at it through the usual historical lenses. I am speaking of a failure of history—we might call it history's "constitutive poverty"—but one it would be wrong to see as other than productive. I feel nervously awake to the possibility that, if responses to catastrophe exist in the present that are discrete and incommensurable (even mutually negating), then they also may have existed in the past. And if only the more resistant of those responses make a ready fit for the project of writing history, there are others it may simply be impossible for history to recover as objects of knowledge.

There is non-appropriable or missed experience that will always evade our attempts to grasp it. To help discern what might be at stake in following out this critical instinct, it might be helpful to approach the problem from a methodological angle.

To try to articulate what I am thinking here, I find Stanley Cavell helpful. He observes that what a historian has to face in knowing the past parallels the experience of the theatergoer: "The epistemology of other minds is the same as the metaphysics of other times and places."[13] When we insist that the past has to be *made* relevant to the present, or understand it as already so relevant, we fall into the typical error of parents and children—"taking difference from each other to threaten, or promise, severance from one another."[14] But we *are* severed. To confirm that is "neither a blessing nor a curse"; it is simply a fact.[15] To deny that, however, is to give up not only knowledge of the position of others, but also "the means of locating one's own."[16] Our charge in dealing with figures from the slave past, whatever our critical orientation, is to make their present *theirs*, and (if I might hijack Cavell's language here) "it is only in this perception of them as separate from me that I make them present. That I make them *other*, and face them."[17]

Recall David Lloyd's compelling case for failed futures. One characteristic of the figures in the past with whom we so desperately crave a connection is that they possessed their own "specific and unreproducible orientation to the future," and our present, rather than represent the fulfillment of that projection, is more likely "the future imposed on the dead by past violence." The restlessness of the dead, the sense that they are still alive to us, Lloyd proposes, "stems from the lack of a future fit for them."[18] The point is to see in our severance from figures in the past, to see in their opacity, the idea that they are present to us in the only way they can be, and thus to be acknowledged, but not to be known. In that severance, in that frustration of our desire to know them, we discover what we might potentially share with them and learn, in turn, in a way we hadn't before, how their condition is like ours. (Slaves are, as perhaps some of us are as well, excluded, denigrated, superseded; they are, as we may ourselves soon be, hidden, forgotten, and silenced.)

Established methods of inquiry and practices of reading have simply not rewarded the scholar curious to journey down these uncertain paths. Although I have found Brown's subsequent essay "Social Death and Political Life in the Study of Slavery" to be both a thought-provoking and forceful assessment of our field's imperatives and tendencies, even his critique seems to mark as unworthy in advance any attempt to go down paths that don't promise redemption.[19]

In the field of Afro-Atlantic slavery, death has emerged as the primary way to describe force in the twilight of critique—death names a fact of human existence transformed by the institutions of slavery into a fundament of political struggle and the very terms of social being. In this regard, "death" has largely supplanted "racism," which now seems too innocuous and imprecise, and it rivals both "class," which seems too dependent on a hermetic conception of the social, and "empire," which seems too quick to want to supersede it. The promotion of death to a place of conceptual prominence in the field can be attributed to the powerful intervention of Orlando Patterson's *Slavery and Social Death* (1982). Patterson describes how, across a number of slave societies, natal alienation, violence, and dishonor structure the "social death" prerequisite to the slave's resurrection in society (what he terms "liminal incorporation").[20] The influence of the social death thesis can be felt across a broad range of critical work, and a number of scholars, seeing productive parallels between Patterson's theory and the theory of "bare life," have invited us to consider some description of social death as a crucial aspect of contemporary social being, from racial personhood to the condition of the stateless. Ruthie Gilmore, for one, sharpens the definition of racism against the whetstone of social death, redescribing the former as "the state-sanctioned production and exploitation of group vulnerabilities toward premature death."[21] Colin

(Joan) Dayan would recognize such death as an internal substrate of living being in the legal fiction of "civil death"—"the state of a person who, though possessing *natural life* has lost all *civil rights*."[22] Though Dayan does Patterson one better by seeing the death engendered by legal authority as suffused with both spiritual and civil dimension, she nonetheless persuasively charts how the "civil death" of the slave functioned as a legal disability made indelible over time, giving rise to effects that persist into our own. Russ Castronovo's writings on "necro-citizenship," Achille Mbembe's genealogy of decolonization as a form of "necropolitics," and many similar arguments follow this itinerary, all with the goal of demonstrating slavery's annihilation of social being and the extent to which slaves in their subordination got a head start on modernity.[23]

Brown has been critical of Patterson's totalizing definition of slavery and has placed at the center of debate the question of whether or not scholars inspired by the theory of social death have hyperbolized its claims for epistemological significance. The tendency, he argues, is for scholars who engage the concept to mistake a theoretical abstraction for a description of the existential condition of the enslaved. In trenchant readings of important books by Saidiya Hartman, Ian Baucom, and Stephanie Smallwood, Brown argues that the overwhelming majority of social death adherents mistake a metaphor for a description of the real. What began in Patterson's work as a distillation of slaveholder ideology gets refined even further into a "logic of slavery" (in the case of Baucom) and "an experience of self" (in the case of the others). In Brown's attempt to understand our collective intellectual moment, what these scholars appear to share is a tendency to take social death to be so total, and the corrosive power of slavery to be so replete, as to leave no trace of "countervailing forces such as the political activity of the weak."[24] They are each in their own way subtly undone by a too strong reliance, as Brown sees it, "on Orlando Patterson's *totalizing* definition of slavery."[25] Let us therefore call this *the totality thesis* (my term admittedly, not Brown's, although its pertinence as a way to name what he describes I will reveal shortly).

Brown offers as an example of the slaves' counterpoint a funerary rite that took place on the deck of the slave ship *Hudibras* in 1786, drawing on this example to make his own (very compelling) case for the metaphysical threat of annihilation as a force that is generative (rather than repressive) of the slaves' culture and politics. Faced with the threat of oblivion, the slaves organized a ceremony to speak to the spirit of a dead female slave, who was the first of their number to die on that particular voyage; the memorial served to interrupt the crew's plan simply to heave her corpse overboard. The cultural significance of this case resides in its providing a glimpse into "what people *made* of death and the dead" in a slave society.[26] Call this *the creativity thesis*.

To be honest, I must admit to feeling a bit stuck. There is truth to the claim of social death theorists that it is difficult, if not impossible, to tease out something that looks like freedom without reproducing the structures of domination that resist and occlude that freedom. Power is superordinate. And yet, at the same time, I find utterly compelling *The Reaper's Garden*'s demonstration of the struggle between members of the plantocracy and the enslaved to harness the affective power of death, as well as the claim that this process generated culture and new knowledge (an entire slave *society*) out of a human catastrophe—what Brown describes as a *mortuary politics*. Subterranean rumblings beneath the deafening clamor of the superordinate. What once looked "nihilistic" appears on second glance to be a sign of the slaves' agency, and cultural practices that had heretofore been branded with the mark of social alienation are translated into indicators of the slaves' resistance to it. So in the case of the *Hudibras*, or the *Zong*, or the *Recovery*, what is wrong with saying that this is what defeat looks like? Why shouldn't we want to see domination for what it is—as engendering and destroying the subject? Why should we want to see it as an obfuscating screen behind which is secreted an irrepressible slave agency?

I have resisted the impulse to engage all of the nuanced particulars of this debate but hope that I have said enough to indicate to you that the entire problematic of slavery and social death has been framed as a choice between totality and creativity. There are clear echoes here of the antinomy between structure and agency that has governed the historiography of slavery, where the former represents a negative power and the latter, its undoing. I think that the choice between totality and creativity also recalls the opposition between containment and subversion, the terms in which critics debated the forces of ideology and resistance within the ambient political culture of the Cold War.[27] In the short form of this debate, according to one of its partisans, "Critics who emphasized possibilities for the elective agency of individual and collective subjects against forms of domination, exclusion, and assimilation energetically contested critics who emphasized the capacity of the . . . modern state . . . to contain apparently subversive gestures, or even to produce them precisely in order to contain them."[28]

Given these Cold War echoes, I would propose that we keep in mind the advice of David Scott, who asks us to consider whether the terms in our debates, which often emerged from unique political contexts, continue to have "the same usefulness, the same salience, the same critical purchase, when the historical conjuncture that originally gave [them] point and purchase has passed?" (This is not a question of absolute truth, he adds, "so much as a question about the *best* truth for our time."[29])

I have cause to question whether the attempt to conceptualize the agency of the enslaved in terms of totality and creativity is "the best truth for our time." I have four issues to raise, in fact:

1. As Slavoj Žižek quips in *Did Somebody Say Totalitarianism?* "The philosophical notion of totality and the political notion of totalitarianism tend to overlap," and the notion of totalitarianism, "far from being an effective theoretical concept, is a kind of stopgap: instead of enabling us to think, forcing us to acquire a new insight into the historical reality it describes, it relieves us of the duty to think." The critical doxa accepts the social as a field of structural indecidability, "and 'totalitarianism' is, at its most elementary, the closure of this undecidability." He finishes, "Any stance that does not endorse the mantra of contingency/displacement/finitude is dismissed as potentially 'totalitarian.'"[30]

2. Patterson is a sociologist who is keen to discern the workings and the import of "structures." It is one of the paradoxes of the social death thesis that it has inspired a broad body of work by scholars who take it as a given that the disarticulation of the social (the sense that it is marked by an irreducible gap or lack) makes it difficult to talk about racism in terms of either "structure" or "totality." Largely post-Foucauldian in orientation, most of these thinkers are simply not invested in either "structure" or "totality" as critical terms of analysis.

3. Brown has returned us to the issue of the agency of the enslaved but in a way that appears to require a set of antinomies that are more trouble than they are worth. "Social death and political life": life and death, being somebody and being no-

body, recovery and mourning, the subject who never dies and the melancholy object that can never be returned to life. But would not a frank look at our own social existence reveal that something *in between* these antinomies is in fact what the social *is*? (A stranger, for example, is neither alive to you in the way family relations are nor as dead as an ancestor.)

4   Both the creativity from catastrophe thesis and the melancholy thesis are born of the idea that death bears a productive (rather than negative) relation to the "creative and self-creative activity through which man creates ... and changes ... his historical, human world and himself" (the Marxist definition of *praxis*).[31] The interest that Brown has sparked suffices to convince me that death is the name we give to force in our current critical conjuncture—that it is a shared methodological assumption across the field. There is broad consensus, in other words, that power is productive, that death is generative of praxis.

So what is the distinction between totality and creativity engineered to achieve? What is at stake in trying to distinguish two positions where there appears to be one? What are the stakes in trying to imagine two distinct itineraries—"social death and political life," totality and creativity? I would suggest that the distinction comes from a desire to keep *a political practice* from collapsing into *a logic of power* and to avoid the consequences that flow from the recognition that power is both external to the subject and the very venue of the subject.

Metalepsis in History

On January 29, 1818, in the final months of a three-year survey of his Jamaican holdings, Matthew "Monk" Lewis scribbled the refrain to a popular slave song in the pages of his journal:

> "Take him to the Gulley! Take him to the Gulley!
> But bringee back the frock and board."—
> "Oh! massa, massa! me no deadee yet!"—
> "Take him to the Gulley! Take him to the Gulley!"
>   "Carry him along!"[32]

Thanks to Lewis, our knowledge of the song's origins runs deep.

The song alludes to the practices of a former proprietor at the Spring-Garden plantation, whose habit it was to send sick and dying slaves to a remote part of the property, called the Gulley, to be "thrown down, and abandoned to [their] fate"—most likely, to be "half devoured by the john-crows, before death had put an end to [their] sufferings."[33] The condemned were taken to their final resting place by their fellow slaves— pallbearers of the living dead. Those condemned to this sorry fate were often clothed only in a tattered frock and foisted atop a plank conscripted for said grim purpose. Lewis reports of one slave who, while in the act of being removed, "screamed out most piteously 'that he was not dead yet'; and implored not to be left to perish in the Gulley in a manner so horrible."[34] His pleas fell on deaf ears when those ears belonged to his master but not when they fell on those of his fellow slaves, who removed him to their quarters and there "nursed him . . . with so much care, that he recovered, and left the estate unquestioned and undiscovered."[35] Lewis's journal entry for that day ends with this twist:

> Unluckily, one day the master was passing through Kingston, when, on turning the corner of a street suddenly, he found himself face to face with the negro, whom he had supposed long ago to have been picked to the bones in the Gulley of Spring-Garden. He immediately seized him, claimed him as his slave, and ordered his attendants to convey him to his house; but the fellow's cries attracted a crowd round them, before he could be dragged away. He related his melancholy story, and the singular manner in which he had recovered his life and liberty; and the public indignation was so forcibly excited by the shocking tale, that [his former owner] was glad to save himself from being torn to pieces by a precipitate retreat from Kingston, and never ventured to advance his claim to the negro a second time.[36]

We cannot know how widespread such inventiveness may have been across the ranks of the enslaved, and it is even harder to comprehend what premature death might have meant for these slaves, how they might have cognized a world out of the simultaneous despair and opportunity that death represented. These difficulties are in fact registered in the way the condemned man's voice is locked up behind its paraphrase in the planter's journal. Lewis reports that the slave "screamed out most piteously" words that, given to us in the third person, he in all likelihood did not in fact scream: "that he was not dead yet." To make an emergency call on your own behalf—to express your own suffering—in a third-person voice is the whorl of conflicting intentions that Lewis retrieves as "slave agency," a sign of the very violence that has left the slave as a fragment in the archive.

As a document of the social, "The Gulley at Spring-Garden" certainly exemplifies a kind of mortuary politics, a sense of death as the terrain of a struggle for power and of social death as a generative force. When exercised on the ground in a slave culture, terror has the power to transform life into death. The gulley serves as a vestibule to death—the horizon of a living death "before death had put an end to [all their] sufferings," its threat served as the ground for *all* of the slaves' being.

Thanks to Lewis's gloss, we know that social death opened up the very parentheses into which the slave escaped "unquestioned and undiscovered." Call this *the metalepsis of the subject*, where the slave makes himself once over from the stuff out of which he had been made (the figure of a figure). But metalepsis is, after all, the trope of disappearance, the trope of obscured cause.

Thus, the song, considered a document of art, seems in its very form to register a refusal to being engendered by this power and to hedge against recovery. With every ecstatic delivery of the ballad, no mention is made of the act of creativity that spawned it, turning the slaves' innovation into an absent cause and making ever more obscure and remote the origins of the metaleptic chain. The song from this vantage seems to point in the direction of those moments in which the social cannot contain a sense of agency, or when agency is expressed as a refusal of the possibilities of social action that have been shaped and organized by colonial power—in short, when the enslaved innovate in the interest of their own oblivion (when they choose it). To some, the song might sound like a celebration of humanistic struggle in the face of social death. To others, it might evince a celebration of what is absent and what is lost, of the irresolute and the irretrievable; of what can never be heard in the sound or what never resolves into sense. "Carry him along," was their refrain. To some this may have meant to "carry him" to his death. To others, it may have meant to "carry him" in your minds as the trace of the disappearance you hope someday yourself to achieve.

I have one final confession to make, but only because it confirms what I have been saying all along: the "Commander in Chief of the *Negroes*" in Bosman's *Description of the Coast of Guinea* was not the one who set off the bomb that destroyed Fort Ruychaver. The suicide bomber was the commander of the fort, Jan de Liefde, an employee of the Dutch West India Company. We need not go into all of the reasons that the company factor blew himself up. What is important to note is that history was set off on the wrong track by an error of translation. It seems that Bosman's first English translator was confused by the Dutch word "van," which could mean both "of" and "by," in the phrase "want het Opperhoofd van de Swarten belegerd zijnde." Albert van Dantzig corrects this to read, not the "Chief *of* the Negroes" who was "besieged by" the Dutch but the "Chief [of the fort], besieged *by* the Negroes . . . , pretended that he wanted to negotiate [and] blew himself and all his Enemies up."[37] Because of this ambiguity, the African's self-immolation has been taken up (say, by those who want real proof of the acts romanticized in abolitionist works such as Aphra Behn's *Oroonoko*) as evidence of the good death, of the death with honor and meaning. The Dutchman who blew himself up must drop out of history for everyday proof of the African martyr spirit to emerge. But the bombing in Guinea wasn't a proof to buttress anyone's thesis of culture or belief, resistance or nihilism. The martyrdom wasn't even a martyrdom, for the African who destroyed himself in the annals of colonial history was only a figure of a figure.

4

| RUMOR IN THE ARCHIVE |

Every great degree of caution in inferring, every skeptical disposition, is a great danger to life. No living being would be preserved had not the opposite disposition—to affirm rather than suspend judgement, to err and make things up rather than wait . . . —been bred to become extraordinarily strong.

FRIEDRICH NIETZSCHE, *The Gay Science*

William Wilberforce, Henry Brougham, Thomas Clarkson, James Stephens: all would have to admit that the bill abolishing the slave trade for which they had fought so hard ten years earlier worked now more like a sieve than a dam. They would have to admit, too, that it had been pure folly to believe, as Wilberforce put it, that "the abolition of the trade, if it could be secured, would be the best remedy for all the diseases of the system."[1] Thus, when in June 1815 Wilberforce introduces a bill to the House of Commons that would extend Parliament's prerogative to include the creation and maintenance of an annual census of the slave population, his is as much an admission of defeat as it is an assertion of sovereign power.[2] West Indian planters and the representatives of their interest fail to see things with quite such an eye for paradox, and on the island of Barbados, in particular, the plantocrats complain bitterly that the bill represents an incursion on their precious local legal autonomy. For months, partisans in the debate vent their frustrations in the newspapers, in legislative assembly, in correspondence with Downing Street, and in their own parlors. As the leaders of the African Institution warned their members in 1816, "We must speak in a whisper, even when we speak at the distance of 6000 miles, of slavery in the West Indies."[3] Few would heed the warning.

On March 30, 1816, the *Barbados Mercury and Bridgetown Gazette* prints on its front page a verbatim transcript of one of the earliest meetings of the Barbados Assembly (held just four months earlier, when the Registry Bill was discussed). The publication of the parliamentary back-and-forth in the columns of the newspaper seems not only ill-considered, but the language itself seems dangerously imprecise. This from the Speaker of the Assembly:

> *Gentlemen*—I am commanded by the President to lay before you a Bill, which has been introduced into the House of Commons, for registering the slaves of the different Islands and Colonies, in order fully to carry into effect the Abolition Act, by preventing the smuggling of Africans.

And this from a proponent of the bill:

> I rise, therefore, to submit, in the form of a motion to the House, the measure which you have recommended; and, in doing so, I think it my unfavorable opportunity to remark upon the dangerous though futile report so prevalent at present, that the real object of the Bill before Parliament, is to promote an emancipation of the slaves, — a report much more likely, in my opinion, to hurt and delude the slaves themselves, than to be detrimental to the interest of the Proprietors.

And this from an opponent:

> We are every third year to deliver in to their Registrar, properly sent us for the purpose, the names, families, size, height, dimensions, &c., &c., of all the negroes on our respective Estates. Is there a default on the part of the resident on the property?—the slave is virtually emancipated.[4]

The very title of the bill startles by its imprecision: "A Bill for effectually preventing the unlawful importation of Slaves, and the holding of Free Persons in Slavery in the British Colonies." "Unlawful . . . holding . . . Free

Persons in Slavery"—six words that could mean so much. Even the semi-literate slave, stealing a moment to scan her master's paper, would need little to fit herself within their signifying folds. In the wake of insurrections on the island of Barbados and elsewhere, various select committees and courts-martial were established to retrieve evidence that some slaves made great efforts to do just that.

King Wiltshire, a slave on the Bayley's plantation, looks forward only to his death when he testifies to the following before the Judge Advocate of the courts martial (and here I quote from the trial transcript): "The opinion amongst the negroes (generally) was, that they were to be freed [and] their freedom was to be given them through a black woman who was a Queen, for whom Mr. Wilberforce acted in England."[5] This report Wiltshire claims to have heard from three free "coloured" men, one of whom, Cain Davis, had told him, specifically, in Wiltshire's words, "that he had seen in the English Newspapers, that the negroes were to be manumitted through the means aforesaid, but that it appeared that the Gentlemen of this Island wished to withhold their Manumissions."[6] Johnny, another slave at Bayley's, is also under sentence of death when the Reverend John Frere Pilgrim encourages him to make a "free and full confession"—what Pilgrim claims to have received would be anything but. Pilgrim testifies:

> Some coloured people who could read, had occasionally . . . brought English Newspapers and read to them, by which they were led to believe that it was the desire of the Prince Regent and the people of England that they should be free, and that they therefore thought themselves free, but that their freedom was unjustly withheld from them by the whites, and therefore they would fight for it.[7]

Almost everyone offers their testimony just as Johnny does, in accordance with British court-martial procedures—"after the evidence had been gone through . . . and the judgment of the Court made up as to their sentence."[8] And despite having every reason to at least hazard what needed to be said to save themselves from execution, almost everyone offered the same testimony: that "they had heard it read in the Papers that they were to be free";[9] that "the King and Mr. Wilberforce had sent out to say that they were all to be freed; but that the whites would not let them have it";[10] that the governor of the island, Sir James Leith, "was on the seas, waiting until they could make a stand, to be their friend";[11] and that, if it came down to a struggle to enforce the word and will of the sovereign, "the

King's troops"—the very agents of the crown who were now taking down their testimony—"would join them."[12] From the mouths of the slaves—allegedly verbatim.

The slaves in the nearby colony of Demerara toil on estates that bear the names Paradise, Success, Triumph, Enterprise, and even Contract. So one might expect them to be considerably more skeptical with regard to language's felicity, disbelieving that there is a saying that might in any significant way also be a doing. But the same rumors percolate to the surface there just seven years after the events in Barbados. The rumors start to appear mere days after the Demerara Court of Policy convenes in July 1823, in the words of the colony's governor, "to carry into effect His Majesty's beneficent views for bettering [the slaves'] condition [through] the abolition of the flogging of females and the carrying Whips to the field."[13] Soon thereafter, the slave Quamina from the Jessup plantation enters the neighboring home of John Smith, a parson with the London Missionary Society, and asks whether he had heard the report that (as the slave phrased it) "the King had sent order to the Governor to free the Slaves."[14] Quamina had been told this just a week earlier by his son Jack, who had heard from the slave Daniel that his master, the colony's Governor John Murray, had been "talk[ing] with some Gentlemen about it."[15] Parson Smith, who would later be tried, convicted, and sentenced to hang by a court-martial on charges of conspiracy in the slave insurrection that soon followed, reassures Quamina that "it was likely some Orders had been sent out to [the] Governor as the Government house wished to make some regulation for the benefit of the Slaves but not to make them free."[16] Closing his journal entry that day, Smith writes, "This answer scarcely satisfied him"—nor, I would add, the hundreds of others who joined Quamina in revolt. This is how the antislavery advocates would sum up what their adversaries labeled "the irritation of mind among the Slaves":

> These poor people, it seems, were led to believe that their liberty was withheld from them, by the suppression of Lord Balthurst's Letter, and the resolutions of the House of Commons, from the 21st July, when they were laid before the Court of Policy, till the 7th August, when the Court passed a vote conformable to the Letter, and by the unaccountable measure of still concealing the new regulations from the slaves themselves.[17]

Governor Murray would hear this directly from the mouths of "the slaves themselves" when, in the opening hours of the insurrection, he encounters an "armed Body of the[se] Insurgents" who assert their desire for "unconditional emancipation" on the grounds that "their good King had sent orders that they should be free."[18] He elaborates in a letter to the undersecretary of state, "They repeatedly said that they knew their good King had sent out their freedom and that being withheld by the Whites they were determined to take it."[19]

Exactly the same was said in Jamaica in 1830 as it became "the policy of His Majesty's Government" to keep up pressure on the colony to introduce "measures of amelioration . . . into the Slave Code."[20] After years of this pressure to alleviate slave conditions, the island's planters turned so vehement and so public in their resistance that the slaves needed little encouragement to turn their masters' paranoia to their own advantage. Many whites groused that any concessions brought emancipation (and the dispossession of their property) inevitably nearer, and collectively they would go as far as to pass provincial resolutions in which they would often plead "rather than submit to this, we beg His Majesty to absolve us from our allegiance." What they sought was not independence but a transfer of their sovereign allegiance to a place whose name could only have struck fear in the hearts of every slave within earshot: America.[21] Opposition such as was witnessed on the island of Jamaica only served to precipitate the slaves' own strategic sense of power.

Choosing to throw the voice of the slave (rather than his own) into the archive, Reverend Peter Duncan testified before a committee of the House of Commons convened to look into the Jamaican revolt:

> Here . . . our masters tell us that the King wants to make us free, and they tell us again that although the King wants to make us free, they will not submit to it, but they will keep us in a state of slavery.[22]

Duncan adds, this time in his own voice:

> I cannot help making the observation, and this I have seen in a thousand instances, that His Majesty has not more loyal subjects, through the wide extent of his dominions, than the religious slaves are in the island of Jamaica; they will do any thing for the King, they revere the very name of the King; and hence, when they suppose that the two parties were at issue, the King upon the one hand and the masters upon the other, there is no difficulty in conceiving which side the slaves would take.[23]

The slave community effervesced with rumors that, based in this strategic sense of the field of power, were nothing short of fictions: that "brown already free, black soon"; that "the King would give no assistance to the white people if they, the negroes, fought for their freedom"; that "the King of England and the Parliament have given Jamaica freedom, and it is held back by the whites"; that freedom was coming in a paper from the king by the hand of the Baptist missionary Thomas Burchell (who had gone to England from his chapel in Montego Bay in May 1831), and that "they did not expect Mr. Burchell until the country was given up [as] he was on sea waiting to bring the gift, freedom."[24] These rumors proved so widespread and so intransigent that the colonial secretary had to issue a circular proclamation, ostensibly from the king, "denying that freedom had been granted or was imminent and enjoining the slaves to remain dutifully quiet" (figure 4.1).[25]

Slaves who long to subvert their masters' authority project an institutionally unfixed king to whom they may deliver a petition begging deliverance. Officials of the crown, eager to buttress their authority at the bleeding edge of empire, read the king's proclamations against revolt in response to black insurgents' falsely speaking and acting in the name of British sovereignty. Inquisitors record slave talk of "rights" and "the English Papers," of "the new laws" that were "coming out" from England, which some understood as a grant of immediate emancipation. These percolations of rumor were riddled with errors that were both factual and conceptual but that nonetheless drove a great deal of the political debate in the plantation zones and metropoles at the colony's outer fringes. The error capable of triggering the most fevered repressive efforts was the assumption, on the part of the slaves, that Britain possessed a monarch to whom they could appeal in the first place, the assumption that the field of imperial sovereignty possessed a standpoint from which they could speak.[26] "Like revolutionaries in France [and other metropoles], black insurgents expressed themselves by speaking and acting—uninvited—in the name of the ... nation, and in so doing they brought about the declarations that officially made them part of that nation."[27]

For certain, the history of Atlantic conspiracy and rebellion is replete with examples of slaves who looked and appealed to friends and powerful allies (such as William Wilberforce, God, their benevolent king or queen) who had decreed their freedom, only to have those decrees withheld by the local regime. It was not at all uncommon in the late eighteenth cen-

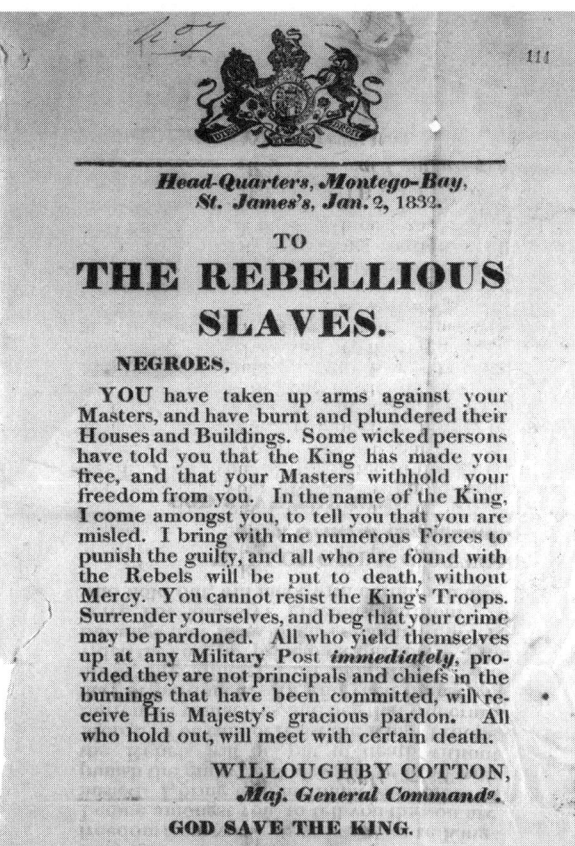

FIGURE 4.1. Willoughby Cotton, "To the Rebellious Slaves" (January 2, 1832). National Archives (United Kingdom), Kew Gardens, Public Records Office, Colonial Office, 137/181.

tury and early nineteenth century for slaves to understand that they had friends and allies in the imperial metropolis. (The fact of the matter, as most well knew, is that they did.) Nor was it uncommon for word to circulate among slaves to the effect that actual decrees had been made by the monarch, Parliament, or the Colonial Office and had been withheld by the local regime.

Proto-

Rumors of a benevolent monarch persistently wash up on the shores of history to befuddle the critical imagination with the enigma of their origins. Let us start from the assumption that these anomalous rumors actually represent evidence that we simply do not understand, evidence that "[we have been] only too eager to assimilate to what we knew all along should have been [the slaves'] goal."[28] Although some scholars have been enticed to classify these rumors as the "naïve lament of the uninitiated," others have looked beneath and behind the signs of inadequacy for evidence of a nascent politics.[29] James Scott has invited us to see the myth of the benevolent monarch as a "weapon of the weak," as an attempt by the slaves to "clothe" their resistance to oppression beneath a gesture of loyalty to the crown. Slaves are engaged in an "art of political disguise" and have left behind, as Scott famously termed it, a "hidden transcript."[30] Whether it is to serve Scott's goal of tearing away the "political disguise" of monarchist prattle or (in the case put forward by Steven Hahn) to pierce rumor's "cloak" of anonymity to reveal what lies underneath, this critical tradition often posits a hiddenness from which the enslaved have to be recovered.[31] Yet, curiously, what the suspicious eye of the historian often finds is only what it set out to look for in the first place—"proto-revolutionaries" in Eugene Genovese's phrase; "proto-peasants" in Michael Craton's; or "proto-politics" in Steven Hahn's—incipient versions of ourselves (and our way of being).[32]

The rumors of a benevolent sovereign are also a kind of prayer, a sorcery, a seduction, a predication that plays out the passage between self-abnegation and self-assertion, between the assumption that "the Lord and the King have given them the gift" and the belief that "if you do not fight for it you will never get it."[33] In this regard, one can hear echoes of what scholars of pre-Soviet Russia describe as "peasant monarchism," or the phenomenon of the good tsar. (*If only he knew about all of the abuses being perpetrated by his minions and his bureaucrats and his police he would surely step in and fix things.*[34]) All the same, this seduction of monarchical power, this claim to "His Majesty's favor" and protection, this earnest taking to heart the idea that they could as slaves avail themselves of sovereign power, that the monarch could hear them, is startlingly difficult to discern from the technology of inquisition, from the summons to speak guilt and to beg pardon. They appeal to the crown, and now, in answer, the crown's ministers stand before them.

What is revealed by this back-and-forth between rumor and inquisition, seduction and repression? Is it the repressive power that is producing the resistance that it had anticipated in the first place, or is it a matter of the stateless calling down a monarchical power to claim it as the subject it is not? Jonathan Elmer might describe the slaves' empty appeal as a "creative nomination" that gives rise to "paradoxes of retroaction."[35] More than a plea that has simply fallen on deaf ears, it represents a plea spoken from a position rendered impossible by the speech act itself, to follow Bryan Wagner's way of thinking—one that constructs a standpoint from which to speak in the very place where that perspective was meant to be foreclosed.[36] Is this, then, the voice of the dominator, the dominated, or the "perfidious contagion of power"?[37] "How much of their original speech had the slaves already lost, even before they came to testify? How much of the whites' ways of talking had the slaves already absorbed?"[38]

But if there is an equal chance of any one of these options being possible, what is the likelihood that none of this was said? How does one leave aside the impression—the possibility, if even remote—that none of this was *said*? How can one write a history of the event in the face of such doubt?

Something odd about these rumors emerges in the attempt to write them down: they start to feel self-canceling, designed to disrupt the context of their preservation. The very act of archiving these rumors *as writing*, which makes them available to us, also makes them more subject to doubt at the level of their ontology. They radiate with a sense of historical impossibility; with a sense, if we might follow Heather Love, of broken intimacy or "failed [and] interrupted connection" born of the awareness that these utterances cannot, may not, possibly do not, finally, belong to the slaves.[39] Once a rumor makes it into an archive, it evidences not the accuracy of its claims but the necessary and melancholy recognition of its own failure—a failure to remain illicit utterance, a failure to succeed at whatever such "loose talk" suggested. There is, as well, a second-order failure that is quite difficult to separate from the first: once a rumor makes it into the archive, it becomes hard to believe it was ever a rumor at all.

Rumors wither under measures of truth and falsity like flowers under hot water. Under such circumstances it remains prudent to approach without touching your object, to work *asymptotically*, so to speak, to follow what Brent Hayes Edwards calls a "queer practice of the archive," making multiple advances toward those objects that cannot be pinned down, that "elude the tenets of empiricism and documentation."[40] In this practice, Edwards proposes, the "orchestrated fragments echo the fragmentation of the archive itself," and I wish to mirror that practice.[41]

Subjective to Subjunctive

Brendan McConville argues in *The King's Three Faces*, his account of pre–Revolutionary America's persistent Anglophilia, that provincials in the Thirteen Colonies possessed a deeply subjective understanding of imperial sovereignty, one figured in the image of a benevolent and loving king.[42] For inhabitants of the home islands, "The Glorious Revolution's constitutional settlement located sovereignty in the King-in-Parliament and more or less settled the balance of power in the government."[43] Political patronage and a fear of Europe's Catholic powers combined to secure allegiance to this order of authority. Provincials, however, possessed a different worldview, one shaped by royal rites and a print culture that celebrated Britain's Protestant princes and came to understand the 1688 settlement and the Hanoverian dynasty very differently. "They saw the national settlement as establishing the Protestant succession and a Protestant political culture built around a cult of benevolent monarchy," McConville writes. "Parliament had no symbolic role in imperial political rituals, its history was poorly understood, and it was diminished in political discussions."[44] Colonists who fought more esteemed adversaries for property and power on the empire's fringes trafficked in subjective understandings of king and constitution as part of their overall strategy. The king of their imperial imagination stood apart from the British state: king above Parliament, king as father, king as constitutional broker. "The logic imparted by royal political culture convinced many provincials that the monarch existed constitutionally apart from Parliament and was a location of sovereignty in his own right."[45] The imagined king is saved from being implicated in the law as an exception to it—with the ability to correct the law's deficiencies and rein in those who exceeded the law's authority.[46]

Although prohibited from print culture and largely ignorant of royal rites, slaves were no less a part of this cult of monarchy. "As unlikely as it may seem," McConville writes, "the same legal system that punished defiant slaves might have been a conduit for subversive royal beliefs to spread to enslaved populations.... Somehow, the existing power structure came to educate enslaved peoples ... about the benevolent nature of their monarchs, and they thus came to dream of a father-monarch that could deliver them from their mundane local pharaohs."[47] How this happened, he concludes, "the actual progression that painted the king's face on the porcelain of protest and rebellion, is partly hidden" from our view.[48] When Elisa Tamarkin posits that the black disposition toward Britain was informed by "a rather causeless enthusiasm, a psychological *fixe*," she intensifies the sense of mystery at the origin of this fixation.[49]

Consider, then, this address from the crown to the "Body of Revolted Negroes" in Demerara in 1823:

> Heads under which you are authorized to communicate with the Body of Negroes, said to be assembled or any other Body of Revolted Negroes you may fall in with.
>
> FIRST—Your Revolt has already proved to you, your weakness.
>
> SECOND—It is true that the Court of Policy, in conjunction with your Masters, were desirous of amending your state, by making certain Regulations favourable to your comforts.
>
> As a first step to this, the flogging of women and the carrying the whip or other instrument of punishment in the field, were about to be immediately abolished—and a LAW was in preparation to that effort.
>
> Other improvements were to have followed, if deemed such as you could be deserving to receive.
>
> You have now forfeited all claim to favour, and the only hope that the measures intended will not be stopped for ever, depends on your immediate and unconditional return to your duty.
>
> You must lay down your arms, and come in within twenty four hours—and your Governor will extend what mercy is possible to you.
>
> Depend however on this, that whatever commands the King sends here, always have been and always will be strictly obeyed.

The idea that slaves were the subjects of George III and thus allowed a right to protection from the crown was largely resigned to the margins of abolitionist discourse, which makes the direct address of the sovereign to this "Body of Negroes" a peculiar thing.[50] No less curious are the ways in which the rhetoric of the text participates in the construction of the reality it seeks to deny. *About to be abolished, in preparation to that effect:* an intention thwarted, an anticipated deliverance. *Now forfeited all claim to favor, what mercy is possible to you:* an acknowledgment indefinitely postponed. This is a reality without ontology, present only as an effect of its deferral and denial. This holding the world in abeyance gives rise to an idol we have seen before—that of a king apart, king divorced from the local state apparatus, king above court and master. But now, because of such talk, "king" holds the place of the subjunctive.

Written on the Wind

"Every colored person, and every friend of their persecuted race, kept their eyes wide open," Harriet Jacobs writes in *Incidents in the Life of a Slave Girl*. "Every evening I examined the newspapers carefully, to see what Southerners had put up at the hotels. I did this for my own sake . . . ; I wished also to give information to others, if necessary; for if many were 'running to and fro,' I resolved that 'knowledge should be increased.'"[51] What Jacobs has set out to describe here, simply and in line with the politics of abolition, is the pragmatic and clandestine knowledge in circulation among slave informants and their white sympathizers—called variously "gossip" or "rumor"—but, as Susan Scott Parrish has astutely observed, talk of the "many" who were "running to and fro" plugs this knowledge into a prophetic narrative structure whose purpose is to work that knowledge toward the end of divine deliverance.[52] Rumor is nothing without its epic ambitions.

In the final dream of the Book of Daniel, the divine spirit promises that the war between the king of the north and the king of the south will end in a kind of last-minute review session:

> At that time shall arise Michael, the great prince who has charge of your people. And there shall be a time of trouble, such as never has been since there was a nation till that time; but at that time your people shall be delivered, every one whose name shall be found written in the book. And many of those who slept in the dust of the earth shall awake, some to everlasting life, and some to shame and everlasting contempt. . . . But you, Daniel, shut up the words, and seal the book, until the time of the end. Many shall run to and fro, and knowledge shall increase. (Daniel 12:1–4)

This last line adorns the frontispiece to Francis Bacon's *Instauratio Magna* (or *Great Renewal* [1620]), the founding work of the New Science. The end time that Daniel augurs signified for Bacon and his circle a state-sponsored, English-led turn from the closed systems of the classical Mediterranean world to the disinterested pursuit of universal knowledge that had been inspired by the newly discovered treasures of the Atlantic world—a reform of knowledge that would bring about Christ's return. Slave knowledge—the knowledge possessed by that new world treasure (or rather, by those appraised as such)—undoes the Baconian ideal. Again quoting Parrish: "[Jacobs] enunciated—by reinterpreting the New Science's scriptural quote—the impossibility of open 'disinterested' knowledge in a society with an extreme imbalance of power" and showed "how both the slave's and the slaveholder's knowledge was forced by the unnatural institution of slavery to become 'cunning,'" which colonials associated with "the possession of secret knowledge."[53]

"Cunning" is certainly one of Jacobs's favorite words. However, all indications are that, understanding the term in its archaic meaning, she means to privilege knowledge's *practical* (over its hidden) aspect. The most common locutions in *Incidents* (italicized for emphasis) provide an extraordinary sense of the ubiquity and the openness of practical knowledge in the form of everyday speech:

— "*I once heard* her father allude to her attachment to me." (32)
— "*I had been told* that she once chased a white gentleman with a loaded pistol." (47)
— "*A rumor went abroad* that his coffin was filled with money." (72)
— "*They hear such talk* as should never meet youthful ears, or any other ears." (80)
— "She had told him pretty plainly what she thought of his character, and there was considerable gossip in the neighborhood about our affairs, *to which the open-mouthed jealousy of Mrs. Flint contributed not a little.*" (82)
— "I have told you that Dr. Flint's persecutions and his wife's jealousy had given rise to *some gossip in the neighborhood.*" (84)
— "Aunt Nancy brought me *all the news she could hear* at Dr. Flint's." (176)
— "*The opinion was often expressed* that I was in the Free States." (177)

This "open-mouthed" prattle speaks volumes concerning the structure of knowledge in a slave culture, but to unexpected effect. Jacobs's writing argues *against* the idea that in slave societies the pursuit of knowledge shifted from open and disinterested (as members of the Royal Society had hoped) to secret and self-interested (as members of the planter class may have imagined and required).

For Jacobs, as for Michael Taussig, there is no such thing as a secret; it is an invention that comes out of the *open secret*—"that which is generally known, but cannot be articulated," or a conscious knowing of what not to know.[54] Jacobs claims precisely this status for knowledge in southern slave districts. "The secrets of slavery are concealed like those of the Inquisition," she writes. "My master was, to my knowledge, the father of eleven slaves. But did the mothers dare to tell who was the father of their children? Did the other slaves dare to allude to it, except in whispers among themselves? No, indeed!" (55). We are being invited to see the world the slaveholders made as one of an active not knowing that made a display of hiddenness, which display could only carry the empty promise of a future revelation. Jacobs marshals this powerful form of social knowledge toward the end of her own deliverance.

The letters famously penned by her narrative surrogate, Linda Brent, conceal her actual location while, at the same time, presenting an intentional subject who speaks from the non-place of representation. Her letters are a version of the open secret, a display of hiddenness. Any forensic approach to those epistolary dispatches, any attempt to recover a subject from that non-place, is destined to fail (whether that was the objective pursued by Dr. Flint and his surrogates or by literary historians).[55] The emptiness—the hollowed-out ontology—is pivotal to liberation and to meaning. Call this Jacobs's "agency of the letter."

Rumor runs on this same mechanism. It, too, is language without a subject, language that comes from no place. "Running to and fro," it produces more than it conceals—projects an intentional subject as the empty origin of its being. One wonders, then, why Jacobs is so quick to attribute the following call for deliverance to "the enormous lies [slaveholders] tell their slaves." Here is her memorable account of slave rumor:

> Intelligent slaves are aware that they have many friends in the Free States. Even the most ignorant have some confused notions about it. They knew that I could read; and I was often asked if I had seen any thing in the newspapers about white folks over in the big north, who were trying to get their freedom for them. Some believe that the abolitionists have already made them free, and that it is established by law, but that their masters prevent the law from going into effect. One

woman begged me to get a newspaper and read it over. She said her husband told her that the black people had sent word to the queen of 'Merica that they were all slaves; that she didn't believe it, and went to Washington city to see the president about it. They quarreled; she drew her sword upon him, and swore that he should help her to make them all free.... That poor, ignorant woman thought that America was governed by a Queen, to whom the President was subordinate. I wish the President was subordinate to Queen Justice. (69–70)

The typology should be familiar: a ruler who has proclaimed some great change in the lives of her subjects finds that her wishes have been thwarted by unfaithful subordinates. But the more familiar the rumor should seem—the more literary—the less we may be inclined to see it as having a life wholly independent of the text. In Jacobs's *Incidents*, uptake exerts a very delicate (but nonetheless transformative) pressure on origins, and there is ever the possibility that the Book of Daniel exerts some of this pressure, befuddling rumor's intentionality and our sense of its origin. The rumor of a benevolent "queen of 'Merica" in her struggle with an obstinate president recapitulates enough of Daniel's apocalyptic war between "the king of the north" and "the king of the south" to give us pause.[56] The epic struggle between "the demon Slavery" (84) and a benevolent royal comes to an end when the latter arrives proffering deliverance in the form of a text ("Some believe that . . . it is established by law" and "begged me to get a newspaper and read it over"). Genette described metalepsis as a "taking hold of (telling) by changing level," and the fantasy of an American queen, dropping into the text when and where she does, seems to do just that.[57] But if that is the case, who is the agent of deliverance here: slaves who have predicated their own rumors, the remote queen that they have figured, or Jacobs herself? Has Jacobs recorded or invented the rumor? Literate when her fellows aren't, able to "shut up the words, and seal the book" at will, Jacobs involves herself in the slaves' deliverance as agent of the apocalypse. The effect is to leave their language stuck between paraphrase and paratext (rumor, as metalepsis, creates a "zone between text and off-text, a zone not only of transition but of transaction").[58] To the extent that Jacobs provides the rumor with material textual support, it becomes a different kind of object, one that reacts to its uptake into discourse—neither originary speech nor literary invention, but something approximating their transaction.

Think of Jacobs as performing for her readers the simultaneity of sourcing and originality and by way of that simultaneity allowing us to see rumor for what it is: a writing circling an absence, independent of intention. Jacobs in this sense anticipates Gayatri Spivak's observation that rumor is "primordially (originarily) errant, always in circulation with no assignable source," and her further assertion that the mistake of both the colonial authorities and the historians who have relied on their diligent recordkeeping has been "to take rumour for speech, to impose the requirements of speech in the narrow sense upon something that draws its strength from participation in writing in the general sense."[59] Rumor, Spivak summarizes, is the "picture of writing."

Rumor's Ontology

The archive takes its name from the Greek *archon*, the "ruler" or "chief magistrate" who operated the system of law in ancient democracies, and takes its meaning more directly from the private residence (*arkheion*) in which the official documents that spoke the law were said to reside. The archon mediated the relation between master and servant as a primeval one, what the jurist William Blackstone understood as the first of the "great relations" of private life, and the one on which all other forms of personal relationship were based (e.g., parent and child, husband and wife).[60] As Carolyn Steedman clarifies, the archon dealt with slaves not as people but "only as aspects of their owners' property and personality."[61] Much the same was true in modern Anglo-American chattel slavery, where organs of state such as the court often denied the enslaved the right and means to speak for themselves. The archive affirms the principle, expressed succinctly by Congressman Francis Wilkinson Pickens on the eve of civil war in an argument against slaves' testimony, that "the slave could only be known through his master."[62]

It has been one of the defining purposes of the archive to posit the slave as knowable while also rendering inaccessible some aspect of either her voice or her intention—to preserve and suppress in the name of governance. This paradox is one of the reasons we tend to think of the archive of slavery as degraded and so much of slave history as irretrievably lost. It also goes a considerable way toward explaining why the moans, stutters, and shouts that inaugurate the black tradition tend to be foregrounded as a failure of speech—what has been described, variously, as the paradoxical record of an "eloquent absence" and a "telling inarticulacy."[63] One need only recall Frederick Douglass's recollection of the slaves' "wildsongs," which registered in his ears as an "unmeaning jargon." Such nonsense attested to a state in which, to paraphrase Fred Moten, the overlooked found itself bound up with the overseen: "Certain experiences of being tracked, managed, cornered in seemingly open space are inextricably bound to an aesthetically and politically dangerous supplementarity, an internal exteriority waiting to get out, as if the prodigal's return were to leaving itself."[64] Recall, too, Édouard Glissant's quietly prescient observation, in *Caribbean Discourse*, that "history has its dimension of the *unexplorable*," a phrase that premises the idea that black culture in the archive is "not lost or found, but undiscovered."[65] These reflections illuminate some of the ways in which black culture tends to deconstruct the contexts of its preservation: "blackness has been associated with a certain sense of decay, even when that decay is invoked in the name of a certain (fetishization of) vitality."[66] *Rumor in the archive:* an appearance made possible only in its disappearance; an aspiration registered at the moment of its suppression; a power that reaffirms itself by liquidating its sources. We are looking at something like a Deleuzean "fold," that "not-external outside" and "not-internal inside" that allows us to think differentiation, orientation, position, and therefore power in terms not of subject and object but of ceaseless self-relation.[67] One imperative is to approach rumors in the archive from the perspective of what is produced by that self-relation rather than what is and isn't preserved in it.

Rumor's paraphrase, translation, and transcription amplifies, rather than dampens, its semantic instability. Rumor rendered as a mode of archival *writing* makes said writing a manifestation of (and not merely a window onto) the fragile status of the enslaved—an expression of their political, even existential, uncertainty. The words left behind by Caribbean slaves are neither evidence irredeemably corrupted by the sovereign power that extracted them nor the verbatim speech through which we can recover subjects lost to history. These words are, rather, exactly what they appear to be: "impossible speech" that oscillates between loyalty and insurgency, speech and paraphrase, fact and prophecy, confession and coercion, and, in that sense, reflects back to us the deeply felt uncertainty of the enslaved. Attention to the rumors on the surface of the archive challenges our conception of the archive as a repository of latent voices and requires that we reconsider whether the story of slavery can ever be narrated "from below" if our aim is to register what is inaccessible in the voice of the enslaved.

What I have been calling a *metaleptic history* means to preserve just that sense of indeterminacy. According to Stephan Palmié, any such inquiry should be motivated by a trenchant critical question: "What right do we have to subject the indeterminacy—perhaps deeply felt uncertainty, ambivalence, and vacillation—that marked the lives and thought of those who died in negating the certainties on which our own world is built to forms of determinism that replicate (if through conscious inversion) the certainties of their executioners?"[68] This is more than a question of reproducing the perspective of the dominated, though it is certainly that.

A close model might be Lisa Lowe's "history hesitant"—a philosophy of history that strives for "modest and mundane" rather than "eternal [and] teleological" ends.[69] Deriving her sense of historical "hesitation" from "Sociology Hesitant" (1905), W. E. B. DuBois's posthumous critique of sociological positivism, Lowe proposes a hesitant historical writing that does not rush to recover what has been lost as such to history. It is a counterpoint to recovery projects that, in seeking to reverse an erasure caused by "the categories and narratives privileged by official accounts and archives," also risk reproducing the very forms of erasure that are "the signature of the regime of liberal freedom."[70] Hesitation "halts the desire for recognition by the present social order and staves off the compulsion to make visible within current epistemological orthodoxy."[71] As method, hesitation involves the deeply counterintuitive commitment to writing a history that is out of sync with its own time, a history that needs to preserve (if we recall the thoughts of David Lloyd cited earlier) something of the restlessness of the dominated: "Only in remaining out of joint with the times to which the dead are lost is there any prospect of a redress that would not be concomitant with the desire to lay the dead to rest. For the restlessness of the dead stems from the lack of a future fit for them, and only the unfitting can address the ghosts that rise like vapors through the disjointed frame of the present."[72] To place ourselves out of joint, we must strain to hear what is alien in the voice of the enslaved. This involves a necessary refusal to translate that foreignness back into our native tongue.

Impossible Speech

I want to make one last approach toward my object, this time under the guidance of Michel de Certeau's "Vocal Utopias," a peculiar bit of writing on the subject of glossolalia. It would be an understatement to say that de Certeau writes allusively about glossolalia (that is the essay's chief peculiarity), which is just what my critical practice calls for. An attempt to paraphrase de Certeau's thoughts may thus be worth the effort.

Glossolalia is a *trompe-l'oreille*, a mimesis of language that can be fabricated "when one knows its phonetic rules"; it orchestrates speech but only in the absence of meaningful statements, only as nonsense (*l'insensé*).[73] Examples of glossolalia include everything from infantile phonations ("eenie meenie minie moe") to neologisms and alliterations, from "speaking in tongues" and "ecstatic utterance" to glottal noises, the Dadaists' phonetic poetry, and approximations of pop music (try googling "Prisencolinensinainciusol"). Glossolalia represents the mumbling, babbling beginnings of speech, but as a theoretical vocal space in which "speech can say itself" (33)—a "vocal utopia"—those origins are an illusion. De Certeau provides a number of reasons for why this origin of speech always evades our attempts to know it.

The questions inside every glossolalic utterance—"How does one start to speak?" (33); where does speech begin and where does it end?—are questions glossolalia also makes impossible to answer. "Every glossolalia combines something prelinguistic, related to a silent origin, or to the 'attack' of the spoken word, and something postlinguistic, made from the excesses, the overflows, and the wastes of language" (33). Further, glossolalia's origins are illusory. It is a speech that begins but comes from no place, de Certeau suggests, because of the way it *stages* the act of communication. "Glossolalia 'rehearses' [*répète*] infantile phonations" (39). It is, in his words, "like a laboratory procedure" (30), "like a simulation of lunar landing" (30), a *"théâtre"* (both a playhouse and a military theater of operation) or an "opera" of enunciation "on the stage" of verbal exchange (30). "Glossolalia would be the phenomenon that *isolates* this opera and *authorizes* it. . . . The fiction of language sets the stage on which a simulation of speech is produced" (30). Finally, like a "cry" or a "confession," glossolalia presents itself as an "imperative" or a "need," and this "'attack' of the spoken word" is aimed primarily to draw out interpretation, to solicit it, a théâtre designed to lure it into a trap:

> [Glossolalia] excites an unwearying impulse to decrypt and to decipher that always supposes a meaningful organization behind the sequence of sounds.... In face of the glossolalic chain, the hermeneutic work mobilizes its scientific apparatus.... Interpretation searches for meaning, and it finds it because it expects it to be there, because interpretation relies on the conviction that especially where meaning appears to be absent, it is hidden someplace, present "all the same." (33–34)

Glossolalia forces interpretation to show itself; it dupes interpretation into pursuing a meaning "in those non-sense places where it postulates 'secret languages'" (34), "the places where it becomes possible and necessary *to write*" (34, emphasis added). In postulating "that somewhere there is speech" (34), positing that "meaning must be . . . *elsewhere*, outside the scene of speech" (36), glossolalia only befuddles interpretation, luring it into seeking out a hidden meaning where one does not reside. That irrecoverable meaning is glossolalia's fiction, its "fable" of origin (40), its "spirit."[74] Because meaning is absent, glossolalia and interpretation relate "in the mode of equivocation" (36). Glossolalia needs "the referent of interpretation to exile itself from meaning"; explanation uses glossolalia "to confirm its own principles" (36). For the reasons de Certeau sets forth (blind origins, speech's staging, the interpretive imperative), glossolalia involves a negation, or an awareness of not saying something. It predicates a metalepsis or litotes: "plays out at a distance" the transition "from a *can not say* . . . to a *can say* . . . by way of a *can say nothing*" (30–31).

At risk of projecting too rigid a "form" onto rumor, let me propose a kind of thought experiment. In this experiment, I ask that you run the rumored expressions we've encountered in the archive through the filter not of gossip or conspiratorial talk (a controlled *network* of speakers and hearers), but that of glossolalia ("a mumble that escapes the control of speakers" [30]). Rumor isn't a literal glossolalia, of course; it is, in this case, an infelicity or parallel kind of babbling, sputtering nonsense [*l'insensé*]—an "experience of being *infans*" (40), as de Certeau proposes, of being speechless *and* at the beginnings of speech:

Brown already free, black soon.

They repeatedly said that they knew their good King had sent out their freedom and that being withheld by the Whites they were determined to take it.

The King's troops would join them.

Our masters tell us that the King wants to make us free, and they tell us again that although the King wants to make us free, they will not submit to it, but they will keep us in a state of slavery.

She said her husband told her that the black people had sent word to the queen of 'Merica that they were all slaves; that she didn't believe it, and went to Washington city to see the president about it.

The King's troops would join them; they would band shoulder to shoulder with the rebel slaves.

I mean for you to sense how such errors and infelicities ("like a cry or a confession") present an imperative or a need, an injunction for the archive to do its "hermeneutic work" (34). Rumor's mistakes set a place "where it becomes . . . necessary to write" and in that way mislead interpretation into a confirmation of its own principles ("that especially where meaning appears to be absent, it is hidden someplace, present 'all the same'"). Again, the reciprocity between rumor and the archive is in this mode of equivocation. Rumor needs the archive to register its very existence. The archive, for its part, uses rumor to affirm its authority.[75] The scribes seek to hear a meaning, but meaning finds itself undone by a rival sense of otherworldliness:

They were to be freed [and] their freedom was to be given them through a black woman who was a Queen, for whom Mr. Wilberforce acted in England.[76]

A black woman was the Queen (allow me to finish the thought for you) *of England.*

Mistaken to a degree that taxes the mind—about American sovereignty, race and British royalty, the difference between sovereignty and intentionality, the truth of their own subjection—the slaves' rumors must have sounded to their masters like utter nonsense. And while any call to retain the perception of such rumors as nonsense risks "replicat[ing] . . . the certainties of their executioners," as Palmié put it, nonsense preserves something of the intransmissible, or what cannot be accessed in the voice of the enslaved.

Strain to hear what is alien in the voice of the enslaved.

Assume that, from within the slaves' locutions, one might extract a sense of the future to which they found themselves fit. What would that world actually look like? In what world are their white masters subject to a black queen? On the basis of what sorts of perceptions were they imagining such things? From what perspective could such things even be imagined? To refuse to make sense of nonsense, to refuse to translate that foreignness back into our native tongue, requires grammatologically *choosing* the babbling, sputtering nonsense of an anarchic, scatological writing in the archive over its protective uplift into the realm of dead, but valued (in being reflective or self-reflective) speech.

Strain to hear what is alien in the voice of the enslaved.

It is entirely possible, of course, that little within these rumors registers as nonsense to your ears. To amplify the sense of the absurd just a bit, I would invite you to feel a measure of the théâtre in the babble, in the sense to which de Certeau alludes, of both dramatic space and military theater of operation. The slaves' intentions do not so much matter; what matters is how rumor registers as a metalepsis. Recall that narrative metalepsis involves "a 'transgressive' invasion of the diegesis . . . by something that should be extradiegetic," as when the author of the novel you're reading turns out to be a character in it, or that novel turns out to be a novel within the novel (*Don Quixote*), or when novels skip from level to level, "characters escaped from a painting, a book, a press clipping, a photograph, a dream, a memory, a fantasy, etc." (Robbe-Grillet).[77] Metalepsis produces "effect[s] of strangeness" whose intensity demonstrates "the importance of the boundary they tax their ingenuity to overstep."[78] Slave rumor dilates this work of metalepsis and inverts it, staging the intrusion into one spatiotemporal universe (call it "the colonial scene" or "slaveholder ideology") of something that by rights should exist only outside of it: "the black people had sent word to the queen of 'Merica that they were all slaves"; "their freedom was to be given them through a black woman who was a Queen." Rumor's effect of strangeness exaggerates the sense *of a boundary*; it produces the sense that we are inside an aesthetic form. Like glossolalia, rumor "'rehearses' [*répète*] . . . beginnings of speech," a naïve speech, in a military staging of more mature "linguistic operations to come" (39). But it is only by way of a dramatic sense of théâtre, which persists as long as we are willing to hear the nonsense, that we are able to *feel* that the slaves have imagined another world, figured its threshold, and are prepared to "tax their ingenuity to overstep" it—"taking hold of (telling) by changing level." Their "impossible speech," which can have arrived for us only in the very force of this otherworldly assertion of a future of non-belonging, cannot and ought not be invoked in the name of historical recovery.

I have one last effect of strangeness for you, which you may find "either comical . . . or fantastic."[79]

Coda

They killed Martin Luther King!

ANONYMOUS, Los Angeles, 1992

A colleague once told me that, shortly after the jury announced its verdict in the Rodney King case, shouts of "They killed Martin Luther King!" could be heard on the streets of Los Angeles. The rumor hung around my office, taunting me over the course of writing this book; it seemed to reflect back so many of the qualities of the material I had been writing about: the infelicity; the untimeliness; the obviousness; the idea of history as a living memory of past atrocities that become primary players on the stage when a new outrage occurs; the nonsense. It may have been that it was said just once, or it may have been said many times. It may have been spoken by one person alone, or it may have been spoken by many. We will never know. Parse my Google search every way to Sunday (for "MLK," "LA uprising," "Rodney King") and I still fail to uncover any trace of the rumor. I resigned myself to muster up a few familiar scholarly moves and call it a day: *it would be hard to say it* never *happened, but the best we can do is admit to a lack of evidence* (or something of the sort). No uses for this rumor. *My* forensic imagination had hit a digital brick wall—that is, until I stumbled upon this, from Paul Mooney's *Masterpiece* standup routine from 1994:

> See, I lived through two riots, so I know what's up. First riot, niggaz was on our own. Second time, the Mexicans helped us. I gotta give it up to the Mexicans. Them mothafuckas helped us. Mexicans went crazy. They was out there cryin' "They killed Martin Luther Kiiiing!" And I was out there hollerin' "*Rodney* King, mothafuckas! Rodney Kiiiing!"[80]

Is this our evidence? Was the rumor a trenchant living memory or a racist joke? Was it reality or fiction? Or had a mistranslation occurred at some point, inverting reality and fiction? The rumor now looks like a classic metalepsis: "Present effect attributed to a remote cause. . . . The remote cause, because several causal steps intervene between it and the result, seems less like a cause than a metaphor substituted for a cause."[81] Every repetition makes it harder for you to believe that it occurred *and* leaves you open to the possibility that it may have occurred.

In one of her memoirs, Maya Angelou writes about her surprise at finding herself in Los Angeles in 1965 at the time of the assassination of Malcolm X and in New York a few years later at the time of the assassination of Martin Luther King.[82] She observes "noticeable differences" between "this current turmoil [in 1968] and the Watts Uprising" (187). In Los Angeles, "rage had ruled," she says. Watts was on fire, from which fact she learns for the first time that "odor travels faster and farther than sound" (64). How different things would be on the evening of April 4, 1968. On that night, following King's assassination, she writes, "a lamentation would rise and hold tremulously in the air, then slowly fall out of hearing range just as another would ascend" (187). Angelou walked the streets of Harlem overhearing strangers ask other strangers, "Why? Why?" (187). She enters a diner at random and notices that the place has been deserted, save for one customer. Helping herself to a cup of coffee, Angelou turns to him and asks, "May I help you?" His response befuddles: "No, baby, nobody can help me. Nobody can help nobody. You know this is all about Malcolm" (190). We hear her thoughts: "What? . . . Malcolm?" The customer explains:

> See, they killed him not far from here, and we didn't do anything. Lot of people loved Malcolm, but we didn't show it, and now even people who didn't agree with Reverend King, they out here, just to show we do know how to care for somebody. Half of this is for Malcolm X, a half for Martin King and a half for a whole lot of others. (190)

Expecting to hear "the awful despair at Martin Luther King's death," Angelou writes, "Malcolm's name shocked me" (190).[83]

I never would have imagined it possible to describe Paul Mooney and Maya Angelou as the bearers of similar critical insights, but they do seem to share something in the way their texts mirror the rumor in question. In both cases, the question of rumor's status as reality or fiction is put aside. What matters are the rhetorical effects: the same mistranslation that triggers action; the sense of an utterance that, both causal *and not*, bears a peculiar status in relation to the event.

Angelou's shock remains the crucial element here, providing a length of Ariadne's thread. Her shock approximates the uneasiness someone like Jorge Luis Borges might feel in encountering metaleptic intrusions—say, when a novelist such as Cervantes takes pleasure in confusing "the world of the reader and the world of the book": "These inversions suggest that if the characters of a fictional work can be readers or spectators, we, its readers or spectators, can be fictitious."[84] When characters step out of their realm into that of the reader, when we encounter rhetorical matter that just seems out of place, one easily feels a sense of vertigo, an "effect of strangeness." And as Genette gives us to understand these inversions, they are troubling because they seem to suggest that "the extradiegetic is perhaps always diegetic and that the narrator and his narrates—you and I—perhaps belong to some narrative."[85] The move in which characters become more real is easy enough to accept (however mysterious the mechanism), but one writer protests the falsity in Borges's assertion: "It's hard for me to understand how I would go about considering myself fictitious."[86] He has my sympathy, but perhaps puzzling out that particular conundrum isn't where our attention should lie. Perhaps, in the case of a rumor's intrusion into a time and space in which it does not belong, the question of how we become fictitiousness isn't the one we should be posing.

"They killed Martin Luther King!" It may be a racist joke, but we are in no position to say it was solely that, or even originally that. We can't dismiss it as rumor entirely—a mistranslation, in circulation, on the streets of Los Angeles, in the summer of 1992, that triggers collective action. All we can really say is that it's here and it now holds *us*. One must go to great lengths to discount that effect, so rather than mourn the lack of evidence, it now seems that we have to ponder, on the assumption that this *is* our evidence, what kind of evidence it is. Evidence *of what*? I don't know how to answer these questions. I don't know whether there can be an answer to such questions. What I would propose is that how you answer these questions will largely depend on how it feels to you to be held by this rumor (by its strangeness, whether comic, fantastic, or some other affect), which, like the "impossible speech" of the enslaved, can have arrived for us only in the force of its otherworldly assertion and (as I've said) neither can nor ought to be invoked in the name of historical recovery. We call these objects into being, then, and can feel held by them without owning or being owned in terms of identity, identification, or the need for it all to add up to something in terms of a collective identity.

I began this book with the idea that a forensic imagination has been directed toward the archive in service of recovering a "we" at the point of "our" violent origin—a project that we now see often manifests in either a cult of death or a cult of voice. What is at stake in the form of refusal for which I have been advocating is not so much a recuperative valorization of idle chatter as a refusal of the metaphysics its exalted other underwrites and the sense of belonging it is said to guarantee. What "we" share is the open secret of "our" impossibility, which is both held in and conveyed by the several itineraries charted in this book of disappearing subjects and disappearing works. To echo David Walker, James Baldwin, and the anticommunitarian strains we have attempted to sound from the first page, it is not the recovery of an impossible community but, rather, the making of a world that will no longer have me that is at stake. I said, too, that whatever blackness or black culture is, it cannot be indexed to a "we"—or if it is, that "we" can only be structured by and given in its own negation and refusal. There is no mutuality, no witnessing, no acknowledgment to be discovered in the archive (understood, as one final reminder, not as a repository, but as a Foucauldian "knot of conflicted interdependence"). In the archive, we discover not who we are but how "we" are not.

ACKNOWLEDGMENTS

A friend of mine (an editor at a major press) once gave me a simple bit of advice: every good book should be structured around a paradox. He was referring to arguments, ideas, and, you know, contents, but to someone who has written a book deeply skeptical of the "we" of black studies, I suppose one of its paradoxes is that it should have one. That collective includes Anjali Arondekar, Jennifer Ashton, Andrew Ayers, Mieke Bal, Lauren Berlant, Jennifer Devere Brody, Marshall Brown, Vincent Brown, Tina Campt, Joseph Cleary, Lou Cubba, Nan Z. Da, Colin (Joan) Dayan, Nadia Ellis, Jed Esty, Jennifer Fleissner, Christopher Freeburg, Catherine Gallagher, Eric Ganther, Thomas Germaine, Saidiya Hartman, Charles Hirschkind, Neils Hooper, Mary Johnson, Amy Kashiwabara, Richard Kaye, Doug Krehbiel, David Kurnick, Jonathan Lamb, Heather Love, Colleen Lye, Sharon Marcus, Saba Mahmood, David Marriot, D. A. Miller, Fred Moten, Tim Murphy, Chris Nealon, Tavia Nyong'o, Sam Otter, Neil Penick, Leigh Raiford, Michael Ralph, Darieck Scott, David Scott, Namwali Serpell, Anita Sokolsky, Kathleen Stewart, Elisa Tamarkin, Bryan Wagner, Julia Bryan Wilson, Tobias Barrington Wolff, and Damon Young. Hidden among this list of names is a congeries entitled the Black Room, a group that has taught me much about the power of intellectual generosity. I am incredibly grateful, too, to have had my enthusiasm for this project reflected back to me in the engagements and in the work of specific students, including Brandon Callender, Monica Huerta, Sarah Johnson, Ismail Muhammad, and, at the University of Chicago, James Duesterberg and Jean Thomas Tremblay.

A number of friends and interlocutors are also held in gratitude for their invitations to colloquy: Lloyd Pratt and David Corbett Peters of the Rothermere American Institute, Oxford University, and the Courtauld Institute, London, respectively; Donald Pease for the invitation to speak at the 2015 Futures of American Studies Institute, Dartmouth College; Jennifer Morgan and members of New York University's Working Group on Slavery, Freedom, and the Archive

(2009–11); Walter Benn Michaels, Kenneth Warren, and the Seminar in American Literature at the Scholl Center for American History and Culture, Newberry Library, Chicago; Toril Moi, who invited me to speak at "Beyond Critique: Reading after the Hermeneutics of Suspicion," Center for the Study of Philosophy, Arts, and Literature, Duke University; Grace (Jos) Lavery and Jessica Rosenberg, who convened the American Comparative Literature Association's seminar "Ornament, Utility, Waste: At the Limits of Aesthetic Capital"; Lauren Goodlad, who organized the Ends of History Conference at the University of Illinois, Urbana-Champaign; and audiences at Brown University; City University of New York; Dartmouth College; Duke University; Friedrich-Alexander Universität (Erlangen, Germany); New York University; Rutgers University; the University of California, Santa Cruz; the University of Chicago; the University of Maryland, College Park; the University of Pennsylvania; the University of Washington, Seattle; Vanderbilt University; Williams College; and Yale University. Thank you to Mark Bradford and El Anatsui for their generosity. Finally, to Laylah Ali, Anjuli Raza Kolb, Gage McWeeny, John Limon, Christopher Pye, David Smith, Anita Sokolsky, and my other friends and mentors at Williams College, thank you for bestowing me with the honor to serve as the Mary Bundy Scott Visiting Professor in the Department of English.

Lauren Berlant and Lee Edelman took an interest in this project at a pivotally important moment. My anonymous readers at Duke University Press were able to see what this book was about, both ethically and intellectually, and encouraged revisions that sharpened its claims; their engagements have impacted my thinking at a very profound level. Without the kindness and commitment of senior editor Courtney Berger, and the steady rigors of Christopher Catanese, Sandra Korn, and Stephanie Gomez Menzies, this book would still be sitting on my desk. I am deeply grateful for the depth, and sympathy, and generosity with which everyone at the press (and their proxies) have engaged my work.

For understanding what this book was about, in addition, at a very personal level, I owe a huge debt of gratitude to Sharon Marcus and Heather Love, both of whom have been fantastic interlocutors and encouraged me to take risks. And, finally, to Paul Rogers, to whom this book is dedicated, thank you for years of holding my ideas and reflecting them back to me in the most generous effort to forge an aesthetic life—a *we* in the face of its impossibility.

Parts of chapter 1 appeared as "Come and Gone," *Small Axe*, no. 48 (November 2015): 186–204. Chapter 2 was originally published as "On Failing to Make the Past Present," *Modern Language Quarterly* 73, no. 3 (September 2012), "Realisms after Modernisms: Views from the Literary Periphery" special issue, ed. Joe Cleary, Jed Esty, and Colleen Lye.

NOTES

INTRODUCTION

1. When I speak of the omnipresence of futurism in queer politics I am thinking in particular of the critique of "reproductive futurity" in Lee Edelman, *No Future: Queer Theory and the Death Drive* (Durham, NC: Duke University Press, 2004). In what follows, my reflections on fathers, sons, and failures of reproduction deliberately echo Edelman's eloquent statement of the antisocial thesis in queer theory.

2. The ideational tilt in queer theory can be detected in a long-standing debate over the value of utopia as measured against "antisociality" (the inescapable antagonisms of queer life), a debate in which "optimism" and "utopia" have frequently appeared as keywords. Some signature appearances (although this list is far from exhaustive) include Lauren Berlant, *Cruel Optimism* (Durham, NC: Duke University Press, 2011); Lauren Berlant and Lee Edelman, "Sex without Optimism," in *Sex, or the Unbearable* (Durham, NC: Duke University Press, 2014), 1–34; José Muñoz, *Cruising Utopia: The Then and There of Queer Futurity* (New York: New York University Press, 2009), a text that is deeply indebted to Ernst Bloch's *The Principle of Hope* (Cambridge, MA: MIT Press, 1995 [1954]); and Michael Snediker, *Queer Optimism: Lyric Personhood and Other Felicitous Persuasions* (Minneapolis: University of Minnesota Press, 2009).

3. The title of Raoul Peck's *I Am Not Your Negro* distills (and, not insignificantly, euphemizes) James Baldwin's measurably more barbed assertion that "what white people have to do is try and find out in their own hearts why it was necessary to have a 'nigger' in the first place, because I'm not a nigger, I'm a man. But if you think I'm a nigger, it means you need him. The question that you've got to ask yourself. . . . If I'm not the nigger here and you invented him, you the white people invented him, then you've got to find out why": James Baldwin, interviewed by Kenneth Clark, "Perspectives: The Negro and the American Promise" (WGBH-TV, Boston, 1963).

4. James Baldwin, *Remember This House* (incomplete ms.); reprinted in James Baldwin and Raoul Peck, *I Am Not Your Negro* (New York: Vintage, 2017), 30–31.

5. The Grenada Revolution (led by Maurice Bishop and the New Jewel Movement) lasted from March 13, 1979, to October 19, 1983, when the US military invaded the island. My professor, Dessima Williams, had been exiled because of Ronald Reagan's overthrow of the island's government: see David Scott, *Omens of Adversity: Tragedy, Time, Memory, Justice* (Durham, NC: Duke University Press, 2014).

6. James Baldwin, "Notes of a Native Son," in *Notes of a Native Son* (Boston: Beacon, 1955), 106. James Weldon Johnson also homes in on this impossible responsibility in *Along This Way* (New York: Penguin, 1990 [1933]), 56:

> The question of the child's future is a serious dilemma for Negro parents. Awaiting each colored child are cramping limitations and buttressed obstacles in addition to those that must be met by youth in general; and this dilemma approaches suffering in proportion to the parents' knowledge of and the child's ignorance of these conditions. Some parents up to the last moment strive to spare the child the bitter knowledge; the child of less sensitive parents is likely to have this knowledge driven in upon him from infancy. And no parent may definitely say which is the wiser course, for either of them may lead to spiritual disaster for the child.

7. Baldwin, "Notes of a Native Son," 90.

8. Baldwin, "Notes of a Native Son," 85, 98, 104.

9. Ismail Muhammad, "The Misunderstood Ghost of James Baldwin," *Slate*, February 15, 2017, accessed February 16, 2017, http://www.slate.com/articles/arts/books/2017/02/how_critics_have_misunderstood_james_baldwin_s_influence_on_today_s_great.html.

10. Baldwin, "Notes of a Native Son," 85.

11. Eve Kosofsky Sedgwick, "Paranoid Reading, Reparative Reading, or, You're So Paranoid, You Probably Think This Essay Is about You," in *Touching Feeling: Affect, Pedagogy, Performativity* (Durham, NC: Duke University Press, 2003), 147.

12. I mark this anticipation of severance *queer* on account of its affinities with the thesis of "antirelationality." The antisocial thesis in queer theory, as originally formulated by Leo Bersani, assumes "a potentially revolutionary inaptitude—perhaps inherent in gay desire—for sociality as it is known." This inaptitude is a threat to the social because "insofar as we fail to reproduce the family in a recognizable form, queers fail to reproduce the social": see Leo Bersani, *Homos* (Cambridge, MA: Harvard University Press, 1995), 76. See also Tim Dean, "The Antisocial Homosexual," *PMLA* 121, no. 3 (2006): 826.

Over the past three decades, Toni Morrison and Nathaniel Mackey have also offered some of the richest and most sustained explorations into these concerns. I discuss Morrison in chapter 2. For Mackey's inscription of Afro-diasporic experience as "wounded kinship," see Nathaniel Mackey, "Sound and Sentiment, Sound and Symbol," *Callaloo* 30 (1987): 29–54. Nadia Ellis presents an eloquent weave of these queer and diasporic critical traditions, building a case for the idea that "diasporic consciousness is at its most potent when it is, so to speak, unconsummated"—and, at such times, she adds, its most "paradigmatic": Nadia Ellis, *Territories of the Soul: Queered Belonging in the Black Diaspora* (Durham, NC: Duke University Press, 2015), 2. Ellis's book has broken important ground in the critique of race and belonging, and in *None Like Us* I am attempting to build on that ground.

13. It is, as Hortense Spillers might say, "as if neither time nor history, nor historiography and its topics, show movement": see Hortense J. Spillers, "Mama's Baby, Papa's Maybe: An American Grammar Book," in *Black, White, and in Color: Essays on American Literature and Culture* (Chicago: University of Chicago Press, 2003), 208.

14. Elizabeth A. Povinelli, "On Suicide, and Other Forms of Social Extinguishment," in *Theory Aside*, ed. Jason Potts and Daniel Stout (Durham, NC: Duke University Press, 2014), 88.

15. Povinelli, "On Suicide, and Other Forms of Social Extinguishment," 88.

16. Now would be a good time to admit to my (no longer) secret love of Queen's "Bohemian Rhapsody," a coming-out anthem for sure, but in my view, in addition, a hymn to severance as the essence of queer art—to letting oneself be consumed with the pleasures of what the choice of severance (from the mother, in the song's imaginary) involves.

17. Povinelli, "On Suicide, and Other Forms of Social Extinguishment," 88.

18. "Antiblackness" has circulated in the quite recent (theoretical) past as one name for the project of questioning the origin and ontology of blackness (the other name for it is "afro-pessimism"). In one way to phrase the question, does the position that sets itself against blackness (call it "racism," call it "white supremacy") precede or follow it? In another formulation, this one from Fred Moten, "If . . . the black cannot be an other for another black, if the black can only be an other for a white, then is there ever anything called black social life?" I am sympathetic to this line of interrogation, but my objective is to remove the question of antiblackness to the registers of rhetoric and relation. See Jared Sexton, "The Social Life of Social Death: On Afro-Pessimism and Black Optimism," in *Time, Temporality and Violence in International Relations: (De)fatalizing the Present, Forging Radical Alternatives*, ed. Anna M. Agathangelou and Kyle D. Killian (New York: Routledge, 2016), esp. 67, 72–73; Fred Moten, "The Case of Blackness," *Criticism*, vol. 50, no. 2 (Spring 2008): esp. 178.

19. David Walker, *Appeal to the Coloured Citizens of the World*, ed. Peter P. Hinks (University Park, PA: The Pennsylvania State University Press, 2012 [1829]), 3.

20. Sexton claims that, for all of the back and forth within black studies between optimism and pessimism, one "agreed upon" point is the idea that "black life is not social life in the universe formed by the codes of state and civil society, of citizen and subject, of nation and culture, of people and places, of history and heritage.... Black life is not lived in the world that the world lives in, but underground, in outer space.... [B]lack life is not social, or rather black life is *lived* in social *death*, which is also *social* death": Sexton, "The Social Life of Social Death," 69. This claim feels almost too stark, too absolute to be an object of universal assent, although I share with Sexton his sense of the breadth of its reach in the sense that it forms a point at which many of the field's "arguments ... begin, but cannot (yet) proceed": Sexton, "The Social Life of Social Death," 69. Sexton captures one of the meanings I intend when I speak of being *unfit for history*.

21. Leo Bersani, "Is the Rectum a Grave?" in *Is the Rectum a Grave? and Other Essays* (Chicago: University of Chicago Press, 2010), 25; Robyn Wiegman, "Sex and Negativity; or, What Queer Theory Has for You," *Cultural Critique* 95 (Winter 2017), 220.

22. Wiegman, "Sex and Negativity," 236.

23. Wiegman, "Sex and Negativity," 236.

24. Jonathan Goldberg, "The History That Will Be," *GLQ* 1 (1995): 388. Heather Love offers a model for drawing together these strands of the social and the historical: Heather Love, *Feeling Backward: Loss and the Politics of Queer History* (Cambridge, MA: Harvard University Press, 2007). See also Valerie Traub, "The New Unhistoricism in Queer Studies," *PMLA* 128, no. 1 (2013): 21–39.

25. Georg Wilhelm Friedrich Hegel, *Philosophy of History*, trans. J. Sibree (New York: Colonial Press, 1900), 98–99. For a statement of the tenets behind the claim that "the Negro is ... a man without a past," see the opening chapter in Melville J. Herskovits, *The Myth of the Negro Past* (Boston: Beacon, 1941).

26. Arthur Schomburg, "The Negro Digs Up His Past," in *The New Negro*, ed. Alain Locke (New York: Athenaeum, 1925), 231. Schomburg's essay sits within a discourse of "vindicationism," a tradition of Black Nationalist and Pan-Africanist writings from at least the second half of the nineteenth century that rebut claims of the inferiority of blacks to whites: see David Scott, *Conscripts of Modernity: The Tragedy of Colonial Enlightenment* (Durham, NC: Duke University Press, 2004), 79–87; Robert Hill, "C. L. R. James: The Myth of Western Civilization," in *Enterprise of the Indies*, ed. George Lamming (Port of Spain: Trinidad and Tobago Institute of the West Indies, 1999), 255–59.

27. The "recovery imperative" names the desire "to recover black subjects from archives structured by violence and colonial dispossession": Laura Helton, Justin Leroy, Max A. Mishler, Samantha Seeley, and Shauna Sweeney, "The Question of Recovery: An Introduction," *Social Text* 33, no. 4 (December 2015), 1.

28. Michel Foucault, *The Archaeology of Knowledge*, trans. A. M. Sheridan Smith (New York: Pantheon, 1972), 12.

29. Foucault, *The Archaeology of Knowledge*, 12.

30. Foucault, *The Archaeology of Knowledge*, 12.

31. Lisa Lowe, "History Hesitant," *Social Text* 33, no. 4 (December 2015), 85.

32. Anjali Arondekar, *For the Record: On Sexuality and the Colonial Archive in India* (Durham, NC: Duke University Press, 2009); Ann Cvetkovich, *An Archive of Feelings: Trauma, Sexuality, and Lesbian Public Cultures* (Durham, NC: Duke University Press, 2003); Helton et al., "The Question of Recovery," 1; Ann Laura Stoler, *Along the Archival Grain: Epistemic Anxieties and Colonial Common Sense* (Princeton, NJ: Princeton University Press, 2009); Diana Taylor, *The Archive and the Repertoire: Performing Cultural Memory in the Americas* (Durham, NC: Duke University Press, 2003).

33. Vincent Brown, *The Reaper's Garden: Death and Power in the World of Atlantic Slavery* (Cambridge, MA: Harvard University Press, 2008), 28. Brown offers a precise articulation of the problem: "The numbers tell an impressive story, but it is easy to forget that they represent the logic of markets better than they do the experience of enslavement": Brown, *The Reaper's Garden*, 28.

34. Helton et al., "The Question of Recovery," 1.

35. Brown, *The Reaper's Garden*, 59.

36. Brown, *The Reaper's Garden*, 260.

37. Stephan Palmié, *Wizards and Scientists: Explorations in Afro-Cuban Modernity & Tradition* (Durham, NC: Duke University Press, 2002), 83, 97.

38. Saidiya Hartman, "Venus in Two Acts," *Small Axe*, no. 26 (June 2008): 2.

39. Anjali Arondekar, "Without a Trace," in Arondekar, *For the Record*, 1, 4.

40. In *The Archaeology of Knowledge*, Foucault understands the archive as an expression of his thesis on power. He challenges us to regard the archive as something held less in libraries than in language—something less certain than a *tradition* but better defined than the *oblivion* that (in his words) "opens up to all new speech the operational field of its freedom." The archive is a generative system "that establishes statements as events and things," the rules of a practice "that enables statements both to survive and to undergo regular modification": see Foucault, *The Archaeology of Knowledge*, 128–30.

41. Sigmund Freud, "Mourning and Melancholia," in *The Standard Edition of the Collected Psychological Works*, vol. 14, ed. James Strachey (London: Hogarth, 1957), 243–258.

42. Anne Cheng, *The Melancholy of Race: Psychoanalysis, Assimilation, and Hidden Grief* (New York: Oxford University Press, 2001), xi. The body of work that would fall under the sign of melancholy is too diverse and too broad to enumerate here, but important works, in addition to *The Melancholy of Race*, include Ian Baucom, *Specters of the Atlantic: Finance Capital, Slavery, and the*

Philosophy of History (Durham, NC: Duke University Press, 2005); Paul Gilroy, *The Black Atlantic: Modernity and Double Consciousness* (Cambridge, MA: Harvard University Press, 1993); Paul Gilroy, *Darker than Blue* (Cambridge, MA: Harvard University Press, 2010); Paul Gilroy, *Postcolonial Melancholia* (New York: Columbia University Press, 2005); Hartman, "Venus in Two Acts"; Saidiya Hartman, "The Time of Slavery," *South Atlantic Quarterly* 101, no. 4 (2002): 757–77; David Kazanjian and David Eng, eds., *Loss: The Politics of Mourning* (Berkeley: University of California Press, 2003); Christina Sharpe, *Monstrous Intimacy: Making Post-slavery Subjects* (Durham, NC: Duke University Press, 2010) and *In the Wake: On Blackness and Being* (Durham, NC: Duke University Press, 2016); Michel-Rolph Trouillot, *Silencing the Past: Power and the Production of History* (Boston: Beacon, 1995). Key literary texts are Fred D'Aguiar's *Feeding the Ghosts* (London: Chatto and Windus, 1997); Toni Morrison, *Beloved* (New York: Penguin, 2000); M. NourbeSe Philip, *Zong!* (Middletown, CT: Wesleyan University Press, 2008); Dereck Walcott, *Omeros* (New York: Farrar, Straus and Giroux, 1990).

There is a great deal of overlap between these works and work that questions whether slavery is over, whether it represents a historical object that has been overcome, although the following make little to no claim to melancholy as a method: Michelle Alexander, *The New Jim Crow: Mass Incarceration in the Age of Colorblindness* (New York: New Press, 2010); Dennis Childs, *Slaves of the State: Black Incarceration from the Chain Gang to the Penitentiary* (Minneapolis: University of Minnesota Press, 2015); Barnor Hesse, "Escaping Liberty: Western Hegemony, Black Fugitivity," *Political Theory* 42, no. 3 (2014): 288–313; Jared Sexton, *Amalgamation Schemes: Antiblackness and the Critique of Multiracialism* (Minneapolis: University of Minnesota Press, 2008); Katherine McKittrick, *Demonic Grounds: Black Women and the Cartographies of Struggle* (Minneapolis: University of Minnesota Press, 2006).

43. Édouard Glissant, *Poetics of Relation*, trans. Betsy Wing (Ann Arbor: University of Michigan Press, 1997), 143–44.

44. Baucom, *Specters of the Atlantic*, 132, 258.

45. Baucom, *Specters of the Atlantic*, 132.

46. Hence, Baucom refers to Jacques Derrida's "mourning without limit."

47. Baucom, *Specters of the Atlantic*, 218.

48. Baucom, *Specters of the Atlantic*, 218.

49. Alan Liu, "The New Historicism and the Work of Mourning," in Alan Liu, *Local Transcendence: Essays on Postmodern Historicism and the Database* (Chicago: University of Chicago Press, 2008), 162. Marjorie Levinson pointed to the method of "negative allegory," or "allegory by absence," in the introduction to *Wordsworth's Great Period Poems: Four Essays* (Cambridge: Cambridge University Press, 1986), 8–13.

50. Michel Foucault, "The Life of Infamous Men," in *Michel Foucault: Power,*

Truth, Strategy, ed. Meaghan Morris and Paul Patton (Sydney, Australia: Feral Publications, 1979), 76–91.

51. As early as 2000, Catherine Gallagher and Stephen Greenblatt described Foucault's essay as "a little-read text," although over the course of the next decade and a half it would become a touchstone in queer and slave historiography, its impact felt less in the frequency of its citation than in the prominence achieved by the books and essays for which it has served as a model: see Catherine Gallagher and Stephen Greenblatt, "Counterhistory and the Anecdote," in *Practicing New Historicism* (Chicago: University of Chicago Press, 2000), 66–70. In the field of Atlantic slavery, see Saidiya Hartman, *Lose Your Mother: A Journey Along the Atlantic Slave Route* (New York: Farrar, Straus and Giroux, 2007), 137; Hartman, "Venus in Two Acts," 2; Marisa Fuentes, *Dispossessed Lives: Enslaved Women, Violence, and the Archive* (Philadelphia: University of Pennsylvania Press, 2016), 127–29. In the field of queer theory, see Carolyn Dinshaw, *Getting Medieval: Sexualities and Communities, Pre- and Postmodern* (Durham, NC: Duke University Press, 1999), 136–42; Brent Hayes Edwards, "The Taste of the Archive," *Callaloo* 35, no. 4 (2010): 946; Love, *Feeling Backward*, 46–49; Chris Nealon, *Foundlings: Lesbian and Gay Historical Emotion Before Stonewall* (Durham, NC: Duke University Press, 2001), 20–22; Kevin Ohi, *Henry James and the Queerness of Style* (Minneapolis: University of Minnesota Press, 2011), 144–45. Giorgio Agamben also views the essay as fundamental to Foucault's thought: see Giorgio Agamben, "The Author as Gesture," in *Profanations* (New York: Zone, 2007), 62–66.

52. Michel Foucault, "La vie des hommes infâmes," *Les Cahiers du Chemin* 29 (January 15, 1977) : 12–29. The title has also been translated as "Lives of Infamous Men": see Michel Foucault, "Lives of Infamous Men," *Michel Foucault: Power*, ed. James D. Faubion (New York: New Press, 2000), 157–75. My citations are to the translation.

53. Foucault, "Lives of Infamous Men," 161–64.

54. Foucault, "Lives of Infamous Men," 157; Agamben, "The Author as Gesture," 66.

55. Gallagher and Greenblatt, "Counterhistory and the Anecdote," 68; Agamben, "The Author as Gesture," 66.

56. Foucault, "Lives of Infamous Men," 157–59, emphases added.

57. Michael Taussig, *The Nervous System* (New York: Routledge, 1992).

58. Baucom, *Specters of the Atlantic*, 218.

59. Hartman, "Venus in Two Acts," 4 (citing Vena Das, *Life and Words: Violence and the Descent into the Ordinary* [Berkeley, CA: University of California Press, 2007], 17).

60. Love, *Feeling Backward*, 48–49.

61. Dinshaw, *Getting Medieval*, 138.

62. Gallagher and Greenblatt, "Counterhistory and the Anecdote," 70.

63. Eve Sedgwick, "Paranoid Reading and Reparative Reading; or, You're So Paranoid, You Probably Think this Introduction Is about You," in *Novel Gazing: Queer Readings in Fiction* (Durham, NC: Duke University Press, 1997), 1–2.

64. Gallagher and Greenblatt, "Counterhistory and the Anecdote," 70–71; Love, *Feeling Backward*, 40.

65. Mark Seltzer, "The Official World," *Critical Inquiry* 37, no. 4 (2011): 726.

66. Louise Fradenburg and Carla Freccero, *Premodern Sexualities* (New York: Routledge, 1996), viii.

67. Colin [Joan] Dayan, *The Law Is a White Dog: How Legal Rituals Make and Unmake Persons* (Princeton, NJ: Princeton University Press, 2011), xiii.

68. I am riffing on what the philosopher Bernard Williams called "wrongful life," or the situation in which one is born with a certain disadvantage that under a different set of circumstances would not have come about. Williams aims to work out the validity of a structure of grievance, with human genetics as his sample set. I do not mean to imply that African Americans bear a strongly genetic defect or anything analogous to it. I am thinking homologously of race as a social disadvantage or slavery as a historical injury. I mean only to suggest the logical constraints of the situation in which a person (or, in this case, a people) is inseparable from a certain disadvantage or injury, which situation with respect to African Americans appears to persist in the literary and archival universe explored in *None Like Us*: see Bernard Williams, "Resenting One's Own Existence," *Making Sense of Humanity* (Cambridge: Cambridge University Press, 1995), 224–232.

69. Michael Ralph, *The Forensics of Capital* (Chicago: University of Chicago Press, 2015), 13. In Ralph's formulation, a *forensic* is a calculus or protocol for predicating a subject (a "calculus used to adjudicate social standing"; "political belonging is shaped by strategies for securing political recognition—by protocols for assessing the integrity of a person or polity"). Ralph derives his sense of forensics from the work of William Pietz, who describes the idea as follows: "Modern forensics is a science of 'hybrids' in the sense that its task is to translate a culture's knowledge of physical causality into the rather different language of social causation that establishes legal liability": see William Pietz, "Material Considerations: On the Historical Forensics of Contract," *Theory, Culture and Society* 19, nos. 5–6 (December 2002): 36.

70. Bryan Wagner, *Disturbing the Peace: Black Culture and the Police Power after Slavery* (Cambridge, MA: Harvard University Press, 2009), 1.

71. Foucault located an "aesthetics of existence" (an "elaboration of one's own life as a personal work of art") in pre-Christian antiquity, although he found reason to encourage its renewed search near the end of his life: see Michel Foucault, "An Aesthetics of Existence," in *Philosophy, Politics, Culture: Interviews and Other Writings of Michel Foucault*, ed. Lawrence D. Kritzman (New York: Routledge, 1988), 49; Michel Foucault, "On the Genealogy of Ethics: An Over-

view of Work in Progress," in Michel Foucault, *Ethics, Subjectivity and Truth*, ed. Paul Rabinow (New York: New Press, 1997), 262.

72. Theodor W. Adorno, "Toward a Theory of the Artwork," in *Aesthetic Theory*, ed. Gretel Adorno and Rolf Tiedemann, trans. Robert Hullot-Kentor (London: Bloomsbury Academic, 2013), 243.

73. In *Dialectic of Enlightenment*, Odysseus presents as cultural progenitor of the idea of mimesis as assimilation and contiguity, for in bartering his way through the threats presented by the various deities and monsters he encounters along his way he survives these threats by cunningly adapting to them. The gods, in turn, in agreeing to the terms of barter, "are overthrown by the very system by which they are honored." Thus, in Odysseus's encounter with Polyphemus, his two contradictory responses, of both answering to his name, and disowning it, function in essence as one: "He acknowledges himself to himself by denying himself under the name Nobody; he saves his life by losing himself." Odysseus "abases himself." In him, "the self does not constitute the fixed antithesis to adventure, but in its rigidity molds itself [*sich anschmiegen*] only by way of that antithesis: being an entity only in the diversity of that which denies all unity . . . Odysseus loses himself in order to find himself." What is true for the epic hero is true for the work of art—and, to my way of thinking, for the critic; see Theodor W. Adorno and Max Horkheimer, *Dialectic of Enlightenment*, trans. John Cumming (New York: Continuum, 1997 [1944]), 47–49, 59–60.

74. Michel de Certeau, "Vocal Utopias: Glossolalias," *Representations* 56 (Autumn 1996): 31.

75. Terri Snyder, "Suicide, Slavery, and Memory in North America," *Journal of American History* 97, no. 1 (June 2010): 50–51.

76. Constantin Fasolt, *The Limits of History* (Chicago: University of Chicago Press, 2004), 143.

77. *The Report from a Select Committee of the House of Assembly, Appointed to Inquire into the Origin, Causes, and Progress, of the Late Insurrection* (Barbados: W. Walker, 1818).

78. Edwards, "The Taste of the Archive," 970.

1. MY BEAUTIFUL ELIMINATION

1. Jonathan Curiel, "At the de Young, a Stunning Work of Recycled Bottle Tops," *SF Weekly*, July 30, 2010, accessed April 22, 2013, http://blogs.sfweekly.com/shookdown/2010/07/at_the_de_young_a_stunning_wor.php. The work Curiel describes, *Hovor II* (2004), hangs in the De Young Museum in San Francisco.

2. Holland Cotter, "A Million Pieces of Home," *New York Times*, February 8, 2013, accessed February 11, 2013, http://www.nytimes.com/2013/02/10/arts/design/a-million-pieces-of-home-el-anatsui-at-brooklyn-museum.html.

3. Kwame Anthony Appiah, "Discovering El Anatsui," in *El Anatsui: When I Last Wrote to You about Africa*, ed. Lisa M. Binder, (New York: Museum for African Art, 2010), 63. The work Appiah describes is *Sasa* (2004).

4. For an outstanding take on the attraction to light in contemporary African diasporic art practice, see Krista Thompson, *Shine: The Visual Economy of Light in African Diasporic Aesthetic Practice* (Durham, NC: Duke University Press, 2015).

5. Appiah, "Discovering El Anatsui," 63.

6. Cotter, "A Million Pieces of Home."

7. Curiel, "At the de Young, a Stunning Work of Recycled Bottle Tops." The epiphanic signals the presence of something like a categorical imperative, a response everyone *ought* to have to the object—effects produced not for any particular person or by any particular object, but by its matter. A *categorical* imperative because any individual perceptual experience of the object, to be perceptual, must carry with it the suspicion that it is a property of the object, both evidence of its autonomy and an assertion of that autonomy. Perception is itself the artwork's medium. The suggestion is that the experience is not in fact (or even uniquely) mine but rather impersonal, consisting of a perspective that can account for me and for you, and for everyone and no one in particular. Hence, I account for the experience of no *particular* object in these opening paragraphs, refuse to specify a when or a where of this encounter—hence, too, the second-person "you," who is neither simply me (because who would care?) nor "the viewer" or "the subject" (because how would you know?).

8. We might describe an Anatsui as "ready-made" or "found object" art, although the artist demurs from describing his works in the language of modernism, preferring the less resonant art-history term "repurposed." The "readymade," a term coined by Marcel Duchamp, described an object that possesses a certain aesthetic autonomy, an object complete in itself whose plasticity has not been altered by the artist. Anatsui's emphasis is less on autonomy than on exhaustion, for "repurposed" implies a sense that the material has reached the end of its use value and has been frozen or immured within the artwork: See Lisa M. Binder, "El Anatsui: Transformations," *African Arts* 41, no. 2 (Summer 2008): 27, 36; Brandon Reintjes, "Installing Anatsui: The Politics of Economics in Global Contemporary Art," master's thesis, University of Louisville, Kentucky, May 2009, 45.

9. Lisa M. Binder, "Introduction," in *El Anatsui: When I Last Wrote to You about Africa*, ed. Lisa M. Binder (New York: Museum for African Art, 2010), 18.

10. Robert Storr, "The Shifting Shapes of Things to Come," in Binder, *El Anatsui*, 62.

11. Storr, "The Shifting Shapes of Things to Come," 62. Yambo Ouologuem, *Le devoir de violence* (London: Secker and Warburg, 1971).

12. Storr, "The Shifting Shapes of Things to Come," 57–62.

13. Jonathan Crary, *Suspensions of Perception* (Cambridge, MA: MIT Press, 1999), 9, 155. For example, in Georges Seurat's pointillist *Parade de cirque* (1888), "The representational features of the painting (the figures, the architectural setting) have a perceptual coherence that is unrelated to the individual touches of color out of which they are constituted." The three musicians to the left of the composition take their shape from dots of orange, blue, and yellow-orange paint, but these discrete points of color "have nothing in common with our experience of those figures suffused in a shimmering hazy violet." In gestalt, the sensory apprehension of a form "alternate[s] temporally with a perception of more elementary sensations": Crary, *Suspensions of Perception*, 156–57.

14. Adorno states on the artwork's irrelevance and incompleteness, "Each artwork, as a structure, perishes in its truth content; through it the artwork sinks into irrelevance, something that is granted exclusively to the greatest artworks. The historical perspective that envisions the end of art is every work's idea. There is no artwork that does not promise that its truth content, to the extent that it appears in the artwork as something existing, realizes itself and leaves the artwork behind simply as a husk": Theodor W. Adorno, "Toward a Theory of the Artwork," in *Aesthetic Theory*, ed. Gretel Adorno and Rolf Tiedemann, trans. Robert Hullot-Kentor (London: Bloomsbury Academic, 2013),180, 241.

15. Theodor W. Adorno and Max Horkheimer, *Dialectic of Enlightenment* (1944), trans. John Cumming (New York: Continuum, 1997).

16. Adorno's mimetic project is "intended to anticipate a new non-dominating mode of relation to inner and external nature": Seyla Benhabib, *Critique, Norm, and Utopia: A Study of the Foundations of Critical Theory* (New York: Columbia University Press, 1986), 11. The natural world presents a surfeit of models of this type of mimesis (see the introduction, footnote 73, for the one exception). Examples include the chameleon who "always taking on the color of its surroundings . . . never seems to be 'itself'"; the witch doctor who "imitating the wild animal in order to appease it . . . attempt[s] to become part of the same order from which the threat emanates"; and homeopathic and other types of inoculation in which the patient receives a drug "that causes symptoms resembling those of the disease being treated": see Michael Cahn, "Subversive Mimesis: Theodor W. Adorno and the Modern Impasse of Critique," in *Mimesis in Contemporary Theory: An Interdisciplinary Approach*, vol. 1, ed. Mihai Spariosu (Philadelphia: John Benjamins, 1984), 54. The anthropologist Michael Taussig describes Adorno's project as a "sensuous" mimesis: Michael Taussig, *Mimesis and Alterity: A Particular History of the Senses* (New York: Routledge, 1993), 44–47.

17. Ernst van Alphen, *Art in Mind: How Contemporary Images Shape Thought* (Chicago: University of Chicago Press, 2005), 2. Largely drawing on theories of the artwork's autonomy indebted to Adorno, Hubert Damisch and Ernst van Alphen argue for a view of the artwork as "an act of thought." Together with Georges Didi-Huberman, they challenge a core axiom of the discipline of art

history—"that the meaning of art can only be formulated historically [and that an] artwork, therefore, is always an expression of the historical period or figure that produced it": Van Alphen, *Art in Mind*, 2. I mean to court the same skepticism in this chapter's argument. Damisch maintains that it is impossible to possess the "period eye" of another time in history (the term is attributed to Michael Baxandall) and that "works of art appear to full advantage only if we deal with them as ways of thinking": see Yve-Alain Bois, Denis Hollier, Rosalind Krauss, and Hubert Damisch, "A Conversation with Hubert Damisch," *October* 85 (Summer 1998): 9. See also Georges Didi-Huberman, *Confronting Images: Questioning the Ends of a Certain History of Art* (University Park: Pennsylvania State University Press, 2009).

18. On film and "thick media effects" as prisms for literary historicism ("how we might shoot [poetry] as a film"), see Alan Liu, "Contingent Methods," in Alan Liu, *Local Transcendence: Essays on Postmodern Historicism and the Database* (Chicago: University of Chicago Press, 2008), esp. 13–19.

19. "A unique handmade object receives from its maker a *spiritual deposit* that Benjamin calls 'aura.' Objects mass produced by machine lack this aura.... The aura is the artifact's historical trace, the footprint that it leaves in time; this mark is erased when it can be replaced by a new copy at any moment": Aaron Kunin, "Artifact, Poetry as," *Princeton Encyclopedia of Poetry and Poetics*, ed. Roland Greene (Princeton, NJ: Princeton University Press, 2012), 88.

20. Walter Benjamin, *The Work of Art in the Age of Its Technological Reproducibility, and Other Writings on Media*, ed. Michael W. Jennings, Brigid Doherty, and Thomas Y. Levin, trans. Edmund Jephcott et al. (Cambridge, MA: Harvard University Press, 2008), 21–23.

21. Liu, *Local Transcendence*, 18.

22. Liu, *Local Transcendence*, 19. Liu also writes, employing more filmic vocabulary, "From the later nineteenth century on, new linguistic, graphic, photographic, filmic, and other media not only updates 'as it really was' into a distinctly modern form of reverie but also provided a new platform for critique. We might instance imagism, cubism, the New Typography, film montage in the style of Sergei Eisenstein, Russian Formalism, the New Criticism, and structural linguistics. All these movements set out in one way or another to make dialectical critique immanent on thick media effects—for example, by making defamiliarization, irony, paradox, and arbitrariness palpable in imagery, picture surface, collage, montage, or signifiers": Liu, *Local Transcendence*, 13.

23. As shall become clear shortly, this chapter makes a case for *punctum* (rather than aura) as historical paradigm.

24. Liu, *Local Transcendence*, 20, 23, emphasis added.

25. Mark Doty writes, "Description is an ART to the degree that it gives us not just the world but the inner life of the witness": Mark Doty, *The Art of Description: World into Word* (Minneapolis: Graywolf, 2010), 65.

26. Michel Foucault, "Friendship as a Way of Life," in *Ethics: Subjectivity and Truth*, ed. Paul Rabinow (New York: New Press, 1997), 137, emphasis added. The double movement of "extinguishment and potentiation" that Elizabeth Povinelli takes as necessary for the creation of "a new social form" would be one way to articulate what I am after here. If I were reading alongside Wittgenstein, I might describe this project of self-divestiture in the language of my "poverty"—that is, the perception that the world "exist[s] in a process of decline . . . beyond recovery by morality" (mine or anyone else's) and that therefore one is to make a virtue of one's secondariness, one's responsiveness, one's capacity merely to read. If I were reading alongside Emerson, I might identify it with his "ontology of dislocations"; the shaking, sliding, and falling in his prose through which the rupture of personal identity is achieved: see Stanley Cavell, "Declining Decline: Wittgenstein as a Philosopher of Culture," in *This New Yet Unapproachable America: Lectures after Wittgenstein after Emerson* (Albuquerque, NM: Living Batch, 1989), 77; and Branka Arsić, *On Leaving: A Reading in Emerson* (Cambridge, MA: Harvard University Press, 2010), 170.

27. Orlando Patterson, "Toward a Future That Has No Past: Reflections on the Fate of Blacks in the Americas," *Public Interest*, no. 27 (1972): 60–61; Édouard Glissant, *Poetics of Relation*, trans. Betsy Wing (Ann Arbor: University of Michigan Press, 1997), 193; Wendy Brown, *States of Injury: Power and Freedom in Late Modernity* (Princeton, NJ: Princeton University Press, 1995).

28. Stephen Best and Saidiya Hartman, "Fugitive Justice," *Representations* 92 (Winter 2005): 5.

29. Best and Hartman, "Fugitive Justice," 5.

30. Frances Ferguson, *Pornography, the Theory* (Chicago: University of Chicago Press, 2004), 38.

31. Ferguson, *Pornography*, 38–39.

32. Liu, *Local Transcendence*, 162.

33. Hegel, *Philosophy of History*, 98.

34. Georg Wilhelm Friedrich Hegel, *Philosophy of Spirit*, trans. A. V. Miller (Oxford: Oxford University Press, 1977), 111–19.

35. Patchen Markell, *Bound by Recognition* (Princeton, NJ: Princeton University Press, 2003), 10–17.

36. Leo Bersani, "Sociality and Sexuality," *Critical Inquiry* 26, no. 4 (Summer 2000): 646.

37. Anita Sokolsky, "The Melancholy Persuasion," in *Psychoanalytic Literary Criticism*, ed. Maud Ellmann (New York: Routledge, 1994), 129.

38. Cedric Robinson, "The Nature of the Black Radical Tradition," in Cedric Robinson, *Black Marxism: The Making of the Black Radical Tradition* (Chapel Hill: University of North Carolina Press, 1983), 167–71.

39. See Jeffrey B. Peires, *The Dead Will Arise: Nongqawuse and the Great Xhosa Cattle-Killing Movement of 1856–7* (Bloomington: Indiana University

Press, 1989), Jennifer Wenzel, *Bulletproof: Afterlives of Anticolonial Prophesy in South African and Beyond* (Chicago: University of Chicago Press, 2009).

40. Robinson, *Black Marxism*, 132–35; R. K. Kent, "Palmares: An African State in Brazil," *Journal of African History* 6, no. 2 (1965): 161–75.

41. Robert I. Rotberg, ed., *Strike a Blow and Die: A Narrative of Race Relations in Colonial Africa by George Simeon Mwase* (Cambridge, MA: Harvard University Press, 1967), 48–49.

42. Robinson, *Black Marxism*, 68, 168–69.

43. Robinson, *Black Marxism*, 170–71.

44. Robinson, *Black Marxism*, 168.

45. Robinson, *Black Marxism*, 168–69.

46. Robinson, *Black Marxism*, 171.

47. David Scott feels skeptical that it is one when he asks, "What makes us think that we can string these words together?" about the critical commonplace "the black radical tradition": see David Scott, "On the Very Idea of a Black Radical Tradition," *Small Axe*, no. 46 (March 2013): 1–6.

48. Robinson takes the phrase "outlandish Africans" (Robinson, *Black Marxism*, 169–70) from Gerald Mullin, *Flight and Rebellion* (New York: Oxford University Press, 1972), 18. Black radicalism reads as "outlandish" in a quite literal sense of reflecting the consciousness of those who remembered another land, those with a superior moral claim on another "home," and, significantly in this regard, Robinson fails to draw a single example of the black radical tradition from the North American context, which absence suggests that creolization effectively snuffed out this revolutionary consciousness.

49. A surrealism *avant la lettre* in Afro-diasporic culture recognized "the imagination as our most powerful weapon"; and the Europeans who would claim the name realized that "entire cultures had methods of thought and communication that transcended the conscious": Robin D. G. Kelley, *Freedom Dreams: The Black Radical Imagination* (Boston: Beacon, 2002), 159–60. See also Franklin Rosemont and Robin D. G. Kelley, eds., *Black, Brown, & Beige: Surrealist Writings from Africa and the Diaspora* (Austin, TX: University of Texas Press, 2009).

50. Stanley Cavell, *The Claim of Reason: Wittgenstein, Skepticism, Morality, and Tragedy* (Oxford: Oxford University Press, 1979), 454.

51. Rei Terada, *Looking Away: Phenomenality and Dissatisfaction, Kant to Adorno* (Cambridge, MA: Harvard University Press, 2009), 2. See also Stanley Cavell, "The Avoidance of Love: A Reading of *King Lear*," in *Disowning Knowledge: In Seven Plays of Shakespeare* (Cambridge: Cambridge University Press, 1987), 39–124.

52. Cavell, *The Claim of Reason*, 454; Paul Standish, "Skepticism, Acknowledgment, and the Ownership of Learning," in *Stanley Cavell and the Education*

of Grownups, ed. Naoko Saito and Paul Standish (New York: Fordham University Press, 2012), 80.

53. Bersani, "Sociality and Sexuality," 646.

54. Terada, *Looking Away*, 4. Erving Goffman's sense of "awayness" also resonates with Terada's "looking away," although her thinking is more phenomenological than sociological: a "kind of inward emigration from the gathering [that] may be called 'away'" to which "strict situational regulations obtain": Erving Goffman, *Behavior in Public Places: Notes on the Social Organization of Gatherings* [New York: Free Press, 1963], 69). See also Mark Seltzer, *The Official World* (Durham, NC: Duke University Press, 2016), 166–69.

55. Terada, *Looking Away*, 3–4.

56. Terada, *Looking Away*, 3–4.

57. I claim for this chapter—indeed, for the entire book—a very local (and quite personal) habitation that approximates what the literary critic Darieck Scott refers to as a "politics without defense," which he defines as a politics "that assimilates to itself racial identities and the history that makes them, knowing and naming the injustice of those identities and histories but choosing not to battle against them but rather to let them, as it were, flow through the self—even overwhelm the self—and yet become transformed." This is an identity "without the customary defenses against history": Darieck Scott, *Extravagant Abjection: Blackness, Power, and Sexuality in the African American Literary Imagination* (New York: New York University Press, 2010), 245–46.

58. Walter Benn Michaels, *The Gold Standard and the Logic of Naturalism* (Berkeley: University of California Press, 1987), 162.

59. I thank Jennifer Ashton for this observation.

60. My claim concerning "striving" assimilates two counterintuitive statements regarding painting and resemblance. The philosopher Nelson Goodman observes that where a painting "denotes" the object it represents, it "resembles" other paintings. "A Constable painting of Marlborough Castle," he writes, "is more like any other picture than it is like the Castle, yet it represents the Castle and not another picture—not even the closest copy." Or, in Michael Leja's paraphrase, "A painting necessarily bears a much stronger resemblance to any other painting than to whatever it depicts." See Nelson Goodman, *Languages of Art: An Approach to a Theory of Symbols* (Indianapolis, IN: Hackett, 1976), 5; Michael Leja, "Touching Pictures in William Harnett," in Michael Leja, *Looking Askance: Skepticism and American Art from Eakins to Duchamp* (Berkeley: University of California Press, 2004), 133.

61. Adorno writes, "Artworks organize what is not organized": Adorno and Tiedemann, *Aesthetic Theory*, 251.

62. Walter Benn Michaels, *The Beauty of a Social Problem* (Chicago: University of Chicago Press, 2015), 85.

63. Jonathan Culler, *On Deconstruction: Theory and Critique after Structuralism* (Ithaca, NY: Cornell University Press, 1982), 193. For a pivotal moment in this critical tradition, see Jacques Derrida's discussion of the *parergon* in Jacques Derrida, *La Vérité en peinture* (Paris: Flammarion, 1978), 63, 71–73.

64. Culler, *On Deconstruction*, 193.

65. Stanley Fish, *Self-Consuming Artifacts: The Experience of Seventeenth-Century Literature* (Berkeley: University of California Press, 1972), 52.

66. Leo Bersani and Ulysse Dutoit, *Arts of Impoverishment: Beckett, Rothko, Resnais* (Cambridge, MA: Harvard University Press, 1993), 93, 105.

67. Walter Benn Michaels, *The Shape of the Signifier: 1967 to the End of History* (Princeton, NJ: Princeton University Press, 2004), 90, 93. The internal quote is from Michael Fried, *Art and Objecthood: Essays and Reviews* (Chicago: University of Chicago Press), 155. Elsewhere, Michaels writes, "What determines the picture as a picture is the establishment of its frame, which will be essential not only to the unity of the work . . . but to the very idea of art": Walter Benn Michaels, "The Force of a Frame: Owen Kydd's Durational Photographs," http://nonsite.org/feature/the-force-of-a-frame.

68. Michaels, *The Beauty of a Social Problem*, 75–77, 198 n. 11. See also Stephen Best, Sharon Marcus, and Heather Love, "Building a Better Description," *Representations* 135 (Summer 2016): 1–21.

69. Michael Fried, "Barthes's *Punctum*," in *Photography Degree Zero: Reflections on Roland Barthes's "Camera Lucida,"* ed. Geoffrey Batchen (Cambridge: MIT Press, 2009), 156.

70. Fried, *Art and Objecthood*, 153.

71. Michaels, *The Shape of the Signifier*, 90; Michaels, *The Beauty of a Social Problem*, 98.

72. That infinity is essentially what Bersani and Dutoit mean by "the untreated, unaestheticized world beyond."

73. Fried, "Barthes's *Punctum*," 148.

74. Michaels, *The Beauty of a Social Problem*, 17.

75. Roland Barthes, *Camera Lucida: Reflections on Photography*, trans. Richard Howard (New York: Hill and Wang, 1981), 26.

76. Barthes, *Camera Lucida*, 26–27.

77. Michaels, *The Beauty of a Social Problem*, 46–47.

78. Michaels, *The Beauty of a Social Problem*, 15–16, emphasis added.

79. I thank James Duesterberg, Jean Thomas Tremblay, and Lauren Berlant for their generous and generative discussions of Anatsui's trompe l'oeil as it relates to Barthes's *punctum* and for calling me back to think more deeply about the "act" of framing as both explicitly theorized in *Camera Lucida* and unconsciously (though no less powerfully) operative in recent examples of the New Materialism.

80. Lacan, as a young intellectual, seeks to escape the life of the mind by joining a crew of fishermen in Brittany. One fisherman, Petit-Jean, points to a sardine can floating in the water, winking and glittering in the sun, "a witness to the canning industry, which we, in fact, were supposed to supply." Joking, he says to Lacan, "You see that can? Do you see it? Well, it doesn't see you!" Though the joke was at Lacan's expense (he was so "out of place in the picture" he could not be seen), he gets the last laugh by reading in the joke the logic of the *gaze*: "If what Petit-Jean said to me, namely, that the can did not see me, had any meaning, it was because in a sense, it was looking at me, all the same. It was looking at me at the level of the point of light, the point at which everything that looks at me is situated": Jacques Lacan, *The Four Fundamental Concepts of Psychoanalysis*, ed. Jacques-Alain Miller, trans. Alan Sheridan (New York: W. W. Norton, 1998), 95.

81. In Manny Farber's formulation, such art "feels its way through walls of particularization, with no sign that the artist has any object in mind other than eating away the immediate boundaries of his art, and turning these boundaries into the conditions of the next achievement." Farber directs his scorn at a particular kind of artist who, in thrall to the "sin of framing," takes small-scale formal achievements and squanders them "in pursuit of the continuity, harmony, involved in constructing a masterpiece . . . , filling every pore of a work with glinting, darting Style and creative Vivacity": Manny Farber, "White Elephant Art and Termite Art" (1962), in *Negative Space: Manny Farber on the Movies*, expanded ed. (New York: Da Capo, 1998), 135.

Anatsui arguably traffics in a similar aesthetic practice. Known for viewing curators and installers as collaborators with whom he shares the authorship of his work, Anatsui insists that the form of any particular object not be viewed as immutable and that it be seen only as the temporary expression of a set of "raw materials"—that is, swatches that can be organized differently each time a work is displayed. (Anatsui says, "I never dictate to people how to display the work—though they're full of interpretational possibilities. You can display the pieces to arrive at all kinds of other meanings": quoted in Gerard Houghton, "The Epitome of Freedom," in *Il mondo vi appartiene*, ed. Caroline Bourgeois [Milan: Electa, 2011], 90.)

82. "It comes to us, with no work of our own; then leaves us prepared to undergo a giant labor": Elaine Scarry, *On Beauty and Being Just* (Princeton, NJ: Princeton University Press, 1999), 53.

83. Heather Love has recuperated "the strain of failure that runs through all modernism" for the critical project of queer theory: see Heather Love, *Feeling Backward: Loss and the Politics of Queer History* (Cambridge, MA: Harvard University Press, 2007), 56. See also Judith Halberstam, *The Queer Art of Failure* (Durham, NC: Duke University Press, 2011). Other forms of the queer object that serve a project of de-realization are Daniel Tiffany's "lyric substance" (a lyr-

icism that points to "the obscurity of its particular medium") and Rei Terada's "looking away" (an attachment to "mere" appearance, to "transient perceptual objects" that are "below or marginal to normal appearance . . . because only they seem capable of noncoercive relation"): Daniel Tiffany, *Infidel Poetics: Riddles, Nightlife, Substance* (Chicago: University of Chicago Press, 2009), 55–56; Terada, *Looking Away*, 3–4.

84. Bersani, "Sociality and Sexuality," 641–56.

85. Bersani, "Sociality and Sexuality," 648–49.

86. Foucault, "Friendship as a Way of Life," 136, 138.

87. Bersani, "Sociality and Sexuality," 642.

88. Bersani, "Sociality and Sexuality," 643, emphasis added.

89. Camelia Elias, *The Fragment: Towards a History and Poetics of a Performative Genre* (Bern: Peter Lang, 2004), 4.

90. Bruno Latour, *Reassembling the Social: An Introduction to Actor-Network-Theory* (New York: Oxford University Press, 2007), 148.

91. Bradford's technique bears some affinities with the technique Max Ernst called *grattage* (graphic frottage), which involved the vigorous scraping and partial removal of dry paint, an early (some consider it the earliest) instance of which is his painting *Forest and Sun* (1927), currently in the collection of the Art Institute of Chicago.

92. On the deconstructive palimpsest, see the translator's preface by Gayatri Chakravorty Spivak in Jacques Derrida, *Of Grammatology* (Baltimore: Johns Hopkins University Press, 1976), xviii. On the Mystic Writing Pad, see Richard Galpin, *Erasure in Art: Destruction, Deconstruction, and Palimpsest*, 1998, chap. 3, para. 9, www.richardgalpin.co.uk/archive/erasure.htm.

93. H. W. Fowler, F. G. Fowler, and J. B. Sykes, *The Concise Oxford Dictionary of Current English* (Oxford, Clarendon, 1976). Palimpsest was often called on to explain "the ways in which the subject is written and overwritten through multiple and contradictory discourses": Bronwyn Davies, *A Body of Writing: 1990–1999* (Walnut Creek, CA: Altamira, 2000), 138. It allowed one to see how the essential and pre-discursive self once imagined by humanism was in fact "still there as one amongst many writings," continuing to take up space and thus shape our interpretation of the self-as-process: Davies, *A Body of Writing*, 138. However, since one image it might confer is that of an *original* writing on a blank parchment, the metaphor could also "hold in place the idea that there is an original prediscursive self . . . that is shaped through discourse": Davies, *A Body of Writing*, 138. There is nothing to stop a reader from reading the metaphor in this way; in fact, such a reading seems inevitable in the situation in which surface and depth are taken to be the terms of a binary, surface is held to "overwrite" or hide depth either behind or beneath it, and depth is understood as ideally expressed in the blankness of the parchment. Palimpsest proved a defining metaphor in the post-structuralist genealogy that shaped me. It provides

a topos of surface and depth that I have felt was in need of rethinking: see Stephen Best and Sharon Marcus, "Surface Reading: An Introduction." *Representations* 108 (Fall 2009): 1–21.

One of the more compelling attempts to rethink the surface-depth binary appears in Foucault's discussion of *surfaces of emergence* in *The Archaeology of Knowledge*. In chapter 3, "The Formation of Objects," Foucault attempts to get a handle on what he calls the "rules of formation" of a discourse—in this case, madness, in which, upon a certain chronological break, a variety of objects, such as behavioral disorders, sexual aberrations, and intellectual deficiencies, congealed into a single register. "Surface of emergence" describes that which is "susceptible to deviation"—that is, "normative," possessing a "margin of tolerance" and "threshold beyond which exclusion is demanded": Michel Foucault, *The Archaeology of Knowledge*, trans. A. M. Sheridan Smith (New York: Pantheon, 1972), 41. Foucault's description of how madness appears in their midst of these surfaces of emergence is both interesting and memorable. He writes, "In these fields of initial differentiation, in the distances, the discontinuities, and the thresholds that appear within it, psychiatric discourse finds a way of limiting its domain, of defining what it is talking about, of giving it the status of an object—and therefore of making it manifest, nameable, and describable" Foucault, *The Archaeology of Knowledge*, 41.

Note here that, in his attempt to describe an order of appearance, Foucault links it not to a logic of disappearance but, rather, to a kind of movement across "distances . . . discontinuities [and] threshold[s]." When he asserts that the discourse of psychiatry *"finds a way* of limiting its domain," that it recoils against its own expansion, the personification of emergence as self-abnegation highlights the extent to which the forces at play here are internal to the surface, and not external to it.

What might we observe of this movement? First, none of it sounds like the excavation or exfoliation that might be appropriate to the layered strata of a palimpsest. Second, in all of this recalcitrant recoil and fumbling across discontinuities and thresholds, one ought to hear the crinkling and folding of a surface layer onto itself, a surface that is infinitely folded and thus comes to contain its own depth. It is here that the Foucauldian fold starts to acquire some of the characteristics of surface that "Surface Reading" meant to accentuate—its intricacy, multiplicity and involution. See also Stephen Best, "*La Foi Postcritique*, on Second Thought," *PMLA* 132, no. 2 (2017): 337–43.

94. Paper will be obliterated in such a way that the revealed color suggests a singular planar surface. String or cord will trace the shape of letters, but when it is sanded, it just as easily obscures as reveals that shape. Neon polyester cord (from Home Depot)—red, orange, yellow, yellow-green, or deep blue—combines with a silicone caulk (also from Home Depot) that, whether it is white, black, or clear, reveals its own color when it is sanded while obscuring the color of the

cord it hides underneath: see Richard Shiff, "Move with Chance," in *Mark Bradford* (New Haven, CT: Yale University Press, 2010), 77.

95. Mieke Bal, *Lili Dujourie—Early Works, 1969–1983* (Munich: Kunstverein München, 1998), 126, emphasis added.

96. Elias, *The Fragment*, 190.

97. Gwendolyn Brooks, "Boy Breaking Glass," in *In the Mecca* (New York: Harper & Row, 1968), 36–37.

98. Marc Crawford, quoted in D. H. Melhem, *Gwendolyn Brooks: Poetry and the Heroic Voice* (Lexington: University Press of Kentucky, 1987), 176.

99. R. Baxter Miller, "'Does Man Love Art?' The Humanistic Aesthetic of Gwendolyn Brooks," in *Black American Literature and Humanism*, ed. R. Baxter Miller (Lexington: University Press of Kentucky, 1981), 107–9, emphasis added.

100. Sokolsky, "The Melancholy Persuasion," 129.

101. Allan Grossman, *The Long Schoolroom: Lessons in the Bitter Logic of the Poetic Principle* (Ann Arbor: University of Michigan Press, 1997), 15–16.

102. Ben Lerner, comment on Allan Grossman, "You're a Poet; Don't You Hate Most Poems?" *The Believer*, accessed 23 June 2015, www.believermag.com/exclusives/?read=interview_lerner.

103. Grossman, *The Long Schoolroom*, 16.

104. Lerner, comment on Grossman, "You're a Poet."

105. Grossman takes *lyric* poetry to be singularly beset by such "bitterness," but I find such effects of the virtual in Brooks's free verse as well. My sense of recursion and the involute in "Boy Breaking Glass" echoes Hortense Spillers's reading of *Maud Martha*, which, in her assessment "prepares the way for . . . the stunning poetry of *In the Mecca*." *Maud Martha*'s title character engages in a "kind of displaced fable-making [in which she] might be seen as the 'true poet' of the narrative and the writer herself the 'imitator' of it": Hortense J. Spillers, "'An Order of Constancy': Notes on Brooks and the Feminine," in *Black, White, and in Color: Essays on American Literature and Culture* (Chicago: University of Chicago Press, 2003), 136–37.

106. According to Daniel Tiffany, poetic materialism is rarely founded on the problematic of the object. Instead, it fashions a new (self-standing?) phenomenalism on the construction of some type of "lyric substance"—that is, on the conversion of its poetic "objects" into a riddling substance that defies the intuitive laws of objects: Daniel Tiffany, *Toy Medium: Materialism and Modern Lyric* (Berkeley: University of California Press, 2000); Tiffany, *Infidel Poetics*.

107. Brooks writes, "'But WHY do These People offend themselves?' / say they who say also 'It's time. / It's time to help / These people'": Gwendolyn Brooks, *Riot: A Poem in Three Parts* (Detroit: Broadside, 1969), 19. See also Daniel Patrick Moynihan, *The Negro Family: The Case for National Action* (Washington, DC: Office of Policy Planning and Research, United States Department of Labor, 1965), also known as the "Moynihan Report."

108. Seltzer, *The Official World*, 165–68. Terada, *Looking Away*, 3–4.

The accent on the minor and the given can be felt across a broad range of practices and fields of inquiry, with one center of gravity in literary and cultural studies: Best and Marcus, "Surface Reading"; Roland Barthes, *The Neutral: Lecture Course at the Collège de France, 1977–1978*, trans. Rosalind E. Krauss and Denis Hollier (New York: Columbia University Press, 2005); Rita Felski, *The Limits of Critique* (Chicago: University of Chicago Press, 2015); Anne-Lise François, *Open Secrets: The Literature of Uncounted Experience* (Stanford, CA: Stanford University Press, 2003); Heather Love, "Close but Not Deep: Literary Ethics and the Descriptive Turn," *New Literary History* 41, no. 2 (Spring 2010): 371–91; Heather Love, "Close Reading and Thin Description," *Public Culture* 25, no. 3 (Fall 2013): 401–34; Sianne Ngai, *Ugly Feelings* (Cambridge, MA: Harvard University Press, 2005); Eve Kosofsky Sedgwick, *Touching Feeling: Affect, Pedagogy, Performativity* (Durham, NC: Duke University Press, 2003); Terada, *Looking Away*; Alex Woloch, *The One versus the Many: Minor Characters and the Space of the Protagonist in the Novel* (Princeton: Princeton University Press, 2003).

109. Seltzer, *The Official World*, 166. Stephen Best, "On Failing to Make the Past Present," *Modern Language Quarterly* 73, no. 3 (September 2012): 454.

110. All quotations from Anne-Lise François, "Late Exercises in Minimal Affirmatives," in *Theory Aside*, ed. Jason Potts and Daniel Stout (Durham, NC: Duke University Press, 2014), 35, 45–46, 45. See also Elizabeth Anker and Rita Felski, eds., *Critique and Postcritique* (Durham, NC: Duke University Press, 2017).

111. Sedgwick, *Touching Feeling*, 8.

112. Sedgwick, *Touching Feeling*, 8.

113. Sedgwick, *Touching Feeling*, 8.

114. Sedgwick, *Touching Feeling*, 8. I detect a desire to explicate a similar set of critical resources in what Wayne Koestenbaum calls "fag limbo"—which, upon his wry assimilation of the word "fag" to its original meaning, "fatigue," describes a sensibility that involves disidentification and critical fatigue, an inability (in his words) "to think through anything but the materials right now in my room, wherever and whatever my room might be, whether bubble or cell or gallery or mausoleum or website": Wayne Koestenbaum, "Fag Limbo," in Wayne Koestenbaum, *My 1980s and Other Essays* (New York: Farrar, Straus and Giroux, 2013), 197.

115. Koestenbaum, "Fag Limbo," 200.

116. Koestenbaum, "Fag Limbo," 200. A masterly example of thinking like a work of art is T. J. Clark, *The Sight of Death: An Experiment in Art Writing* (New Haven, CT: Yale University Press, 2006).

2. ON FAILING TO MAKE THE PAST PRESENT

Epigraph: Alain Corbin, *The Life of an Unknown: The Rediscovered World of a Clog Maker in Nineteenth-Century France*, trans. Arthur Goldhammer (New York: Columbia University Press, 2001), viii.

1. This critical tendency sometimes operates under the term "neoslavery," which was initially coined by Bernard Bell as a way to classify the contemporary historical novel of slavery: see Bernard Bell, *The Afro-American Novel and Its Tradition* (Amherst: University of Massachusetts Press, 1987); Ashraf Rushdy, *Neo-slave Narratives: Studies in the Social Logic of a Literary Form* (New York: Oxford University Press, 1999); Valerie Smith, "Neo-slave Narratives," in *The Cambridge Companion to the African-American Slave Narrative*, ed. Audrey A. Fisch (New York: Cambridge University Press, 2007), 168–88. "Neo-slavery" is distinct scholarship that falls under "slavery by another name"—for example, an interest in forms of debt peonage and burdened obligation that arose in the wake of emancipation. On forms of racial indebtedness, see Douglas Blackmon, *Slavery by Another Name: The Re-enslavement of Black Americans from the Civil War to World War II* (New York: Doubleday, 2008); Saidiya Hartman, "Fashioning Obligation: Indebted Servitude and the Fetters of Slavery," in Saidiya Hartman, *Scenes of Subjection: Terror, Slavery, and Self-Making in Nineteenth-Century America* (New York: Oxford University Press, 1997), 125–63.

2. In *We Who Are Dark: The Philosophical Foundations of Black Solidarity* (Cambridge, MA: Harvard University Press, 2005), Tommie Shelby argues for a reconceptualization of black political solidarity, given that a "thick" sense of racial identity and a "thin" sense of shared historical persecution no longer appear to be sufficient conditions for it.

3. João Biehl, "Vita: Life in a Zone of Social Abandonment," *Social Text 68* 19, no.3 (Fall 2001): 136.

4. Nathaniel Mackey, *Bedouin Hornbook* (Lexington: University Press of Kentucky, 1986), 34.

5. Leo Bersani, *Homos* (Cambridge, MA: Harvard University Press, 1995), 10. Daniel Tiffany, *Infidel Poetics: Riddles, Nightlife, Substance* (Chicago: University of Chicago Press, 2009), 13.

6. Heather Love, *Feeling Backward: Loss and the Politics of Queer History* (Cambridge, MA: Harvard University Press, 2009), 4.

7. David Scott, *Conscripts of Modernity: The Tragedy of Colonial Enlightenment* (Durham, NC: Duke University Press, 2004), 50, 209. See also Reinhart Koselleck, *Futures Past: On the Semantics of Historical Time*, trans. Keith Tribe (Cambridge, MA: MIT Press, 1985).

8. David Lloyd, "The Indigent Sublime: Specters of Irish Hunger," *Representations* 92 (Fall 2005): 152–53.

9. Houston A. Baker Jr., *Blues, Ideology, and Afro-American Literature* (Chicago: University of Chicago Press, 1984); Hazel Carby, *Reconstructing Womanhood: The Emergence of the Afro-American Woman Novelist* (New York: Oxford University Press, 1987); Henry Louis Gates Jr., *The Signifying Monkey* (New York: Oxford University Press, 1988); Valerie Smith, *Self-Discovery and Authority in Afro-American Narrative* (Cambridge, MA: Harvard University Press, 1987); Hortense J. Spillers, "Mama's Baby, Papa's Maybe: An American Grammar Book," *Diacritics* 17, no. 2 (1987): 64–81.

10. Paul Gilroy, *The Black Atlantic: Modernity and Double Consciousness* (Cambridge, MA: Harvard University Press, 1993), 73. Colin (Joan) Dayan faults Gilroy's entire method for the ease with which it transforms slavery into "nothing more than a metaphor": Colin [Joan] Dayan, "Paul Gilroy's Slaves, Ships and Routes: The Middle Passage as Metaphor," *Research in African Literatures* 27, no. 4 (Winter 1996): 7–14. Hers is still the most rigorous critique of the idea of "the black Atlantic."

11. Gilroy, *The Black Atlantic*, 187; Toni Morrison, *Beloved* (New York: Penguin, 2000), 200.

12. Vincent Brown, "History Attends to the Dead," *Small Axe*, no.31 (March 2010): 227. See also Vincent Brown, *The Reaper's Garden: Death and Power in the World of Atlantic Slavery* (Cambridge, MA: Harvard University Press, 2008).

13. Saidiya Hartman, *Lose Your Mother: A Journey Along the Atlantic Slave Route* (New York: Farrar, Straus and Giroux, 2007), 87.

14. Alexander X. Byrd, *Captives and Voyagers: Black Migrants across the Eighteenth-Century British Atlantic World* (Baton Rouge: Louisiana State University Press, 2008); Peter Linebaugh and Marcus Rediker, *The Many-Headed Hydra: Sailors, Slaves, Commoners, and the Hidden History of the Revolutionary Atlantic* (Boston: Beacon, 2000); Cassandra Pybus, *Epic Journeys of Freedom: Runaway Slaves of the American Revolution and Their Global Quest for Liberty* (New York: Beacon, 2006): Marcus Rediker, *The Slave Ship: A Human History* (New York: Viking Penguin, 2007); Joseph Roach, *Cities of the Dead: Circum-Atlantic Performance* (New York: Columbia University Press, 1996); James Sidbury, *Becoming African in America: Race and Nation in the Early Black Atlantic* (New York: Oxford University Press, 2007); Stephanie Smallwood, *Saltwater Slavery: A Middle Passage from Africa to American Diaspora* (Cambridge, MA: Harvard University Press, 2007).

15. Elisa Tamarkin, "Transatlantic Returns," in *A Companion to American Literary Studies*, ed. Caroline F. Levander and Robert S. Levine (Malden, MA: Blackwell, 2011), 266–67.

16. Orlando Patterson, "Toward a Future That Has No Past: Reflections on the Fate of Blacks in the Americas," *Public Interest*, no. 27 (Spring 1972): 48.

17. Eric Slauter, "History, Literature, and the Atlantic World," *William and Mary Quarterly* 65 (3rd series), no. 1 (January 2008): 135.

18. Stanley Cavell, "Finding as Founding: Taking Steps in Emerson's 'Experience,'" in *This New yet Unapproachable America: Lectures after Wittgenstein after Emerson* (Albuquerque, NM: Living Batch, 1989), 84. See Sigmund Freud, "Mourning and Melancholia" (1917), in *The Standard Edition of the Complete Psychological Works of Sigmund Freud*, vol. 14, ed. James Strachey (London: Hogarth, 1957), 239–60. Cavell finds Freud's essay "Transience" (1918) more pertinent to this conceptualization of mourning than the more frequently referenced "Mourning and Melancholia."

19. That "refusal" is pathological for Freud, a suicidal identification that also represents a hatred of the object. For him, there really should be no melancholy, assuming a civilizational process managed by the pleasure principle. Given this sense of the antinomy between mourning and melancholia, it is important to stress that much of the contemporary work on melancholy does not pathologize the dyad in the way that Freud, Wendy Brown, and others do.

20. Slavoj Žižek, "Melancholy and the Act," in *Did Somebody Say Totalitarianism? Five Interventions in the (Mis)use of a Notion* (London: Verso, 2001), 141.

21. Marsha Darling, "In the Realm of Responsibility: A Conversation with Toni Morrison," *Women's Review of Books* (March 1988), 6.

22. Morrison, *Beloved*, 34.

23. Morrison, *Beloved*, 260.

24. Anne-Lise François describes God's promise as an event that "can have no time of its own, only the tense of a hope or memory": Anne-Lise François, *Open Secrets: The Literature of Uncounted Experience* (Stanford, CA: Stanford University Press, 2008), 47.

25. Walter Benn Michaels, *Our America: Nativism, Modernism, Pluralism* (Durham, NC: Duke University Press, 1995), 141.

26. The line, spoken by Gavin Stevens, a character in William Faulkner's *Requiem for a Nun* (New York: Random House, 1951), is often attributed to Faulkner himself.

27. Ian Baucom, *Specters of the Atlantic: Finance Capital, Slavery, and the Philosophy of History* (Durham, NC: Duke University Press, 2005), 150.

28. Baucom, *Specters of the Atlantic*, 29. The traumatic economic convulsion of our present has been so long lasting and of such global reach that it in many respects affirms every base tenet of Atlanticism. The Great Recession has affirmed Baucom's thesis, too—for, coming in the wake of the convulsive events of September 2008 (i.e., the implosion of Morgan Stanley, AIG, collateralized debt obligations, AAA-rated mortgage securities, and a general deleveraging), it also came in the wake of the appearance of *Specters of the Atlantic*, which was published three years earlier.

29. Baucom, *Specters of the Atlantic*, 29.

30. Scott, *Conscripts of Modernity*, 41.

31. Leopold van Ranke, "Preface: Histories of the Latin and Germanic Nations

from 1494–1514," in *The Varieties of History: From Voltaire to the Present*, ed. Fritz Stern (New York: Vintage, 1973), 57.

32. Walter Benjamin, "Theses on the Philosophy of History," in *Illuminations*, ed. Hannah Arendt, trans. Harry Zohn (New York: Schocken, 1969), 255.

33. Kenneth Warren, *What Was African American Literature?* (Cambridge, MA: Harvard University Press, 2011), 82.

34. Colin [Joan] Dayan, *The Law Is a White Dog: How Legal Rituals Make and Unmake Persons* (Princeton, NJ: Princeton University Press, 2011), xiv, xiii.

35. Saidiya Hartman, "The Time of Slavery," *South Atlantic Quarterly* 101, no. 4 (2002): 758.

36. Hartman, "The Time of Slavery," 759–59.

37. Hartman, "The Time of Slavery," 758.

38. Hartman, "The Time of Slavery," 759. As I said, Hartman's formulation is an erstwhile one, as the fundaments to her thought shift significantly in *Lose Your Mother*. In that text, dispossession forms the condition of relation for blacks in the New World and the irredeemable past the grounds of any historiography of slavery. The title alone signals the book's attachment to what I am calling the *abandonment thesis*.

39. Benjamin, "Theses on the Philosophy of History," 257.

40. It is curious what a prominent role Benjamin has been made to play in the recent melancholic turn, not least the function that his "Theses on the Philosophy of History" has served in advancing it, considering his own quite explicit caution against "left melancholy": see esp. Walter Benjamin, "Left-Wing Melancholy" (1931), in *The Weimar Republic Sourcebook*, ed. Anton Kaes, Martin Jay, and Edward Dimendberg (Berkeley: University of California Press, 1994), 304–6; Wendy Brown, "Resisting Left Melancholy," *boundary 2* 26, no. 3 (1999): 22.

41. Leo Bersani, *The Culture of Redemption* (Cambridge, MA: Harvard University Press, 1990), 1. The most full-throated statement of this division appears in Walter Benjamin, "The Work of Art in the Age of Mechanical Reproduction" (1936), in Arendt, *Illuminations*, 217–51.

42. Bersani, *The Culture of Redemption*, 1.

43. Bersani, *The Culture of Redemption*, 53, 55.

44. Bersani, *The Culture of Redemption*, 1. I thank David Kurnick for reminding me of Bersani's critique.

45. Heather Love makes a compelling case that a "descriptive reading" of *Beloved* draws into focus the novel's "critique of historical reclamation," Morrison's expressed commitments to the latter project aside, and it is to this reading that I attribute my first sense that Morrison is more attuned to turning against herself than those inspired by her tend to grant her: see Heather Love, "Close but not Deep: Literary Ethics and the Descriptive Turn," *New Literary History* 41(2010): 371–91.

46. Darling, "In the Realm of Responsibility," 5–6.

47. In the broad study of Afro-Atlantic slavery, death has emerged as the primary way to describe force in the aftermath of ideology critique: see Orlando Patterson, *Slavery and Social Death* (Cambridge, MA: Harvard University Press, 1982); Colin [Joan] Dayan, "Legal Slaves and Civil Bodies," in *Materializing Democracy: Toward a Revitalized Cultural Politics*, ed. Russ Castronovo and Dana Nelson (Durham, NC: Duke University Press, 2002), 53–94; Russ Castronovo, *Necro Citizenship: Death, Eroticism, and the Public Sphere in the Nineteenth-Century United States* (Durham, NC: Duke University Press, 2001); Achille Mbembe, "Necropolitics," trans. Libby Meintjes, *Public Culture* 15, no.1 (2003): 11–40; Giorgio Agamben, *Homo Sacer: Sovereign Power and Bare Life* (Stanford, CA: Stanford University Press, 1998). For a critique of recent extensions of the social death thesis, see Vincent Brown, "Social Death and Political Life in the Study of Slavery," *American Historical Review* (December 2009): 1231–49.

48. Toni Morrison, *A Mercy* (New York: Knopf, 2008), 6. Hereafter, page numbers cited in parentheses in the text refer to this edition.

49. John Updike, "Dreamy Wilderness," *The New Yorker*, November 3, 2008, 112–13.

50. Stanley Cavell, *This New Yet Unapproachable America: Lectures after Wittgenstein after Emerson* (Albuquerque, NM: Living Batch, 1989), 12.

51. While not an endorsement of the death drive, Morrisonian abandonment at the very least taps a resistance to what Lee Edelman terms "reproductive futurism," that is, an organizing principle of communal relation and social viability that sets ideological limits on contemporary political discourse: Lee Edelman, *No Future: Queer Theory and the Death Drive* (Durham, NC: Duke University Press, 2004), 2.

52. Edelman, *No Future*, 4.

53. Cavell, *This New yet Unapproachable America*, 12.

54. Fred Moten glosses Mackey's formulation to mean "a beginning whose origin is never fully recoverable, never operative as the end of any imagined return": Fred Moten, *In the Break: The Aesthetics of the Black Radical Tradition* (Minneapolis: University of Minnesota Press, 2003), 73.

INTERSTICE

1. Toni Morrison, "The Site of Memory," in *Inventing the Truth: The Art and Craft of Memoir*, ed. William Zinsser (Boston, 1987), 109.

2. Jacques Derrida, *Archive Fever: A Freudian Impression*, trans. Eric Prenowitz (Chicago: University of Chicago Press, 1995), 89–91; Jacques Lacan, "The Mirror-Phase as Formative of the Function of the I," in *Écrits: A Selection*, trans. Alan Sheridan (New York: W. W. Norton, 1977), 1–7.

3. John Blassingame, *The Slave Community: Plantation Life in the Antebellum South* (New York: Oxford University Press, 1979 [1972]), esp. 367–82.

4. Peter Linebaugh and Marcus Rediker, *The Many-Headed Hydra: Sailors, Slaves, Commoners, and the Hidden History of the Revolutionary Atlantic* (Boston: Beacon, 2000).

5. For a time, literary critics worked tirelessly to make the slave narrative tradition prima facie evidence of the slave experience, a hard-to-ignore tradition of letters that would rival a ubiquitous and irrepressible song as (in the words of W. E. B. DuBois) "the articulate message of the slave to the world." Key works include Houston A. Baker Jr., *Blues, Ideology, and Afro-American Literature* (Chicago: University of Chicago Press, 1984); Henry Louis Gates Jr., *The Signifying Monkey* (New York: Oxford University Press, 1988), Valerie Smith, *Self-Discovery and Authority in Afro-American Narrative* (Cambridge, MA: Harvard University Press, 1987); Robert Stepto, *From Behind the Veil: A Study of Afro-American Narrative* (Chicago: University of Illinois Press, 1979).

6. Nell Irvin Painter, "Soul Murder and Slavery: Toward a Fully Loaded Cost Accounting," in *Southern History across the Color Line* (Chapel Hill: University of North Carolina Press, 2002), 16, 39.

7. Saidiya Hartman, "Venus in Two Acts," *Small Axe* 26 (June 2008): 3.

8. Lisa Lowe, "History Hesitant," *Social Text* 33, no. 4 (December 2015): 85.

9. Ludwig Wittgenstein, *Philosophical Investigations: The German Text, with an English Translation* (1953), rev. 4th ed., trans. G. E. M. Anscombe, P. M. S. Hacker, and Joachim Schulte (Malden, MA: Wiley-Blackwell, 2009), no. 89.

10. Toril Moi, "'Nothing Is Hidden': From Confusion to Clarity, or Wittgenstein on Critique," in *Critique and Postcritique*, ed. Elizabeth Anker and Rita Felski (Durham, NC: Duke University Press, 2017), 36.

11. Charles Altieri, "Cavell's Imperfect Perfectionism," in *Ordinary Language Criticism: Literary Thinking after Cavell after Wittgenstein*, ed. Kenneth Dauber and Walter Jost (Evanston, IL: Northwestern University Press, 2003), 216.

12. Susan Scott Parrish, *American Curiosity: Cultures of Natural History in the Colonial British Atlantic World* (Chapel Hill: University of North Carolina Press, 2006), 265. Ross Posnock refers to the "buried essence" model of authenticity: Ross Posnock, "'Don't Think, But Look!': W. G. Sebald, Wittgenstein, and Cosmopolitan Poverty," *Representations* 112 (Fall 2010): 138 n. 40.

13. Dominick LaCapra writes, "All history . . . must more or less blindly encounter the problem of a transferential relation to the past, whereby the processes at work in the object of study acquire their displaced analogues in the historian's account. Coming to terms with transference in an exchange with the past may be the issue that confronts historiography with its most engaging and unsettling challenge": Dominick LaCapra, *History and Criticism* (Ithaca, NY: Cornell University Press, 1985), 11. See also Carlo Ginzburg, *The Judge and the Historian: Marginal Notes on a Late-Twentieth-Century Miscarriage of Justice*, trans. Antony Shugaar (London: Verso, 1999).

14. James Sweet has worked to move the study of the slave past away from

a search for identity. He asks, What if "entanglement" (rather than "identity") were the starting point of one's inquiry? What narrative forms would be adequate to describe the entanglements of an Olaudah Equiano or a Domingos Álvares over the course of their movement through the Atlantic world? See James Sweet, "Mistaken Identities? Olaudah Equiano, Domingos Álvares, and the Methodological Challenges of Studying the African Diaspora," *American Historical Review* 114 (April 2009): 305.

15. Paul Ricoeur, *Freud and Philosophy: An Essay on Interpretation*, trans. Denis Savage (New Haven, CT: Yale University Press, 1970), 28–33. On mimesis in critical writing, see Michael Taussig, "The Corn-Wolf: Writing Apotropaic Texts," *Critical Inquiry* 37 (Autumn 2010): 26–33; Michael Taussig, *Defacement: Public Secrecy and the Labor of the Negative* (Palo Alto, CA: Stanford University Press, 1999), 13, 43.

16. Carolyn Steedman, *Dust: The Archive and Cultural History* (New Brunswick, NJ: Rutgers University Press, 2002), back cover.

17. Lee Edelman theorizes the possibility of that withholding in "Against Survival: Queerness in a Time That's Out of Joint," *Shakespeare Quarterly* 62, no. 2 (Summer 2011): 162.

18. Harold Bloom, *A Map of Misreading* (London: Oxford University Press, 1975), 102.

19. Carla Freccero, *Queer/Early/Modern* (Durham, NC: Duke University Press, 2006), 2.

20. Valerie Traub, "The New Unhistoricism in Queer Studies," *PMLA* 128, no. 1 (2013): 30.

21. Richard A. Lanham, *A Handlist of Rhetorical Terms*, 2d ed. (Berkeley: University of California Press, 1991), 99; Traub, "The New Unhistoricism in Queer Studies," 30.

22. Madhavi Menon, *Wanton Words: Rhetoric and Sexuality in English Renaissance Drama* (Toronto: University of Toronto Press, 2004), 85.

23. Traub, "The New Unhistoricism in Queer Studies," 31.

24. Gerard Genette, *Narrative Discourse: An Essay in Method*, trans. Jane E. Lewin (Ithaca, NY: Cornell University Press, 1990), 235 n. 51.

25. Elaine Freedgood, "Fictional Settlements: Footnotes, Metalepsis, the Colonial Effect," *New Literary History* 41, no. 2 (Spring 2010): 398; Genette, *Narrative Discourse*, 234–35. See also Michael Lucey, *Never Say I: Sexuality and the First Person in Collette, Gide, and Proust* (Durham, NC: Duke University Press, 2006), esp. the chapter "Proust's Queer Metalepses."

26. Genette, *Narrative Discourse*, 236.

27. Genette, *Narrative Discourse*, 235–36.

28. Michel de Certeau, "Vocal Utopias: Glossolalias," *Representations* 56 (Autumn 1996): 31.

3. THE HISTORY OF PEOPLE WHO DID NOT EXIST

Epigraphs: Sarah Kane, *4.48 Psychosis*, in *Complete Plays* (London: Methuen, 2001), 244; Leo Bersani and Adam Phillips, *Intimacies* (Chicago: University of Chicago Press, 2008), 122.

1. Willem Bosman, *A New and Accurate Description of the Coast of Guinea* (London: James Knapton, 1705), 8. Hereafter, page numbers cited in parentheses in the text refer to this edition.

2. The first English edition of *A New and Accurate Description of the Coast of Guinea*, published in 1705, was based on a French translation of the original Dutch text (1703).

3. Talal Asad, *On Suicide Bombing* (New York: Columbia University Press, 2007), 74.

4. Søren Kierkegaard, *Fear and Trembling/Repetition: Kierkegaard's Writings*, vol. 6, ed. and trans. Edna H. Hong and Howard V. Hong (Princeton, NJ: Princeton University Press, 1983), 10–14.

5. William Piersen, "White Cannibals, Black Martyrs: Fear, Depression, and Religious Faith as Causes of Suicide among New Slaves," *Journal of Negro History* 62, no. 2 (April 1977): 153.

6. See Ian Baucom, *Specters of the Atlantic: Finance Capital, Slavery, and the Philosophy of History* (Durham, NC: Duke University Press, 2005), 163–66.

7. Constantin Fasolt, *The Limits of History* (Chicago: University of Chicago Press, 2004), 143.

8. The full passage reads, "A historical phenomenon, known clearly and completely and resolved into a phenomenon of knowledge, is, for him who has perceived it, dead: for he has recognized in it the delusion, the injustice, the blind passion, and in general the whole earthly and darkening horizon of this phenomenon, and has thereby also understood its power in history. This power has now lost its hold over him insofar as he is a man of knowledge: but perhaps it has not done so insofar as he is a man involved in life": Friedrich Nietzsche, "On the Uses and Disadvantages of History for Life," in *Untimely Meditations*, ed. Daniel Breazeale (Cambridge: Cambridge University Press, 1997), 67.

9. Nietzsche, "On the Uses and Disadvantages of History for Life," xv.

10. Vincent Brown, "History Attends to the Dead," *Small Axe*, no. 31 (March 2010): 219–27.

11. Vincent Brown, unpublished comments at "Middle Passages: Histories and Poetics," City University of New York Graduate Center, May 2010.

12. Tim Dean, *Unlimited Intimacy: Reflections on the Subculture of Barebacking* (Chicago: University of Chicago Press, 2009), 46–47.

13. Stanley Cavell, "The Avoidance of Love: A Reading of *King Lear*," in *Disowning Knowledge: In Seven Plays of Shakespeare* (New York: Cambridge University Press, 1987), 108.

14. Cavell, "The Avoidance of Love," 108.

15. Cavell, "The Avoidance of Love," 109.

16. Cavell, "The Avoidance of Love," 108.

17. Cavell, "The Avoidance of Love," 109.

18. David Lloyd, "The Indigent Sublime: Specters of Irish Hunger," *Representations* 92 (Fall 2005): 152–53. See also David Scott, *Conscripts of Modernity: The Tragedy of Colonial Enlightenment* (Durham, NC: Duke University Press, 2004); Reinhart Koselleck, *Futures Past: On the Semantics of Historical Time*, trans. Keith Tribe (Cambridge, MA: MIT Press, 1985).

19. Vincent Brown, "Social Death and Political Life in the Study of Slavery," *American Historical Review* (December 2009): 1231–49.

20. Orlando Patterson, *Slavery and Social Death: A Comparative Study* (Cambridge, MA: Harvard University Press, 1982), 45–51.

21. Ruthie Gilmore, "Profiling Alienated Labor," presentation at the Mellon Sawyer Seminar "Redress in Law, Literature, and Social Thought," Humanities Research Institute, University of California, Irvine, February 24, 2003. See also Ruthie Gilmore, *Golden Gulag: Prisons, Surplus, Crisis, and Opposition in Globalizing California* (Berkeley: University of California Press, 2007).

22. Colin [Joan] Dayan, *The Law Is a White Dog: How Legal Rituals Make and Unmake Persons* (Princeton, NJ: Princeton University Press, 2011), 44.

23. The sense that black people got a head start on modernity is affirmed in the sociological thinking of Erving Goffman, who, in "On Cooling the Mark Off," takes up the issue of how institutional structures help persons adapt to failure and loss, or what he terms "social death" (a term that, in his use, bears none of the weight of slavery, but that, upon its assumption by Patterson, begins to): see Erving Goffman, "On Cooling the Mark Off: Some Aspects of Adaptation to Failure," *Psychiatry: Journal of Interpersonal Relations* (1952): 451–63.

24. Brown, "Social Death and Political Life in the Study of Slavery," 1235.

25. Brown, "Social Death and Political Life in the Study of Slavery," 1239.

26. Brown, "History Attends to the Dead," 221.

27. On New Historicism as a response to the designs of the New Left, see Robert J. C. Young, "New Historicism and the Counter Culture," in *Torn Halves: Political Conflict in Literary and Cultural Theory* (New York: St. Martin's Press, 1996), 163–83.

28. Louis Montrose, *The Purpose of Playing: Shakespeare and the Cultural Politics of the Elizabethan Theatre* (Chicago: University of Chicago Press, 1996). In its Americanist vein, the problematic Montrose describes took the shape of a critique of multiculturalism, particularly in its reduction (in the writings of someone like Walter Benn Michaels) to the desire to critique American hegemony from a standpoint outside of the culture. Michaels admonished, famously, that it "seems wrong to think of the culture you live in as the object of your affections: you don't like it or dislike it, you exist in it, and the things you like and

dislike exist in it too." Often, the premises that underlay containment could inspire the most stunning of syllogisms, such as the claim that slavery was not the antithesis of freedom, but the penultimate expression of its core idea (i.e., the bourgeois identification of the self as property), "since only if you identify freedom with self-ownership can being owned by someone else seem an intrinsic abridgement of that freedom": Walter Benn Michaels, *The Gold Standard and the Logic of Naturalism* (Berkeley: University of California Press, 1987), 18, 124.

29. Scott, *Conscripts of Modernity*, 50.

30. Slavoj Žižek, *Did Somebody Say Totalitarianism? Five Interventions in the (Mis)use of a Notion* (London: Verso, 2001), 3–6.

31. Tom Bottomore et al., eds., *A Dictionary of Marxist Thought* (Cambridge, MA: Harvard University Press, 1983), s.v. "Praxis," 384–89.

32. Matthew Lewis, *Journal of a West India Proprietor: Kept during a Residence in the Island of Jamaica*, ed. Judith Terry (New York: Oxford University Press, 1999 [1834]), 203.

33. Lewis, *Journal of a West India Proprietor*, 204.

34. Lewis, *Journal of a West India Proprietor*, 204.

35. Lewis, *Journal of a West India Proprietor*, 204.

36. Lewis, *Journal of a West India Proprietor*, 204.

37. Albert van Dantzig, "English Bosman and Dutch Bosman: A Comparison of Texts," *History in Africa* 2 (1975): 185–216. Van Dantzig's translation of the suicide bombing appears on page 196. For the background story explaining the circumstances that led up to the bombing, see Albert van Dantzig, "The Ankobra Gold Interest," *Transactions of the Historical Society of Ghana* 14 (1973): 176–77.

4. RUMOR IN THE ARCHIVE

Epigraph: Friedrich Nietzsche, *The Gay Science*, ed. Bernard Williams (Cambridge: Cambridge University Press, 2001), 112.

1. *Hansard's Parliamentary Debates*, series 1, vol. 34, June 19, 1816 (London: T. C. Hansard, 1816): 1155.

2. Wilberforce's bill was modeled on James Stephen's earlier Registry Bill, which was put before Parliament in 1812. See James Stephen's pamphlet *Reasons for Establishing a Registry of Slaves in the Colonies* (London: African Institution, 1815). For more recent accounts of the Registry Bill and the response of rebel slaves to it, see Gelien Matthews, *Caribbean Slave Revolts and the British Abolitionist Movement*, (Baton Rouge: Louisiana State University Press, 2006); Michael Craton, *Testing the Chains: Resistance to Slavery in the British West Indies* (Ithaca, NY: Cornell University Press, 1982), 259.

3. "Insurrection in Barbadoes; its Connection with the Registry Bill," *The Christian Observer*, vol. 15, no. 6 (June 1816), 405.

4. *Barbados Mercury and Bridgetown Gazette*, March 30, 1816, 1.

5. "The Examination of King Wiltshire, a Slave Belonging to the Plantation called 'Bayley's,'" in *Report from a Select Committee of the House of Assembly, Appointed to Inquire into the Origin, Causes, and Progress, of the Late Insurrection* (Barbados: W. Walker, 1818), 27.

6. *Report from a Select Committee of the House of Assembly*, 27.

7. "The Deposition of the Rev. John Frere Pilgrim, Rector of the Parish of Saint James," in *Report from a Select Committee of the House of Assembly*, 36.

8. "Examination of Conrade Adams Howell, Lieutenant-Colonel of the St. Michael's or Royal Regiment of Militia," in *Report from a Select Committee of the House of Assembly*, 56–57. On the subject of court martial procedure in English common law, see Rande W. Kostal, *A Jurisprudence of Power: Victorian Empire and the Rule of Law* (New York: Oxford University Press, 2005), 193–209.

9. "The Examination of Cuffee Ned, a Slave Belonging to 'Three Houses' Plantation," in *Report from a Select Committee of the House of Assembly*, 27–28.

10. "Examination of Conrade Adams Howell," 57.

11. "The Deposition of the Rev. Thomas Harrison Orderson, Rector of the Parish of Christ Church," in *Report from a Select Committee of the House of Assembly*, 35.

12. "The Examination of Edward Thomas," in *Report from a Select Committee of the House of Assembly*, 45.

13. General John Murray to R. Wilmot Horton, Undersecretary of State, Downing Street, "Private letter," December 25, 1823, National Archives (United Kingdom), Public Records Office, Colonial Office (hereafter, PRO-CO) 111/39, 128–131.

14. "A Journal Containing Various Occurrences at Le Resouvenir, Demerary. Commenced in March 1817, by John Smith, Missionary," July 25, 1823, PRO-CO 111/46.

15. "A Journal Containing Various Occurrences at Le Resouvenir."

16. "A Journal Containing Various Occurrences at Le Resouvenir."

17. John Murray to the Right Honorable the Earl Bathurst, December 26, 1823, PRO-CO 111/39, 141–142.

18. Governor John Murray to Lord Bathurst, Demerara, August 24, 1823, PRO-CO 111/39, 77.

19. Governor John Murray to R. Wilmot Horton Esquire, Undersecretary of State, Downing Street, December 25, 1823, PRO-CO 111/39, 128–31.

20. *Copy of the Report of a Committee of the House of Assembly of Jamaica, appointed to inquire into the Cause of, and Injury sustained by, the recent Rebellion in that Colony; together with the Examinations on Oath, Confessions and other Documents annexed to that Report* (June 27, 1832), PRO-CO 137/181, 3.

21. The testimony before the House of Commons (*Report from Select Com-

mittee on the Extinction of Slavery throughout the British Dominions: with the Minutes of Evidence, Appendix and Index [Shannon, Ireland: Irish University Press, 1968 (1832)]) is replete with rumors of slave apprehension toward America:

> Rev. Peter Duncan (June 22, 1832): "The coloured people are enthusiastically loyal, and their hatred to America is just as deep and deadly as their attachment to the British Constitution is warm and devoted.... The coloured people are ready to oppose the very first movement of any thing like a step towards America; they will not submit to it; they hate the very name of America, and every thing that is British is dear to them as a body." (131–32)
>
> Rev. William Knibb (July 11, 1832): "The chief cause was, an idea that the planters were going to transfer them to America, in consequence of the free paper having come from the King of England." (244)
>
> Right Hon. Sir James Graham (July 11, 1832): "When you state that the slaves feared they were about to be transferred to America, do you mean that they expected they were to be taken to America, or that the island of Jamaica was about to renounce its allegiance to the Crown of England, and to be incorporated with the United States?"
>
> Rev. Knibb: "I mean the latter." (246)

22. *Report from Select Committee on the Extinction of Slavery throughout the British Dominions*, 131.

23. Reverend Peter Duncan, June 22, 1823, in *Report from Select Committee on the Extinction of Slavery throughout the British Dominions*, 131. It is no surprise that slaves on Caribbean islands would see the law as benevolent since, when the law intervenes in disputes between the planter class and the imperial administration, it often comes in on the side of the administration. See Craton, "Proto-Peasant Revolts? The Late Slave Rebellions in the British West Indies 1816-1832," *Past & Present*, vol. 85, no. 1 (November 1979), 109, 113, which discusses legislation which suggested that freedom was impending, as well as the resistance of colonial legislatures to imperial governance.

24. Confessions of Thomas Dove, Robert Gardner, and William Binham, respectively, in *Copy of the Report of a Committee of the House of Assembly of Jamaica*, 32, 35.

25. Craton, *Testing the Chains*, 296.

26. On the political debate over the idea of slaves as subjects of the crown, see Christopher Brown, "Empire without Slaves: British Concepts of Emancipation in the Age of the American Revolution," *William and Mary Quarterly* 56 (3d series), no. 2 (April 1999): 273–306.

27. Laurent Dubois, *A Colony of Citizens: Revolution and Slave Emancipation in the French Caribbean, 1787–1804* (Chapel Hill: University of North Carolina Press, 2004), 89.

28. Stephan Palmié, *Wizards and Scientists: Explorations in Afro-Cuban Modernity and Tradition* (Durham, NC: Duke University Press, 2002), 94.

29. Srinivas Aravamudan has remarked, regarding the trope of the talking book, that underneath the sign of inadequacy lay a complex set of questions concerning the nature of literacy "and the continuation, through subterranean echoes, of the buzz, murmur, and crackle of multiple resonances": Srinivas Aravamudan, *Tropicopolitans: Colonialism and Agency, 1688–1804* (Durham, NC: Duke University Press, 1999), 287. Steven Hahn has made a strong case for the idea of the slaves' monarchist speech as a "protopolitical" form of speech. "Unable to advance political demands through argument or merit or by rallying their numbers, unable even to represent themselves as political actors because they stood outside of formal politics," he writes, "the slaves instead projected a terrain of struggle in which their aspirations could be advanced and in which they might imagine powerful allies": Steven Hahn, *A Nation under Our Feet: Black Political Struggles in the Rural South from Slavery to the Great Migration* (Cambridge, MA: Harvard University Press, 2003), 60–61.

30. James Scott, *Domination and the Arts of Resistance: Hidden Transcripts* (New Haven, CT: Yale University Press, 1990), 96.

31. Hahn, *A Nation under Our Feet*, 57.

32. Recovery often involves us in a Whiggish and teleological construction of history in which the past was what it was in any given moment for the sake of our being what we are now. This mirroring puts one in mind of Stephen Greenblatt's observation, regarding his vocation, "I began with the desire to speak with the dead [and] came to understand that in my most intense moments of straining to listen all I could hear was my own voice": Stephen Greenblatt, *Shakespearean Negotiations: The Circulation of Social Energy in Renaissance England* (Berkeley: University of California Press, 1988), 1.

33. "Voluntary Confession of Linton, a Prisoner in Savannah la Mar Gaol, under Sentence of Death, March 1832" and "Confession of McKinley, a Prisoner under Sentence of Death in Savanna la Mar Gaol, March 1832, to the Rev. Thomas Stewart," both in *Copy of the Report of a Committee of the House of Assembly of Jamaica*, 29–30, 37.

34. See Daniel Field, *Rebels in the Name of the Tsar* (Boston: Houghton Mifflin, 1976), 1–16, 96. The trope is also referred to in the literature as "naïve monarchism."

35. Jonathan Elmer, "Babo's Razor: or, Discerning the Event in an Age of Differences," *differences* 19, no. 2 (Summer 2008): 59, 68.

36. Bryan Wagner, *Disturbing the Peace: Black Culture and the Police Power after Slavery* (Cambridge, MA: Harvard University Press, 2009). On the tenta-

tive talk of William Knox and others regarding slaves as subjects of George III, see Brown, "Empire without Slaves."

37. Michael Taussig, "The Spirit Queen," in *The Magic of the State* (New York: Routledge, 1997), 5.

38. Viotta da Costa, *Crowns of Glory, Tears of Blood: The Demerara Slave Rebellion of 1823* (New York: Oxford University Press, 1994), 170.

39. Heather Love, *Feeling Backward: Loss and the Politics of Queer History* (Cambridge, MA: Harvard University Press, 2007), 24.

40. Brent Hayes Edwards, "The Taste of the Archive," *Callaloo* 35, no. 4 (2010): 961. Edwards is quoting Shane Vogel, *The Scene of Harlem Cabaret: Race, Sexuality, Performance* (Chicago: University of Chicago Press, 2009), 108.

41. Edwards, "The Taste of the Archive," 961.

42. Brendan McConville, *The King's Three Faces: The Rise and Fall of Royal America, 1660–1776* (Chapel Hill: University of North Carolina Press, 2006).

43. McConville, *The King's Three Faces*, 8.

44. McConville, *The King's Three Faces*, 8.

45. McConville, *The King's Three Faces*, 249.

46. McConville, *The King's Three Faces*, 253.

47. McConville, *The King's Three Faces*, 175–76.

48. McConville, *The King's Three Faces*, 172.

49. Elisa Tamarkin, "Black Anglophilia; or, The Sociability of Antislavery," *American Literary History* 14, no. 3 (Fall 2002): 452.

50. Brown, "Empire without Slaves," 276, 285.

51. Harriet Jacobs [Linda Brent], *Incidents in the Life of a Slave Girl*, edited by Henry Louis Gates, Jr., Schomburg Library of Nineteenth-Century Black Women Writers (New York: Oxford University Press, 1988), 287. Hereafter, page numbers cited in parentheses in the text refer to this edition.

52. Susan Scott Parrish, *American Curiosity: Cultures of Natural History in the Colonial British Atlantic World* (Chapel Hill: University of North Carolina Press, 2005), 263–64.

53. Parrish, *American Curiosity*, 265.

54. Michael Taussig, *Defacement: Public Secrecy and the Labor of the Negative* (Palo Alto, CA: Stanford University Press, 1999), 5. Taussig echoes Jacobs, in many respects: "Wherever there is power, there is secrecy, except it is not only secrecy that lies at the core of power, but public secrecy. . . . There is no such thing as a secret. It is an invention that comes out of the public secret, a limit-case, a supposition, a great 'as if,' without which the public secret would evaporate. To see the secret as secret is to take it at face value, which is what the tension in defacement requires" (7). What Taussig calls the *public secret* I am calling the *open secret*, both in deference to the genealogies of queer theory and in recognition of Jacobs's insistent previousness in recognizing the connection between the open secret and power.

55. Daniel Tiffany suggests that the very history of anonymous publication adheres to the principle of the open secret. He writes, "Disappearance submits to the laws of appearance under the sign of Anon": Daniel Tiffany, *Infidel Poetics: Riddles, Nightlife, Substance* (Chicago: University of Chicago Press, 2009), 30, 149.

56. Lauren Berlant gives a bravura reading of Jacobs's "Queen of 'Merica" rumor as an example of the "royalist strain" in "diva citizenship in "The Queen of America Goes to Washington City: Notes on Diva Citizenship," in *The Queen of America Goes to Washington City: Essays on Sex and Citizenship* (Durham, NC: Duke University Press, 1997), 221–46.

57. Gerard Genette, *Narrative Discourse: An Essay in Method*, trans. Jane E. Lewin (Ithaca, NY: Cornell University Press, 1990), 235n51.

58. Gerard Genette, *Paratexts: Thresholds of Interpretation*, trans. Jane E. Lewin (Cambridge: Cambridge University Press, 1997), 2.

59. Gayatri Spivak, "Subaltern Studies: Deconstructing Historiography," in *Selected Subaltern Studies*, ed. Ranajit Guha and Gayatri Chakravorty Spivak (New York: Oxford University Press, 1988), 23–24.

60. Sir William Blackstone, *Commentaries on the Laws of England, in Four Books* (Dublin: Company of Booksellers, 1775), vol. 1, 422–32.

61. Carolyn Steedman, *Dust: The Archive and Cultural History* (New Brunswick, NJ: Rutgers University Press, 2002), 40.

62. Quoted in William Lee Miller, *Arguing about Slavery: The Great Battle in the United States Congress* (New York: Vintage, 1996), 256. As Steven Hahn has recently observed, slavery was a system "of extreme personal domination in which a slave had no relationship that achieved legal sanction or recognition other than with the master, or with someone specifically designated by the master. Nothing was more central to the character of the institution or more debilitating to the slaves as human beings and political actors": Hahn, *A Nation under Our Feet*, 16.

63. For the term "telling inarticulacy," see Nathaniel Mackey, "Sound and Sentiment, Sound and Symbol," in *Discrepant Engagement: Dissonance, Cross-Culturality, and Experimental Writing* (Cambridge: Cambridge University Press, 1993), 253. Stephan Palmié speaks of "the paradoxical record of an eloquent absence" in *Wizards and Scientists*, 82. For the scream's troubling entailment with critical voice, see Saidiya Hartman, *Scenes of Subjection: Terror, Slavery, and Self-Making in Nineteenth-Century America* (New York: Oxford University Press, 1997), 3–4; Fred Moten, "Resistance of the Object: Aunt Hester's Scream," in Fred Moten, *In the Break: The Aesthetics of the Black Radical Tradition* (Minneapolis: University of Minnesota Press), 1–7.

64. Fred Moten, "Black Op," *PMLA* 123, no. 5 (October 2008): 1745.

65. See Stephen Best, "Neither Lost nor Found: Slavery and the Visual Archive," *Representations* 113 (Winter 2011): 150–63. On the "dimension of the

unexplorable," see Édouard Glissant, *Caribbean Discourse* (Charlottesville: University of Virginia Press, 1989), 66. The reference to the "undiscovered" is taken from Tiffany, *Infidel Poetics*, 162. The uncreation effected by the colonial archive reads, with the help of Stephan Palmié, like a type of apocalypticism. "Created and preserved by the same machinery of power and knowledge that annihilated [the free Afro-Cuban artisan José Antonio] Aponte, the archival record has become the medium through which his ghostly voice—warped and distorted, to be sure, by the noise of multiple interferences, now speaks to us about a world of images that we will never see": Palmié, *Wizards and Scientists*, 83.

66. Fred Moten, "The Case of Blackness," *Criticism* 50, no. 2 (Spring 2008): 177–218.

67. Gilles Deleuze and Félix Guattari, *What Is Philosophy?* trans. Hugh Tomlinson and Graham Burchell (New York: Columbia University Press, 1994), 60.

68. Palmié, *Wizards and Scientists*, 137–38.

69. Lisa Lowe, "History Hesitant," *Social Text* 33, no. 4 (December 2015): 98 n. 1; W. E. B. Du Bois, "Sociology Hesitant," *boundary 2* 27, no. 3 (2000): 39–40.

70. Lowe, "History Hesitant," 98.

71. Lowe, "History Hesitant," 98.

72. David Lloyd, "The Indigent Sublime: Specters of Irish Hunger," *Representations* 92 (Fall 2005): 153.

73. Michel de Certeau, "Vocal Utopias: Glossolalias," *Representations* 56 (Autumn 1996): 29. Hereafter, page numbers in parentheses in the text refer to this article. I thank Jonathan Lamb for his offhanded mention of de Certeau's thoughts on metalepsis. "Vocal Utopias" has proved more important to my thinking in the end than either he or I could have imagined.

74. "The very term *spirit*, which for so many traditions designates the act or the actor of speech, underlines the nonplace of 'that which speaks'": de Certeau, "Vocal Utopias," 31.

75. Colonial archives were as much sites for the recording of prophetic and prospective "non-events," in Ann Stoler's phrase, as for the retrospective documentation of actual ones. Colonial archives often preserved the "records of things that never happened" in the form of portents, visions, and hopes—"the feared, the unrealized, and the ill-conceived," as well as "the expectant and [the] conjured." Colonial archives engendered objects in the very act of sequestration, for they served the process of developing "negative prints" of what stirred official anxiety; if they were records of anything, they were "records of uncertainty and doubt in how people imagined they could and might make the rubrics of rule correspond to a changing imperial world." See Ann Laura Stoler, *Along the Archival Grain: Epistemic Anxieties and Colonial Common Sense* (Princeton, NJ: Princeton University Press, 2009), 1, 4–5, 21–22.

76. "The Examination of King Wiltshire," 27.

77. Michael Lucey, *Never Say I: Sexuality and the First Person in Collette, Gide, and Proust* (Durham, NC: Duke University Press, 2006), 198; Gerard Genette, *Narrative Discourse: An Essay in Method*, trans. Jane E. Lewin (Ithaca, NY: Cornell University Press, 1990), 235.

78. Genette, *Narrative Discourse*, 235.

79. Genette, *Narrative Discourse*, 235.

80. Paul Mooney, *Masterpiece* (1994), accessed July 14, 2017, https://www.youtube.com/watch?v=AC8uwKeFpb4.

81. Richard A. Lanham, *Handlist of Rhetorical Terms*, 2d ed. (Berkeley: University of California Press, 1991), 99.

82. Maya Angelou, *A Song Flung Up to Heaven* (New York: Random House, 2002). Hereafter, page numbers from this volume are cited in parentheses in the text.

83. I thank Tobias Barrington Wolff for bringing this anecdote to my attention.

84. Jorge Luis Borges, "Partial Magic in the *Quixote*," in *Labyrinths: Selected Stories and Other Writings*, ed. Donald Yates and James Irby (New York: New Directions, 1962), 174.

85. Genette, *Narrative Discourse*, 236.

86. David Foster Wallace, *The Story About the Story II*, ed. J. C. Hallman (Portland, OR: Tin House Books, 2013), 33.

BIBLIOGRAPHY

Adorno, Theodor W. *Hegel: Three Studies*, trans. Shierry Weber Nicholsen. Cambridge, MA: MIT Press, 1993.
———. *In Search of Wagner*, trans. Rodney Livingstone. London: NLB, 1981. (Originally published as *Versuch über Wagner* [Berlin: Suhrkamp Verlag, 1952].)
———. *Minima Moralia: Reflections from Damaged Life*, trans. E. F. N. Jephcott. New York: Verso, [1951] 1974.
———. "Toward a Theory of the Artwork." In *Aesthetic Theory*, ed. Gretel Adorno and Rolf Tiedemann, trans. Robert Hullot-Kentor, 241–71. London: Bloomsbury Academic, 2013.
Adorno, Theodor W., and Max Horkheimer. *Dialectic of Enlightenment* (1944), trans. John Cumming. New York: Verso, 1997.
Agamben, Giorgio. "The Author as Gesture." In *Profanations*, 62–66. New York: Zone, 2007.
———. *Homo Sacer: Sovereign Power and Bare Life*. Stanford, CA: Stanford University Press, 1998.
Alexander, Michelle. *The New Jim Crow: Mass Incarceration in the Age of Colorblindness*. New York: New Press, 2010.
Allport, Gordon W., and Leo Postman. *The Psychology of Rumor*. New York: Henry Holt, 1947.
Alphen, Ernst van. *Art in Mind: How Contemporary Images Shape Thought*. Chicago: University of Chicago Press, 2005.
Altieri, Charles. "Cavell's Imperfect Perfectionism." In *Ordinary Language Criticism: Literary Thinking after Cavell after Wittgenstein*, ed. Kenneth Dauber and Walter Jost, 199–229. Evanston, IL: Northwestern University Press, 2003.
Angelou, Maya. *A Song Flung Up to Heaven*. New York: Random House, 2002.
Anker, Elizabeth, and Rita Felski, eds. *Critique and Postcritique*. Durham, NC: Duke University Press, 2017.
Anonymous. *Remarks on the Insurrection in Barbados, and the Bill for the Registration of the Slaves*. London: Ellerton and Henderson, 1816.

Appiah, Kwame Anthony. "Discovering El Anatsui." In *El Anatsui: When I Last Wrote to You about Africa*, ed. Lisa M. Binder, 63–73. New York: Museum for African Art, 2010.

Aravamudan, Srinivas. *Tropicopolitans: Colonialism and Agency, 1688–1804*. Durham, NC: Duke University Press, 1999.

Arondekar, Anjali. *For the Record: On Sexuality and the Colonial Archive in India*. Durham, NC: Duke University Press, 2009.

Arsić, Branka, *On Leaving: A Reading in Emerson*. Cambridge, MA: Harvard University Press, 2010.

Asad, Talal. *On Suicide Bombing*. New York: Columbia University Press, 2007.

Baker, Houston A., Jr. *Blues, Ideology, and Afro-American Literature*. Chicago: University of Chicago Press, 1984.

Bal, Mieke. *Lili Dujourie—Early Works, 1969–1983*. Munich: Kunstverein München, 1998.

Baldwin, James. "Notes of a Native Son." In *Notes of a Native Son*, 85–114. Boston: Beacon, 1955.

———, and Raoul Peck. *I Am Not Your Negro*. New York: Vintage, 2017.

Barthes, Roland. *Camera Lucida: Reflections on Photography*, trans. Richard Howard. New York: Hill and Wang, 1981.

———. *The Neutral: Lecture Course at the Collège de France, 1977–1978*, trans. Rosalind E. Krauss and Denis Hollier. New York: Columbia University Press, 2005.

Baucom, Ian. *Specters of the Atlantic: Finance Capital, Slavery, and the Philosophy of History*. Durham, NC: Duke University Press, 2005.

Bell, Bernard. *The Afro-American Novel and Its Tradition*. Amherst: University of Massachusetts Press, 1987.

Benhabib, Seyla. *Critique, Norm, and Utopia: A Study of the Foundations of Critical Theory*. New York: Columbia University Press, 1986.

Benjamin, Walter. "Left-Wing Melancholy" (1931). In *The Weimar Republic Sourcebook*, ed. Anton Kaes, Martin Jay, and Edward Dimendberg, 304–6. Berkeley: University of California Press, 1994.

———. "Theses on the Philosophy of History." In *Illuminations*, ed. Hannah Arendt, trans. Harry Zohn, 253–64. New York: Schocken, 1969.

———. *The Work of Art in the Age of Its Technological Reproducibility, and Other Writings on Media*, ed. Michael W. Jennings, Brigid Doherty, and Thomas Y. Levin, trans. Edmund Jephcott et al. Cambridge, MA: Harvard University Press, 2008.

———."The Work of Art in the Age of Mechanical Reproduction" (1936). In *Illuminations*, ed. Hannah Arendt, trans. Harry Zohn, 217–51. New York: Schocken, 1969.

Bennett, Jane. *Vibrant Matter: A Political Ecology of Things*. Durham, NC: Duke University Press, 2010.

Berlant, Lauren. *Cruel Optimism*. Durham, NC: Duke University Press, 2011.

———. *The Queen of America Goes to Washington City: Essays on Sex and Citizenship*. Durham, NC: Duke University Press, 1997.

———, and Lee Edelman. *Sex, or The Unbearable*. Durham, NC: Duke University Press, 2014.

Bersani, Leo. *The Culture of Redemption*. Cambridge, MA: Harvard University Press, 1990.

———. *Homos*. Cambridge, MA: Harvard University Press, 1995.

———. "Is the Rectum a Grave?" In *Is the Rectum a Grave? and Other Essays*, 3–30. Chicago: University of Chicago Press, 2010.

———. "Sociality and Sexuality." *Critical Inquiry* 26, no. 4 (Summer 2000): 641–56.

———, and Adam Phillips. *Intimacies*. Chicago: University of Chicago Press, 2008.

———, and Ulysse Dutoit. *Arts of Impoverishment: Beckett, Rothko, Resnais*. Cambridge, MA: Harvard University Press, 1993.

Best, Stephen. "Come and Gone," *Small Axe* no. 48 (November 2015): 186–204.

———. "*La Foi Postcritique*, on Second Thought," *PMLA* 132, no. 2 (2017): 337–43.

———. "Neither Lost nor Found: Slavery and the Visual Archive." *Representations* 113 (Winter 2011): 150–63.

———. "On Failing to Make the Past Present." *Modern Language Quarterly* 73, no. 3 (September 2012): 453–74.

———, and Saidiya Hartman. "Fugitive Justice." *Representations* 92 (Winter 2005): 1–15.

———, and Sharon Marcus. "Surface Reading: An Introduction." *Representations* 108 (Fall 2009): 1–21.

———, Sharon Marcus, and Heather Love. "Building a Better Description." *Representations* 135 (Summer 2016): 1–21.

Biehl, João. "Vita: Life in a Zone of Social Abandonment." *Social Text 68* 19, no. 3 (Fall 2001): 131–49.

Bilder, Mary Sarah. "Salamanders and Sons of God: The Culture of Appeal in Early New England." In *The Many Legalities of Early America*, ed. Christopher L. Tomlins and Bruce H. Mann, 47–77. Chapel Hill: University of North Carolina Press, 2001.

Binder, Lisa M. "El Anatsui: Transformations." *African Arts* 41, no. 2 (Summer 2008): 24–37.

———, ed. *El Anatsui: When I Last Wrote to You about Africa*. New York: Museum for African Art, 2010.

Blackburn, Robin. "The Haitian Revolution as an Episode in the History of Philosophy." Paper presented at University of California, Santa Cruz, October 12, 2006.

———. *The Overthrow of Colonial Slavery, 1776–1848*. London: Verso, 1988.

Blackmon, Douglas. *Slavery by Another Name: The Re-enslavement of Black*

Americans from the Civil War to World War II. New York: Doubleday, 2008.

Blackstone, Sir William. *Commentaries on the Laws of England, in Four Books.* Dublin: Company of Booksellers, 1775.

Blassingame, John. *The Slave Community: Plantation Life in the Antebellum South* (1972). New York: Oxford University Press, 1979.

Bloch, Ernst, *The Principle of Hope.* Cambridge, MA: MIT Press, 1954.

Bloom, Harold. *A Map of Misreading.* London: Oxford University Press, 1975.

Bogues, Anthony. *Black Heretics, Black Prophets: Radical Political Intellectuals.* New York: Routledge, 2003.

Bois, Yve-Alain, Denis Hollier, Rosalind Krauss, and Hubert Damisch. "A Conversation with Hubert Damisch," *October* 85 (Summer 1998): 3–17.

Bonabeau, Eric, Marco Dorigo, and Guy Theraulaz. *Swarm Intelligence: From Natural to Artificial Systems.* New York: Oxford University Press, 1999.

Borges, Jorge Luis. "Partial Magic in the *Quixote.*" In *Labyrinths: Selected Stories and Other Writings,* ed. Donald Yates and James Irby, 171–74. New York: New Directions, 1962.

Bosman, Willem. *A New and Accurate Description of the Coast of Guinea.* London: James Knapton, 1705.

Brooks, Gwendolyn. *In the Mecca.* New York: Harper & Row, 1968.

———. *Riot: A Poem in Three Parts.* Detroit: Broadside, 1969.

Brown. Christopher L. "Empire without Slaves: British Concepts of Emancipation in the Age of the American Revolution." *William and Mary Quarterly* 56 (3d series), no. 2, (April 1999): 273–306.

Brown, Vincent. "History Attends to the Dead." *Small Axe,* no. 31 (March 2010): 219–27.

———. *The Reaper's Garden: Death and Power in the World of Atlantic Slavery.* Cambridge, MA: Harvard University Press, 2008.

———. "Social Death and Political Life in the Study of Slavery." *American Historical Review* (December 2009): 1231–49.

Brown, Wendy. "Resisting Left Melancholy." *boundary 2* 26, no. 3 (1999): 19–27.

———. *States of Injury: Power and Freedom in Late Modernity.* Princeton, NJ: Princeton University Press, 1995.

Buck-Morss, Susan. *Hegel, Haiti, and Universal History.* Pittsburgh, PA: University of Pittsburgh Press, 2009.

Byrd, Alexander X. *Captives and Voyagers: Black Migrants across the Eighteenth-Century British Atlantic World.* Baton Rouge, LA: Louisiana State University Press, 2008.

Cahn, Michael. "Subversive Mimesis: Theodor W. Adorno and the Modern Impasse of Critique." In *Mimesis in Contemporary Theory: An Interdisciplinary Approach,* vol. 1, ed. Mihai Spariosu, 27–64. Philadelphia: John Benjamins, 1984.

Canetti, Elias. *Crowds and Power*, trans. Carol Stewart. New York: Farrar, Straus and Giroux, 1984.

Carby, Hazel. *Reconstructing Womanhood: The Emergence of the Afro-American Woman Novelist*. New York: Oxford University Press, 1987.

Castronovo, Russ. *Necro Citizenship: Death, Eroticism, and the Public Sphere in the Nineteenth-Century United States*. Durham, NC: Duke University Press, 2001.

Cavell, Stanley. "The Avoidance of Love: A Reading of *King Lear*." In *Disowning Knowledge: In Seven Plays of Shakespeare*, 39–124. Cambridge: Cambridge University Press, 1987.

———. *The Claim of Reason: Wittgenstein, Skepticism, Morality, and Tragedy* Oxford: Oxford University Press, 1979.

———. *Disowning Knowledge: In Seven Plays of Shakespeare*. Cambridge: Cambridge University Press, 1987.

———. *This New Yet Unapproachable America: Lectures after Wittgenstein after Emerson*. Albuquerque, NM: Living Batch, 1989.

Césaire, Aimé. *Notebook of a Return to the Native Land*, trans. Clayton Eshleman and Annette Smith. Middletown, CT: Wesleyan University Press, 2001.

Chakrabarty, Dipesh. *Provincializing Europe: Postcolonial Thought and Historical Difference*. Princeton, NJ: Princeton University Press, 2000.

Cheng, Anne. *The Melancholy of Race: Psychoanalysis, Assimilation, and Hidden Grief*. New York: Oxford University Press, 2001.

Childs, Dennis. *Slaves of the State: Black Incarceration from the Chain Gang to the Penitentiary*. Minneapolis: University of Minnesota Press, 2015.

Clark, T. J. *The Sight of Death: An Experiment in Art Writing*. New Haven, CT: Yale University Press, 2006.

Clarkson, Thomas. *An Essay on the Comparative Efficiency of Regulation or Abolition as applied to the Slave Trade*. London: J. Phillips, 1789.

———. *An Essay on the Impolicy of the African Slave Trade*. Philadelphia: Francis Bailey, 1788.

———. *An Essay on the Slavery and Commerce of the Human Species, Particularly the African* (1785). Philadelphia: N. Wiley, 1804.

———. *A Summary View of the Slave-Trade and of the Probable Consequences of its Abolition*. London: J. Phillips, 1788.

———. *The History of the Rise, Progress and Accomplishment of the Abolition of the African Slave-Trade by the British Parliament*. London: John W. Parker, 1839.

———. *Letters on the Slave Trade, and the State of the Natives . . . in Africa*. London: J. Phillips, 1791.

Constable, Marianne. *Just Silences: The Limits and Possibilities of Modern Law*. Princeton, NJ: Princeton University Press, 2007.

Copy of the Report of a Committee of the House of Assembly of Jamaica, Appointed to Inquire into the Cause of, and Injury Sustained by, the Recent Rebellion in That Colony; together with the Examinations on Oath, Confessions and Other Documents Annexed to that Report (June 27, 1832). National Archives (United Kingdom), Public Records Office, Colonial Office 137/181.

Corbin, Alain, *The Life of an Unknown: The Rediscovered World of a Clog Maker in Nineteenth-Century France*, trans. Arthur Goldhammer. New York: Columbia University Press, 2001.

Costa, Viotta da. *Crowns of Glory, Tears of Blood: The Demerara Slave Rebellion of 1823*. New York: Oxford University Press, 1994.

Crary, Jonathan. *Suspensions of Perception*. Cambridge, MA: MIT Press, 1999.

Craton, Michael. "Proto-Peasant Revolts? The Late Slave Rebellions in the British West Indies 1816–1832," *Past & Present*, vol. 85, no. 1 (November 1979): 99–125.

———. *Testing the Chains: Resistance to Slavery in the British West Indies*. Ithaca, NY: Cornell University Press, 1982.

Culler, Jonathan. *On Deconstruction: Theory and Critique after Structuralism*. Ithaca, NY: Cornell University Press, 1982.

Cvetkovich, Ann. *An Archive of Feelings: Trauma, Sexuality, and Lesbian Public Cultures*. Durham, NC: Duke University Press, 2003.

D'Aguiar, Fred. *Feeding the Ghosts*. London: Chatto and Windus, 1997.

Dantzig, Albert van. "The Ankobra Gold Interest." *Transactions of the Historical Society of Ghana* 14 (1973): 169–85.

———. "English Bosman and Dutch Bosman: A Comparison of Texts." *History in Africa* 2 (1975): 185–216.

Darling, Marsha. "In the Realm of Responsibility: A Conversation with Toni Morrison." *Women's Review of Books* (March 1988): 5–6.

Das, Vena. *Life and Words: Violence and the Descent into the Ordinary*. Berkeley: University of California Press, 2007.

Davies, Bronwyn. *A Body of Writing: 1990–1999*. Walnut Creek, CA: Altamira, 2000.

Dayan, Colin [Joan]. *Haiti, History, and the Gods*. Berkeley: University of California Press, 1995.

———. *The Law Is a White Dog: How Legal Rituals Make and Unmake Persons*. Princeton, NJ: Princeton University Press, 2011.

———. "Legal Slaves and Civil Bodies." In *Materializing Democracy: Toward a Revitalized Cultural Politics*, ed. Russ Castronovo and Dana Nelson, 53–94. Durham, NC: Duke University Press, 2002.

———. "Paul Gilroy's Slaves, Ships and Routes: The Middle Passage as Metaphor." *Research in African Literatures* 27, no. 4 (Winter 1996): 7–14.

Dean, Tim. "The Antisocial Homosexual." *PMLA* 121, no. 3 (2006): 826–28.

———. *Unlimited Intimacy: Reflections on the Subculture of Barebacking*. Chicago: University of Chicago Press, 2009.

de Certeau, Michel. "Vocal Utopias: Glossolalias." *Representations* 56 (Autumn 1996): 29–47.
Delany, Samuel. "Historifying Marginal Practices." In *Time and the Literary*, ed. Karen Newman, Jay Clayton, and Marianne Hirsch, 239–58. New York: Routledge, 2002.
Deleuze, Gilles, and Félix Guattari. *What Is Philosophy?* trans. Hugh Tomlinson and Graham Burchell. New York: Columbia University Press, 1994.
Derrida, Jacques. *Archive Fever: A Freudian Impression*, trans. Eric Prenowitz. Chicago: University of Chicago Press, 1995.
———. *Of Grammatology*. Baltimore, MD: Johns Hopkins University Press, 1976.
———. *La Vérité en peinture*. Paris: Flammarion, 1978.
Didi-Huberman, Georges. *Confronting Images: Questioning the Ends of a Certain History of Art*. University Park: Pennsylvania State University Press, 2009.
Dinshaw, Carolyn. *Getting Medieval: Sexualities and Communities, Pre- and Postmodern*. Durham, NC: Duke University Press, 1999.
Downes, Paul. *Democracy, Revolution, and Monarchism in Early-American Literature*. Cambridge: Cambridge University Press, 2003.
Doty, Mark. *The Art of Description: World into Word*. Minneapolis, MN: Graywolf, 2010.
Drake, St. Clare. *The Redemption of African and Black Religion*. Chicago: Third World, 1977.
Du Bois, W. E. B. "Sociology Hesitant." *boundary 2* 27, no. 3 (2000): 37–44.
Dubois, Laurent. *A Colony of Citizens: Revolution and Slave Emancipation in the French Caribbean, 1787–1804*. Chapel Hill: University of North Carolina Press, 2004.
———. *Avengers of the New World: The Story of the Haitian Revolution*. Cambridge, MA: Harvard University Press, 2005.
Dumesle, Hérard. *Voyage dans le nord d'Haiti, ou révélations des lieux et des monuments historiques*. Aux Cayes, Haiti: L'imprimerie du gouvernement, 1824.
Edelman, Lee. "Against Survival: Queerness in a Time That's out of Joint." *Shakespeare Quarterly* 62, no. 2 (Summer 2011): 148–69.
———. *No Future: Queer Theory and the Death Drive*. Durham, NC: Duke University Press, 2004.
Edwards, Brent Hayes. "The Taste of the Archive." *Callaloo* 35, no. 4 (2010): 944–72.
Edwards, Bryan. *The History Civil and Commercial of the British Colonies in the West Indies*, vol. 1. London: John Stockdale, 1801.
Elias, Camelia. *The Fragment: Towards a History and Poetics of a Performative Genre*. Bern: Peter Lang, 2004.
Ellis, Nadia. *Territories of the Soul: Queered Belonging in the Black Diaspora*. Durham, NC: Duke University Press, 2015.

Elmer, Jonathan. "Babo's Razor: or, Discerning the Event in an Age of Differences." *differences* 19, no. 2 (Summer 2008): 54–81.

Emerson, Ralph Waldo. "Experience" (1844). In *Ralph Waldo Emerson: Essays and Lectures*, 469–92. New York: Library of America, 1983.

Farber, Manny. "White Elephant Art and Termite Art" (1962). In *Negative Space: Manny Farber on the Movies*, expanded ed., 134–44. New York: Da Capo, 1998.

Fasolt, Constantin. *The Limits of History*. Chicago: University of Chicago Press, 2004.

Faulkner, William. *Requiem for a Nun*. New York: Random House, 1951.

Felski, Rita. *The Limits of Critique*. Chicago: University of Chicago Press, 2015.

Ferguson, Frances. *Pornography, the Theory*. Chicago: University of Chicago Press, 2004.

Field, Daniel. *Rebels in the Name of the Tsar*. Boston: Houghton Mifflin, 1976.

Fish, Stanley. *Self-Consuming Artifacts: The Experience of Seventeenth-Century Literature*. Berkeley: University of California Press, 1972.

Fleissner, Jennifer. "Historicism Blues." *American Literary History* 25, no. 4 (Winter 2013): 699–717.

Foucault, Michel. "An Aesthetics of Existence." In *Philosophy, Politics, Culture: Interviews and Other Writings of Michel Foucault*, ed. Lawrence D. Kritzman, 47–56. New York: Routledge, 1988.

———. *The Archaeology of Knowledge*, trans. A. M. Sheridan Smith. New York: Pantheon, 1972.

———. "Friendship as a Way of Life." In *Ethics: Subjectivity and Truth*, ed. Paul Rabinow, 135–40. New York: New Press, 1997.

———. "The Life of Infamous Men." In *Michel Foucault: Power, Truth, Strategy*, ed. Meaghan Morris and Paul Patton, 76–91. Sydney, Australia: Feral Publications, 1979.

———. "Lives of Infamous Men." In *Michel Foucault: Power*, ed. James D. Faubion, 157–75. New York: New Press, 2000.

———. "On the Genealogy of Ethics: An Overview of Work in Progress." In *Ethics, Subjectivity and Truth*, ed. Paul Rabinow, 253–80. New York: New Press, 1997.

———. *The Order of Things*. New York: Random House, 1970.

———. "La vie des hommes infâmes." *Les Cahiers du Chemin* 29 (January 15, 1977): 12–29.

Fradenburg, Louise, and Carla Freccero. *Premodern Sexualities*. New York: Routledge, 1996.

François, Anne-Lise. "Late Exercises in Minimal Affirmatives." In *Theory Aside*, ed. Jason Potts and Daniel Stout, 34–55. Durham, NC: Duke University Press, 2014.

———. *Open Secrets: The Literature of Uncounted Experience*. Stanford, CA: Stanford University Press, 2003.

Freccero, Carla. *Queer/Early/Modern*. Durham, NC: Duke University Press, 2006.

Freedgood, Elaine. "Fictional Settlements: Footnotes, Metalepsis, the Colonial Effect." *New Literary History* 41, no. 2 (Spring 2010): 393–411.

Freud, Sigmund. "Mourning and Melancholia" (1917). In *The Standard Edition of the Complete Psychological Works of Sigmund Freud*, vol. 14, ed. James Strachey, 239–60. London: Hogarth, 1957.

Fried, Michael. *Art and Objecthood: Essays and Reviews*. Chicago: University of Chicago Press.

———. "Barthes's *Punctum*." In *Photography Degree Zero: Reflections on Roland Barthes's "Camera Lucida,"* ed. Geoffrey Batchen, 144–57. Cambridge: MIT Press, 2009.

Fuentes, Marisa. *Dispossessed Lives: Enslaved Women, Violence, and the Archive*. Philadelphia: University of Pennsylvania Press, 2016.

Gallagher, Catherine, and Stephen Greenblatt. "Counterhistory and the Anecdote." In *Practicing New Historicism*, 49–74. Chicago: University of Chicago Press, 2000.

Gates, Henry Louis, Jr. *The Signifying Monkey*. New York: Oxford University Press, 1988.

Geggus, David. "La cérémonie de Bois-Caïman." *Chemins Critiques* 2, no. 3 (May 1992): 59–78.

Genette, Gerard. *Narrative Discourse: An Essay in Method*, trans. Jane E. Lewin. Ithaca, NY: Cornell University Press, 1990.

———. *Paratexts: Thresholds of Interpretation*, trans. Jane E. Lewin. Cambridge: Cambridge University Press, 1997.

Gilmore, Ruthie. *Golden Gulag: Prisons, Surplus, Crisis, and Opposition in Globalizing California*. Berkeley, CA: University of California Press, 2007.

Gilroy, Paul. *The Black Atlantic: Modernity and Double Consciousness*. Cambridge, MA: Harvard University Press, 1993.

———. *Darker than Blue*. Cambridge, MA: Harvard University Press, 2010.

———. *Postcolonial Melancholia*. New York: Columbia University Press, 2005.

Ginzburg, Carlo. *The Judge and the Historian: Marginal Notes on a Late-Twentieth-Century Miscarriage of Justice*, trans. Antony Shugaar. London: Verso, 1999.

Glissant, Édouard. *Caribbean Discourse*. Charlottesville: University of Virginia Press, 1989.

———. *Poetics of Relation*, trans. Betsy Wing. Ann Arbor: University of Michigan Press, 1997. (Originally published as *Poétique de la relation* [Paris: Gallimard, 1990].)

Goffman, Erving. *Behavior in Public Places: Notes on the Social Organization of Gatherings*. New York: Free Press, 1963.

———. *Forms of Talk*. Philadelphia: University of Pennsylvania Press, 1981.

———. "On Cooling the Mark Off: Some Aspects of Adaptation to Failure." *Psychiatry: Journal of Interpersonal Relations* (1952): 451–63.

Goldberg, Jonathan. "The History That Will Be." *GLQ* 1 (1995): 385–403.

Goodman, Nelson. *Languages of Art: An Approach to a Theory of Symbols*. Indianapolis: Hackett, 1976.

Goveia, Elsa V. *Slave Society in the British Leeward Islands at the End of the Eighteenth Century*. Westport, CT: Greenwood, 1965.

———. *A Study on the Historiography of the British West Indies to the End of the Nineteenth Century*. Washington, DC: Howard University Press, 1980.

———. *The West Indian Slave Laws of the 18th Century*. London: Caribbean Universities Press, 1970.

Greenblatt, Stephen. *Shakespearean Negotiations: The Circulation of Social Energy in Renaissance England*. Berkeley: University of California Press, 1988.

Grossman, Allan. *The Long Schoolroom: Lessons in the Bitter Logic of the Poetic Principle*. Ann Arbor: University of Michigan Press, 1997.

Guha, Ranajit. "On Some Aspects of the Historiography of Colonial India." In *Subaltern Studies I: Writings on South Asian History and Society*, ed. Ranajit Guha, 1–8. Delhi: Oxford University Press, 1982.

———. "The Prose of Counter-Insurgency." In *Subaltern Studies 2: Writings on South Asian History and Society*, ed. Ranajit Guha, 45–84. Delhi: Oxford University Press, 1983.

Hacking, Ian. *Historical Ontology*. Cambridge, MA: Harvard University Press, 2002.

Hahn, Steven. *A Nation under Our Feet: Black Political Struggles in the Rural South, from Slavery to the Great Migration*. Cambridge, MA: Harvard University Press, 2003.

———. "'Extravagant Expectations' of Freedom: Rumour, Political Struggle, and the Christmas Insurrection Scare of 1865 in the American South." *Past and Present*, no. 157 (November 1997): 122–58.

Halberstam, Judith. *The Queer Art of Failure*. Durham, NC: Duke University Press, 2011.

Hansard's Parliamentary Debates. Series 1, vol. 34, June 19, 1816. London: T. C. Hansard, 1816.

Hartman, Saidiya. *Lose Your Mother: A Journey along the Atlantic Slave Route*. New York: Farrar, Straus and Giroux, 2007.

———. *Scenes of Subjection: Terror, Slavery, and Self-Making in Nineteenth-Century America*. New York: Oxford University Press, 1997.

———. "The Time of Slavery." *South Atlantic Quarterly* 101, no. 4 (2002): 757–77.

———. "Venus in Two Acts." *Small Axe*, no. 26 (June 2008): 1–14.

Hegel, Georg Wilhelm Friedrich. *Philosophy of History*, trans. J. Sibree. New York: Colonial Press, 1900.

———. *Philosophy of Spirit*, trans. A. V. Miller. Oxford: Oxford University Press, 1977.

Helton, Laura, Justin Leroy, Max A. Mishler, Samantha Seeley, and Shauna Sweeney. "The Question of Recovery: An Introduction." *Social Text 125* 33, no. 4 (December 2015): 1–16.

Herskovits, Melville J. *The Myth of the Negro Past*. Boston: Beacon, 1941.

Hesse, Barnor. "Escaping Liberty: Western Hegemony, Black Fugitivity." *Political Theory* 42, no. 3 (2014): 288–313.

Hill, Robert. "C. L. R. James: The Myth of Western Civilization." In *Enterprise of the Indies*, ed. George Lamming, 255–59. Port of Spain: Trinidad and Tobago Institute of the West Indies, 1999.

Hinks, Peter H. *To Awake My Afflicted Brethren: David Walker and the Problem of Antebellum Slave Resistance*. University Park, PA: Pennsylvania State University Press, 1997.

Hoffman, François. "Histoire, mythe et idéologie: La cérémonie du Bois-Caïman." *Études Creoles: Culture, langue, société* 13, no. 1 (1990): 9–34.

Houghton, Gerard. "The Epitome of Freedom." In *Il mondo vi appartiene. The World Belongs to You. Le monde vous appartient.*, ed. Caroline Bourgeois, 88–90. Milan: Electa, 2011.

"Insurrection in Barbadoes; its Connection with the Registry Bill," *The Christian Observer*, vol. 15, no. 6 (June 1816), 403–14.

Jacobs, Harriet [Linda Brent]. *Incidents in the Life of a Slave Girl*, edited by Henry Louis Gates, Jr. Schomburg Library of Nineteenth-Century Black Women Writers. New York: Oxford University Press, 1988 [1861].

Johnson, Michael. "Denmark Vesey and His Co-Conspirators." *William and Mary Quarterly* 58, no. 4 (October 2001): 915–76.

Johnson, Walter. "On Agency." *Journal of Social History* 37, no. 1 (2003): 113–24.

Johnson, James Weldon. *Along This Way* (1933). New York: Penguin, 1990.

Jordan, Winthrop. "The Charleston Hurricane of 1822: Or, the Law's Rampage." *William and Mary Quarterly* 54, no. 1 (January 2002): 175–78.

Kane, Sarah. *4.48 Psychosis*. In *Complete Plays*, 203–45. London: Methuen, 2001.

Kazanjian David. "Hegel, Liberia." *diacritics* 40, no. 1 (2012): 6–41.

———, and David Eng, eds. *Loss: The Politics of Mourning*. Berkeley: University of California Press, 2003.

Kelley, Robin D. G. *Freedom Dreams: The Black Radical Imagination*. Boston: Beacon, 2002.

Kent, R. K. "Palmares: An African State in Brazil." *Journal of African History* 6, no. 2 (1965): 161–75.

Kierkegaard, Søren. *Fear and Trembling/Repetition: Kierkegaard's Writings*, vol. 6, ed. and trans. Edna H. Hong and Howard V. Hong. Princeton, NJ: Princeton University Press, 1983.

Knox, William, *Three Tracts respecting the Conversion and Instruction of the Free Indians, and Negro Slaves in the Colonies; Addressed to the Venerable Society for the Propagation of the Gospel in the Foreign Parts*. London, 1768.

Koestenbaum, Wayne. *My 1980s and Other Essays*. New York: Farrar, Straus and Giroux, 2013.

Koselleck, Reinhart. *Futures Past: On the Semantics of Historical Time*, trans. Keith Tribe. Cambridge, MA: MIT Press, 1985.

Kostal, Rande W. *A Jurisprudence of Power: Victorian Empire and the Rule of Law*. New York: Oxford University Press, 2005.

Kunin, Aaron. "Artifact, Poetry as." In *Princeton Encyclopedia of Poetry and Poetics*, ed. Roland Greene, Stephen Cushman, Clare Cavanagh, Jahan Ramazani, and Paul Rouzer, 87–89. Princeton, NJ: Princeton University Press, 2012.

Lacan, Jacques. *The Four Fundamental Concepts of Psychoanalysis*, ed. Jacques-Alain Miller, trans. Alan Sheridan. New York: W. W. Norton, 1998.

———. "The Mirror-Phase as Formative of the Function of the I." In *Écrits: A Selection*, trans. Alan Sheridan, 1–7. New York: W. W. Norton, 1977.

LaCapra, Dominick. *History and Criticism*. Ithaca, NY: Cornell University Press, 1985.

Lanham, Richard A. *A Handlist of Rhetorical Terms*, 2d ed. Berkeley: University of California Press, 1991.

Latour, Bruno. *Reassembling the Social: An Introduction to Actor-Network-Theory*. New York: Oxford University Press, 2007.

———. "Why Has Critique Run Out of Steam? From Matters of Fact to Matters of Concern." *Critical Inquiry* 30 (Winter 2004): 225–48.

Leja, Michael. *Looking Askance: Skepticism and American Art from Eakins to Duchamp*. Berkeley: University of California Press, 2004.

Lepore, Jill. *New York Burning: Liberty, Slavery, and Conspiracy in Eighteenth-Century Manhattan*. New York: Vintage, 2006.

Levinson, Marjorie. "What Is New Formalism?" *PMLA* 122, no. 2 (March 2007): 558–69.

———. *Wordsworth's Great Period Poems: Four Essays*. Cambridge: Cambridge University Press, 1986.

Lewis, Matthew. *Journal of a West India Proprietor: Kept during a Residence in the Island of Jamaica* (1834), ed. Judith Terry. New York: Oxford University Press, 1999.

Ligon, Richard. *A True and Exact History of the Island of Barbados*. London: Humphrey Moseley, 1657.

Linebaugh, Peter, and Marcus Rediker. *The Many-Headed Hydra: Sailors, Slaves, Commoners, and the Hidden History of the Revolutionary Atlantic*. Boston: Beacon, 2000.

Liu, Alan. *Local Transcendence: Essays on Postmodern Historicism and the Database*. Chicago: University of Chicago Press, 2008.

———. "The New Historicism and the Work of Mourning." In *Local Transcendence: Essays on Postmodern Historicism and the Database, 157–65. Chicago: University of Chicago Press, 2008.

Lloyd, David. "The Indigent Sublime: Specters of Irish Hunger." *Representations* 92 (Fall 2005): 152–85.

Love, Heather. "Close but Not Deep: Literary Ethics and the Descriptive Turn." *New Literary History* 41, no. 2 (Spring 2010): 371–91.

———. "Close Reading and Thin Description." *Public Culture* 25, no. 3 (Fall 2013): 401–34.

———. *Feeling Backward: Loss and the Politics of Queer History*. Cambridge, MA: Harvard University Press, 2007.

Lowe, Lisa. "History Hesitant." *Social Text* 33, no. 4 (December 2015): 85–107.

Lucey, Michael. *Never Say I: Sexuality and the First Person in Collette, Gide, and Proust*. Durham, NC: Duke University Press, 2006.

Mackey, Nathaniel. *Bedouin Hornbook*. Lexington: University Press of Kentucky, 1986.

———. "Sound and Sentiment, Sound and Symbol." *Callaloo* 30 (1987): 29–54.

———. "Sound and Sentiment, Sound and Symbol." In *Discrepant Engagement: Dissonance, Cross-Culturality, and Experimental Writing*, 231–59. Cambridge: Cambridge University Press, 1993.

Menon, Madhavi. *Wanton Words: Rhetoric and Sexuality in English Renaissance Drama*. Toronto: University of Toronto Press, 2004,

Markell, Patchen. *Bound by Recognition*. Princeton, NJ: Princeton University Press, 2003.

Matthews, Gelien. *Caribbean Slave Revolts and the British Abolitionist Movement*. Baton Rouge: Louisiana State University Press, 2006.

Mbembe, Achille. "Necropolitics," trans. Libby Meintjes. *Public Culture* 15, no.1 (2003): 11–40.

McConville, Brendan. *The King's Three Faces: The Rise and Fall of Royal America, 1660–1776*. Chapel Hill: University of North Carolina Press, 2006.

McKittrick, Katherine. *Demonic Grounds: Black Women and the Cartographies of Struggle*. Minneapolis: University of Minnesota Press, 2006.

Melhem, D. H. *Gwendolyn Brooks: Poetry and the Heroic Voice*. Lexington, KY: University Press of Kentucky, 1987.

Michaels, Walter Benn. *The Beauty of a Social Problem*. Chicago: University of Chicago Press, 2015.

———. *The Gold Standard and the Logic of Naturalism*. Berkeley: University of California Press, 1987.

———. *Our America: Nativism, Modernism, Pluralism*. Durham, NC: Duke University Press, 1995.

———. *The Shape of the Signifier: 1967 to the End of History*. Princeton, NJ: Princeton University Press, 2004.

Miller, R. Baxter, ed. *Black American Literature and Humanism*. Lexington: University Press of Kentucky, 1981.

Miller, William Lee. *Arguing about Slavery: The Great Battle in the United States Congress*. New York: Vintage, 1996.

Moi, Toril. "'Nothing Is Hidden': From Confusion to Clarity, or Wittgenstein on Critique." In *Critique and Postcritique*, ed. Elizabeth Anker and Rita Felski, 31–49. Durham, NC: Duke University Press, 2017.

Montrose, Louis. *The Purpose of Playing: Shakespeare and the Cultural Politics of the Elizabethan Theatre*. Chicago: University of Chicago Press, 1996.

Morrison, Toni. *A Mercy*. New York: Knopf, 2008.

———. *Beloved*. New York: Penguin, 2000.

———. "The Site of Memory." In *Inventing the Truth: The Art and Craft of Memoir*, ed. William Zinsser, 83–102. Boston: Houghton Mifflin, 1995.

Moten, Fred. "Black Op." *PMLA* 123, no. 5 (October 2008): 1743–47.

———. "The Case of Blackness." *Criticism* 50, no. 2 (Spring 2008): 177–218.

———. *In the Break: The Aesthetics of the Black Radical Tradition*. Minneapolis: University of Minnesota Press, 2003.

Moynihan, Daniel Patrick. *The Negro Family: The Case for National Action*. Washington, DC: Office of Policy Planning and Research, US Department of Labor, 1965.

Mullin, Gerald. *Flight and Rebellion*. New York: Oxford University Press, 1972.

Muhammad, Ismail. "The Misunderstood Ghost of James Baldwin," *Slate*, February 15, 2017. http://www.slate.com/articles/arts/books/2017/02/how_critics _have_misunderstood_james_baldwin_s_influence_on_today_s_great.html.

Muñoz, José. *Cruising Utopia: The Then and There of Queer Futurity*. New York: New York University Press, 2009.

Nealon, Chris. *Foundlings: Lesbian and Gay Historical Emotion before Stonewall*. Durham, NC: Duke University Press, 2001.

Ngai, Sianne. *Ugly Feelings*. Cambridge, MA: Harvard University Press, 2005.

Nietzsche, Friedrich. *The Gay Science*, ed. Bernard Williams. Cambridge: Cambridge University Press, 2001.

———. "On the Uses and Disadvantages of History for Life." In *Untimely Meditations*, ed. Daniel Breazeale, 57–123. Cambridge: Cambridge University Press, 1997.

Ohi, Kevin. *Henry James and the Queerness of Style*. Minneapolis: University of Minnesota Press, 2011.

Ouologuem, Yambo. *Le devoir de violence*. London: Secker and Warburg, 1971.

Painter, Nell Irvin. "Soul Murder and Slavery: Toward a Fully Loaded Cost Accounting." In *Southern History across the Color Line*, 15–39. Chapel Hill: University of North Carolina Press, 2002.

Palmié, Stephan. *Wizards and Scientists: Explorations in Afro-Cuban Modernity and Tradition*. Durham, NC: Duke University Press, 2002.

Parrish, Susan Scott. *American Curiosity: Cultures of Natural History in the Colonial British Atlantic World*. Chapel Hill: University of North Carolina Press, 2006.

Patterson, Orlando. "Slavery and Slave Revolts: A Sociohistorical Analysis of the First Maroon War, 1665–1740." In *Maroon Societies: Rebel Slave Communities in the Americas*, ed. Richard Price, 246–92. Baltimore: Johns Hopkins University Press, 1996.

———. *Slavery and Social Death: A Comparative Study*. Cambridge, MA: Harvard University Press, 1982.

———. "Toward a Future That Has No Past: Reflections on the Fate of Blacks in the Americas." *Public Interest*, no. 27 (1972): 25–62.

Pearson, Edward, ed. *Designs against Charleston: The Trial Record of the Denmark Vesey Conspiracy of 1822*. Chapel Hill: University of North Carolina Press, 1999.

Peires, Jeffrey B. *The Dead Will Arise: Nongqawuse and the Great Xhosa Cattle-Killing Movement of 1856–7*. Bloomington: Indiana University Press, 1989.

Philip, M. NourbeSe. *Zong!* Middletown, CT: Wesleyan University Press, 2008.

Piersen, William. "White Cannibals, Black Martyrs: Fear, Depression, and Religious Faith as Causes of Suicide among New Slaves." *Journal of Negro History* 62, no. 2 (April 1977): 147–59.

Pietz, William. "Material Considerations: On the Historical Forensics of Contract." *Theory, Culture and Society* 19, nos. 5–6 (December 2002): 35–50.

Posnock, Ross. "'Don't Think, But Look!': W. G. Sebald, Wittgenstein, and Cosmopolitan Poverty." *Representations* 112 (Fall 2010): 112–39.

Povinelli, Elizabeth A. "On Suicide, and Other Forms of Social Extinguishment." In *Theory Aside*, ed. Jason Potts and Daniel Stout, 78–93. Durham, NC: Duke University Press, 2014.

Pybus, Cassandra. *Epic Journeys of Freedom: Runaway Slaves of the American Revolution and Their Global Quest for Liberty*. New York: Beacon, 2006.

Ralph, Michael. *The Forensics of Capital*. Chicago: University of Chicago Press, 2015.

Ranke, Leopold van. "Preface: Histories of the Latin and Germanic Nations from 1494–1514." In *The Varieties of History: From Voltaire to the Present*, ed. Fritz Stern, 57–60. New York: Vintage, 1973.

Rediker, Marcus, *The Slave Ship: A Human History*. New York: Viking Penguin, 2007.

Reintjes, Brandon. "Installing Anatsui: The Politics of Economics in Global Contemporary Art." Masters thesis, University of Louisville, Kentucky, May 2009.

Report from a Select Committee of the House of Assembly Appointed to Inquire into the Origin, Causes, and Progress of the Late Insurrection. Barbados: W. Walker, 1818.

Report from Select Committee on the Extinction of Slavery throughout the British Dominions, with the Minutes of Evidence, Appendix and Index (1832). Shannon, Ireland: Irish University Press, 1968.

Ricoeur, Paul. *Freud and Philosophy: An Essay on Interpretation*, trans. Denis Savage. New Haven, CT: Yale University Press, 1970.

Roach, Joseph, *Cities of the Dead: Circum-Atlantic Performance.* New York: Columbia University Press, 1996.

Robinson, Cedric. *Black Marxism: The Making of the Black Radical Tradition.* Chapel Hill: University of North Carolina Press, 1983.

Rosemont, Franklin and Robin D. G. Kelley, eds., *Black, Brown, & Beige: Surrealist Writings from Africa and the Diaspora.* Austin, TX: University of Texas Press, 2009.

Rotberg, Robert I., ed. *Strike a Blow and Die: A Narrative of Race Relations in Colonial Africa by George Simeon Mwase.* Cambridge, MA: Harvard University Press, 1967.

Rushdy, Ashraf. *Neo-slave Narratives: Studies in the Social Logic of a Literary Form.* New York: Oxford University Press, 1999.

Sarat, Austin. *Speech and Silence in American Law.* Cambridge: Cambridge University Press, 2010.

Scarry, Elaine. *On Beauty and Being Just.* Princeton, NJ: Princeton University Press, 1999.

Schomburg, Arthur. "The Negro Digs Up His Past." In *The New Negro*, ed. Alain Locke, 231–37. New York: Athenaeum, 1925. (Originally published in *Survey Graphic* 6, no. 6 [March 1925]: 670–73.)

Scott, Darieck. *Extravagant Abjection: Blackness, Power, and Sexuality in the African American Literary Imagination.* New York: New York University Press, 2010.

Scott, David. *Conscripts of Modernity: The Tragedy of Colonial Enlightenment.* Durham, NC: Duke University Press, 2004.

———. *Omens of Adversity: Tragedy, Time, Memory, Justice.* Durham, NC: Duke University Press, 2014.

———. "On the Very Idea of a Black Radical Tradition." *Small Axe*, no. 46 (March 2013): 1–6.

———. "That Event, This Memory: Notes on the Anthropology of African Diasporas in the New World." *Diasporas* 1: 261–84.

Scott, James. *Domination and the Arts of Resistance: Hidden Transcripts.* New Haven, CT: Yale University Press, 1990.

Scott, Julius. *The Common Wind: Currents of Afro-American Communication in the Era of the Haitian Revolution.* Ph.D. dissertation, Duke University, Durham, NC, 1986.

Sedgwick, Eve Kosofsky. "Paranoid Reading and Reparative Reading; or, You're So Paranoid, You Probably Think This Introduction Is about You." In *Novel Gazing: Queer Readings in Fiction*, 1–37. Durham, NC: Duke University Press, 1997.

———. "Paranoid Reading, Reparative Reading, or, You're So Paranoid, You Probably Think This Essay Is about You." In *Touching Feeling: Affect, Pedagogy, Performativity*, 123–51. Durham, NC: Duke University Press, 2003.

———. *Touching Feeling: Affect, Pedagogy, Performativity*. Durham, NC: Duke University Press, 2003.

Seltzer, Mark. "The Official World." *Critical Inquiry* 37, no. 4 (2011): 724–53.

———. *The Official World*. Durham, NC: Duke University Press, 2016.

Sexton, Jared. *Amalgamation Schemes: Antiblackness and the Critique of Multiracialism*. Minneapolis: University of Minnesota Press, 2008.

———. "The Social Life of Social Death: On Afro-Pessimism and Black Optimism." In *Time, Temporality and Violence in International Relations: Defatalizing the Present, Forging Radical Alternatives*, ed. Anna M. Agathangelou and Kyle D. Killian, 61–75. New York: Routledge, 2016.

Sharp, Granville. *An Essay on Slavery, Proving from Scripture Its Inconsistency with Humanity and Religion . . .* Burlington, NJ: Isaac Collins, 1773.

———. *A Representation of the Injustice and Dangerous Tendency of Tolerating Slavery; or of Admitting the Least Claim of Private Property in the Persons of Men, in England*. London: Benjamin White, 1769.

———. *The Just Limitation of Slavery in the Laws of God, Compared with the Unbounded Claims of the African Traders and British American Slaveholders . . .* London: Benjamin White, 1776.

Sharpe, Christina. *In the Wake: On Blackness and Being*. Durham, NC: Duke University Press, 2016.

———. *Monstrous Intimacy: Making Post-slavery Subjects*. Durham, NC: Duke University Press, 2010.

Shelby, Tommie. *We Who Are Dark: The Philosophical Foundations of Black Solidarity*. Cambridge, MA: Harvard University Press, 2005.

Shibutani, Tamotsu. *Improvised News: A Sociological Study of Rumor*. New York: Bobbs-Merrill, 1966.

Shiff, Richard. "Move with Chance." In *Mark Bradford*, 75–93. New Haven, CT: Yale University Press, 2010.

Sidbury, James. *Becoming African in America: Race and Nation in the Early Black Atlantic*. New York: Oxford University Press, 2007.

———. *Ploughshares into Swords: Race, Rebellion, and Identity in Gabriel's Virginia, 1730–1810*. Cambridge: Cambridge University Press, 1997.

———. "Reading, Revelation, and Rebellion: The Textual Communities of Gabriel, Denmark Vesey, and Nat Turner." In *Nat Turner: A Slave Rebellion in History and Memory*, ed. Kenneth Greenberg, 119–33. New York: Oxford University Press, 2003.

Simmel, Georg. "The Sociology of Secrecy and of Secret Societies." *American Journal of Sociology* 11, no. 4 (January 1906): 441–98.

Slauter, Eric. "History, Literature, and the Atlantic World." *William and Mary Quarterly* 65 (3d series), no. 1 (January 2008): 135–61.

Slotkin, Richard. "Narratives of Negro Crime in New England, 1675–1800." *American Quarterly* 25 (1973): 3–31. (Reprinted in Paul Finkelman, ed., *Articles on American Slavery, Volume 11: Law, the Constitution, and Slavery* [New York: Garland, 1989], 489–517.)

Smallwood, Stephanie. *Saltwater Slavery: A Middle Passage from Africa to American Diaspora.* Cambridge, MA: Harvard University Press, 2007.

Smith, Valerie. "Neo-slave Narratives." In *The Cambridge Companion to the African-American Slave Narrative*, ed. Audrey A. Fisch, 168–88. New York: Cambridge University Press, 2007.

———. *Self-Discovery and Authority in Afro-American Narrative.* Cambridge, MA: Harvard University Press, 1987.

Snediker, Michael. *Queer Optimism: Lyric Personhood and Other Felicitous Persuasions.* Minneapolis: University of Minnesota Press, 2009.

Snyder, Terri. "Suicide, Slavery, and Memory in North America." *Journal of American History* 97, no. 1 (June 2010): 39–62.

Sokolsky, Anita. "The Melancholy Persuasion." In *Psychoanalytic Literary Criticism*, ed. Maud Ellmann, 128–40. New York: Routledge, 1994.

The Speech of Mr. Wilberforce . . . on a Motion for the Abolition of the Slave Trade in the House of Commons May the 12th, 1789. London: J. Owen, 1789.

Spillers, Hortense J. "'An Order of Constancy': Notes on Brooks and the Feminine." In *Black, White, and in Color: Essays on American Literature and Culture*, 131–51. Chicago: University of Chicago Press, 2003.

———. "Mama's Baby, Papa's Maybe: An American Grammar Book." *Diacritics* 17, no. 2 (1987): 64–81.

———. "Mama's Baby, Papa's Maybe: An American Grammar Book." In *Black, White, and in Color: Essays on American Literature and Culture*, 203–29. Chicago: University of Chicago Press, 2003.

Spivak, Gayatri. "Subaltern Studies: Deconstructing Historiography." In *Selected Subaltern Studies*, ed. Ranajit Guha and Gayatri Chakravorty Spivak, 3–34. New York: Oxford University Press, 1988.

Standish, Paul. "Skepticism, Acknowledgment, and the Ownership of Learning." In *Stanley Cavell and the Education of Grownups*, ed. Naoko Saito and Paul Standish, 73–85. New York: Fordham University Press, 2012.

Steedman, Carolyn. *Dust: The Archive and Cultural History.* New Brunswick, NJ: Rutgers University Press, 2002.

Stephen, James. *Reasons for Establishing a Registry of Slaves in the Colonies.* London: African Institution, 1815.

Stepto, Robert. *From Behind the Veil: A Study of Afro-American Narrative.* Chicago: University of Illinois Press, 1979.

Stoler, Ann Laura. *Along the Archival Grain: Epistemic Anxieties and Colonial Common Sense*. Princeton, NJ: Princeton University Press, 2009.

Substance of the Debates on a Resolution for Abolishing the Slave Trade, Which Was Moved in the House of Commons on the 10th June 1806, and in the House of Lords on the 24th June 1806. London: Phillips and Fardon, 1806.

Sweet, James. "Mistaken Identities? Olaudah Equiano, Domingos Álvares, and the Methodological Challenges of Studying the African Diaspora." *American Historical Review* 114 (April 2009): 279–306.

Tamarkin, Elisa. "Black Anglophilia; or, The Sociability of Antislavery." *American Literary History* 14, no. 3 (Fall 2002): 444–78.

———. "Transatlantic Returns." In *A Companion to American Literary Studies*, ed. Caroline F. Levander and Robert S. Levine, 264–78. Malden, MA: Blackwell, 2011.

Taussig, Michael. "The Corn-Wolf: Writing Apotropaic Texts." *Critical Inquiry* 37 (Autumn 2010): 26–33.

———. *Defacement: Public Secrecy and the Labor of the Negative*. Palo Alto, CA: Stanford University Press, 1999.

———. *Mimesis and Alterity: A Particular History of the Senses*. New York: Routledge, 1993.

———. "The Spirit Queen." In *The Magic of the State*, 3–15. New York: Routledge, 1997.

Taylor, Diana. *The Archive and the Repertoire: Performing Cultural Memory in the Americas*. Durham, NC: Duke University Press, 2003.

Terada, Rei. *Looking Away: Phenomenality and Dissatisfaction, Kant to Adorno*. Cambridge, MA: Harvard University Press, 2009.

Thompson, Krista. *Shine: The Visual Economy of Light in African Diasporic Aesthetic Practice*. Durham, NC: Duke University Press, 2015.

Tiffany, Daniel. *Infidel Poetics: Riddles, Nightlife, Substance*. Chicago: University of Chicago Press, 2009.

———. *Toy Medium: Materialism and Modern Lyric*. Berkeley: University of California Press, 2000.

Traub, Valerie. "The New Unhistoricism in Queer Studies." *PMLA* 128, no. 1 (2013): 21–39.

Trouillot, Michel-Rolph. *Silencing the Past: Power and the Production of History*. Boston: Beacon, 1995.

Turner, Patricia. *I Heard It through the Grapevine: Rumor in African-American Culture*. Berkeley: University of California Press, 1993.

Vogel, Shane. *The Scene of Harlem Cabaret: Race, Sexuality, Performance*. Chicago: University of Chicago Press, 2009.

Wade, Richard C. *Slavery in the Cities: The South, 1820–1860*. New York: Oxford University Press, 1964.

———. "The Vesey Plot: A Reconsideration." *Journal of Southern History* 30 (1964): 143–61.

Wagner, Bryan. *Disturbing the Peace: Black Culture and the Police Power after Slavery*. Cambridge, MA: Harvard University Press, 2009.

Walcott, Dereck. *Omeros*. New York: Farrar, Straus and Giroux, 1990.

Walker, David, *Appeal to the Coloured Citizens of the World*, ed. Peter P. Hinks. University Park, PA: The Pennsylvania State University Press, 2012 (1829).

Wallace, David Foster. *The Story about the Story II*, ed. J. C. Hallman. Portland, OR: Tin House Books, 2013.

Warren, Kenneth. *What Was African American Literature?* Cambridge, MA: Harvard University Press, 2011.

Wenzel, Jennifer. *Bulletproof: Afterlives of Anticolonial Prophesy in South African and Beyond*. Chicago: University of Chicago Press, 2009.

White, Ed. *The Backcountry and the City: Colonization and Conflict in Early America*. Minneapolis: University of Minnesota Press, 2005.

———. "The Value of Conspiracy Theory." *American Literary History* (2002): 1–31.

White, Luise. *Speaking with Vampires: Rumor and History in Colonial Africa*. Berkeley: University of California Press, 2000.

Wiegman, Robyn. "Sex and Negativity; or, What Queer Theory Has for You." *Cultural Critique* 95 (Winter 2017): 219–43.

Williams, Bernard. "Resenting One's Own Existence." In *Making Sense of Humanity*, 224–32. Cambridge: Cambridge University Press, 1995.

Williams, Eric, ed. *Documents on British West Indian History, 1807–1833*. Port of Spain: PNM Publishing Company, 1952.

Wittgenstein, Ludwig. *Philosophical Investigations: The German Text, with an English Translation* (1953), rev. 4th ed., trans. G. E. M. Anscombe, P. M. S. Hackerm and Joachim Schulte. Malden, MA: Wiley-Blackwell, 2009.

———. "Remarks on Frazer's *Golden Bough*." In *Philosophical Occasions, 1912–1951*, ed. James C. Klagge and Alfred Nordmann, 118–55. Indianapolis, IN: Hackett, 1993.

Woloch, Alex. *The One versus the Many: Minor Characters and the Space of the Protagonist in the Novel*. Princeton, NJ: Princeton University Press, 2003.

Wood, Gordon. "Conspiracy and the Paranoid Style: Causality and Deceit in the Eighteenth Century." *William and Mary Quarterly* 39 (July 1982): 401–41.

Young, Robert J. C. "New Historicism and the Counter Culture." In *Torn Halves: Political Conflict in Literary and Cultural Theory*, 163–83. New York: St. Martin's Press, 1996.

Žižek, Slavoj. *Did Somebody Say Totalitarianism? Five Interventions in the (Mis)use of a Notion*. London: Verso, 2001.

———. "Melancholy and the Act." In *Did Somebody Say Totalitarianism? Five Interventions in the (Mis)use of a Notion*, 141–52. London: Verso, 2001.

INDEX

abandonment, 64–65; in *A Mercy*, 72–80
abstraction, 51–55
acknowledgment, 9, 11, 19–20, 25, 32, 40–43, 63–65, 96, 99, 117, 132
Adorno, Theodor, 23, 33, 145n14, 145n16; Max Horkheimer and, 33
aesthetic of the intransmissible, 22–26
aesthetics, 23–26, 33, 36, 45–46, 127–29; apocalypticism in, 22, 37; obscurantist, 74–75, 77; self-consuming form and, 34, 57–61; surrealist, 42
"aesthetics of existence," 22, 142n71
affect, 7, 18–20, 61, 101, 131; affective history, 24, 37–38, 40, 66–67, 71, 73, 79
afropessimism, 22, 137n18, 138n20. *See also* Sexton, Jared
Alphen, Ernst van, 33, 145n17
Anatsui, El: *Fading Cloth*, 48–50; framing in, 44–49; gestalt in, 32–33; *Hovor II*, 29–31; literality in, 32; *négraille* (nigger trash) and, 31; *trompe l'oeil* and, 44, 49–50
Angelus Novus (Klee), 35–36
antiblackness, 8, 137n18. *See also* social death
antirelationality, 51, 64–65, 135n1. *See also* Bersani, Leo
antisocial thesis, 10, 135n2, 136n12; antirelationality and, 51, 64–65
Aravamudan, Srinivas, 168n29

archive, 14–15, 83–85, 89–90, 122–24, 139n40; black culture and, 11–13, 22, 87–88, 123; archival disfiguration, 13–17, 171n75; forensic imagination and, 21, 41, 86, 120, 129, 132
Arondekar, Anjali, 14
art as thought, 33, 145n17
Asad, Talal, 93
attunement, 61
aura, 34–36, 146n19. *See also* Benjamin, Walter; Liu, Alan
"awayness," 149n54. *See also* Goffman, Erving; Terada, Rei

Bal, Mieke, 54
Baldwin, James, 2–3, 4–8. *See also* failure: of reproduction (paternal)
Barthes, Roland, 48, 61, 150n79
Baucom, Ian, 15–16, 66, 70
belonging, 1–3, 9, 11, 42–43, 64, 132, 136n12; grammar and, 9, 128–29; in *A Mercy*, 74–77. *See also* unbelonging
Beloved (Morrison), 68–70, 72–74, 78–79
Benjamin, Walter, 34–36, 70–72, 159n40
Bersani, Leo, 10, 46, 50–52, 64, 72, 96
black ascesis, 37, 59–61, 77; black radical tradition and, 42
Black Atlantic, 16, 66–68, 157n10. *See also* slavery

black radical tradition, 40–42, 50, 148n47, 148n48; "appearance in disappearance" and, 42, 51–52; John Chilembwe and, 41; Palmares and, 41; Xhosa and, 40. *See also* Robinson, Cedric
Blackstone, William, 122
black studies, 1–3, 11–12, 17, 25, 68; traumatic model of black history, 5–6, 20–22
Blassingame, John, 84
Bosman, Willem, 92–94
"Boy Breaking Glass" (Brooks), 55–62
Bradford, Mark, 22–23, 87; immurement in, 54–55; *PARATE*, 52; *Paris Is Burning*, 53; surface and depth in, 52–55; *A Truly Rich Man Is One Whose Children Run into His Arms Even When His Hands Are Empty*, 54–55
Brent, Linda. *See* Jacobs, Harriet
Brooks, Gwendolyn, 22, 55–62
Brougham, Henry, 107
Brown, Vincent, 13, 66, 96–103
Brown, Wendy, 38, 55, 158n19, 159n40

Carretta, Vincent, 86
Castronovo, Russ, 100
Cavell, Stanley, 42–44, 77, 98, 147n26, 158n18
Clark, Kenneth, 135n3
Clarkson, Thomas, 107
Crawford, Marc, 57
Culler, Jonathan, 45–46

Damisch, Hubert, 33, 145n17
Dayan, Colin (Joan), 15, 71, 99–100, 157n10
death drive, 160n51
de Certeau, Michel, 24, 90, 125–29, 171n73
Derrida, Jacques, 53, 83
Didi-Huberman, Georges, 33, 145n17

Dinshaw, Carolyn, 19–20
disaffiliation, 4, 7, 98
Douglass, Frederick, 123
DuBois, W. E. B., 124
Dutoit, Ulysse, 46, 150n72

Edwards, Brent Hayes, 26, 115
Elmer, Jonathan, 115

"fag limbo," 155n114
failure: of address, 74–75, 122–23; of archival recovery, 17–20, 23, 115; black ascesis as, 37; Bradford's art of, 23, 34, 52; Goffman and, 164n23; of reproduction (maternal), 72–80; of reproduction (paternal), 3–8, 135n1; queer objects, 50–52, 151n83; semantic, 89–90; virtual poetry (Grossman) and, 58
Farber, Manny, 151n81
Fasolt, Constantin, 25
Fire Next Time, The (Baldwin), 5
Fish, Stanley, 46
forensic imagination, 21, 41, 86, 120, 129, 132
Foucault, Michel, 12, 14, 17–20, 22, 37, 51, 139n40, 141n51, 142n71, 152n93
fragment: archival, 105; and El Anatsui, 49; and Mark Bradford, 52–55; and Gwendolyn Brooks, 60; and Michel Foucault, 18; queer practice of the archive and, 115
frame, 44–49, 150n67. *See also* Michaels, Walter Benn; Fried, Michael
François, Anne-Lise, 61
Freud, Sigmund, 15–16, 53, 68, 158n19
Fried, Michael, 47–48; antitheatricality, 48

Gallagher, Catherine, 18–19, 141n51
genealogical isolation, 1–11
Genette, Gerard, 89, 121, 131–32

gestalt, 32, 145n13
Gilmore, Ruthie, 99
Glissant, Édouard, 15, 38, 55, 123
glossolalia, 125–29. *See also* metalepsis
Goffman, Erving, 149n54, 164n23
grattage, 152n91
Greenblatt, Stephen, 18–19, 141n51, 168n32
Grossman, Allan, 58, 154n105

Hartman, Saidiya, 14, 18–19, 66, 71, 84
Hegel, G. W. F., 11, 39
hiddenness, 85–86. *See also* Wittgenstein, Ludwig
historicism, 12, 35–36; discipline (Foucault), 15; tort historicism, 38–39
history of discontinuity, 24

imperial sovereignty, 112–18, 167n26
impossible sociality: "black exception and black exemption," 10; self-exemption, 6
impossible speech, 26, 123, 125–29, 131
infanticide, 15, 73–74

Jacobs, Harriet, 118–22

Kant, Immanuel, 45, 61
Kelley, Robin D. G., 42
Kierkegaard, Søren, 93
Koestenbaum, Wayne, 155n114
Koselleck, Reinhart, 65

Lacan, Jacques, 49, 83
LaCapra, Dominick, 86
Lefebvre, George, 84
"left-wing melancholy," 159n40. *See also* Benjamin, Walter
Lewis, Matthew, 103–5
literalism: 32, 45–47
Liu, Alan, 35–36, 146n22
Lloyd, David, 65, 98–99, 124

Love, Heather, 19–20, 115, 159n45
Lowe, Lisa, 85, 124

Mackey, Nathaniel, 79, 136n12, 160n54
Marcus, Sharon, 47, 152n93, 155n108. *See also* surface reading
Mbembe, Achille, 100
McCarthy, Tom, 46–47
melancholy historicism, 15–17, 20, 24, 68–73, 139n42
melancholy, 15, 37, 40, 57, 65, 85; "left-wing melancholy," 159n40; melancholy historicism, 15–17, 20, 24, 68–73, 139n42; struggle for recognition and, 39–40; witnessing and, 16, 19–20
Mercy, A (Morrison), 72–80
metalepsis, 88–90, 103–6, 121, 126, 128–32; unhistoricism and, 88
Michaels, Walter Benn, 44–48, 150n67, 164n28. *See also* frame; Fried, Michael; literalism; *punctum*
mimesis, 125, 145n16; mimesis *onto* something (*sich anschmiegen ans Andere*), 23, 33, 143n73; Odysseus and, 143n73
Moi, Toril, 85–86
monarchy: cult of monarchy, 116–17; naïve monarchism/peasant monarchism, 114, 120–21. *See also* imperial sovereignty
Morrison, Toni, 22–23, 66, 83; *Beloved*, 68–70; *A Mercy*, 72–80
Moten, Fred, 123, 137n18, 160n54
mourning, 37, 68, 78, 103, 140n46, 158n18, 158n19
mutual acknowledgment, 40, 42–43

negative allegory, 16–17, 39
negative sociability, 10, 51, 64. *See also* antirelationality; antisocial thesis
negativity, 10, 25, 42, 78, 87, 94, 97
Nietzsche, Friedrich, 55, 95, 107, 163n8

nonsense, 123, 127; glossolalia as, 125–6; rumor as, 127–28
nonsovereignty, 40, 48, 59–60; recognition and, 39–42
Notes of a Native Son (Baldwin), 4–6

open secret, 120, 169n54, 170n55; of black sociality, 22, 132

Painter, Nell, 84
palimpsest, 53–54, 152n93
Palmié, Stephan, 14–15, 84, 124, 127, 170n65
paper, 22, 52–54, 153n94; newspaper, 108–9, 118–21. *See also* Bradford, Mark
Patterson, Orlando, 37–38, 67–68, 99–102, 164n23
Pietz, William, 142n69
punctum, 47, 150n79. See also *studium*

queer objects, 50; poetic "objects" as, 154n106
queer theory, 1–2; affect and, 18–20; antisocial thesis and, 10, 135n2, 136n12; queer exemption, 6; severance and, 7–8; unbelonging and, 64, 74; unhistoricism in, 10, 20, 88
queer unhistoricism, 10, 20, 88

Ralph, Michael, 21, 142n69
"ready-made," 144n8
recognition, 11, 23, 39–40, 57, 95, 115, 124, 142n69, 170n62
recovery imperative, 12, 65, 84–87, 124, 138n27, 168n32
relationality, 57; kinship and, 73
rhetoric, 8–9, 24; analepsis, 31; litotes, 8, 126; metalepsis, 88–90, 103–6, 121, 126, 128–32; paralepsis/occultatio, 69
Ricoeur, Paul, 86

Robinson, Cedric, 40, 148n48. *See also* black radical tradition
rumor, 107, 115, 123, 126–32; in Barbados, 108–10; in Demerara, 110–11; as glossolalia, 125–29; in *Incidents in the Life of a Slave Girl*, 118–22; in Jamaica, 111–13; as proto-politics, 113–14, 168n29

Schomburg, Arthur, 11
Scott, Darieck, 149n57
Scott, David, 65, 70, 77, 102, 136n5, 138n26, 148n47
Sedgwick, Eve Kosofsky, 6, 61–62
self-renunciation, 4–9, 23, 37; alienation as, 36–37; black radical tradition and, 41–42
severance, 6–8, 95, 98–99, 136n12; "Bohemian Rhapsody" (Queen), 137n16
Sexton, Jared, 137n18, 138n20
sich anschmiegen ans Andere, 23, 33, 143n73
Slauter, Eric, 68
slavery, 65–67, 83, 94, 99; afterlife of, 1–2, 13–17, 38–39, 63–64, 70–72; and the Black Atlantic, 16, 66–68, 157n10; and black culture, 11, 13, 22, 37, 87–88, 123, 132; "the legacy of slavery," 67–69, 78–80; "neoslavery," 156n1; and the slave trade, 24, 31, 50, 74, 107–9; and social death, 25, 73, 95–96, 99–101, 103–5
social death, 25, 73, 95–96, 99–101, 103–5; in Goffman, 149n54
Sokolsky, Anita, 40
Spivak, Gayatri, 122
Steedman, Carolyn, 87, 122
Stephens, James, 107
Stoler, Ann Laura, 171n75
studium, 48. See also *punctum*
subjectivity, 8; subjection and, 11
suicide, 24–25; social oblivion as, 103–6; subjective suicide (Povinelli), 7; suicide bombing, 92–94

surface reading, 47, 61–62, 95, 152n93, 155n108
surrealism, 42, 148n49

Tamarkin, Elisa, 67, 117
Taussig, Michael, 120, 145n16, 162n15, 169n54. *See also* mimesis
Terada, Rei, 43; looking away, 149n54, 151n83; phenomenophilia, 44
termite art, 49, 151n81
Tiffany, Daniel, 64, 151n83, 154n106. *See also* open secret
tort, 38–39; wrongful injury, 38–39; "wrongful life," 142n68
Traub, Valerie, 10, 88
trauma, 5–6, 15, 39, 67, 70, 77, 158n28
trompe l'oeil, 23, 47, 150n79; in El Anatsui, 44–45, 49–50; and *U.S.A.* (Haberle), 44
trompe l'oreille. *See* glossolalia

unbelonging, 10, 64. *See also* belonging
unhistoricism, 10, 20, 88. *See also* Traub, Valerie

vindicationism, 66, 138n26

Wagner, Bryan, 21, 115
Walcott, Derek, 50
Walker, David, 8–11, 20, 22, 132
"we," 1, 8–9, 11, 13, 19, 21–22, 132, 133
Weigman, Robyn, 10
Wilberforce, William, 107, 112
Williams, Bernard, 142n68
Williams, Dessima, 136n5
Wittgenstein, Ludwig, 85, 147n26
"wrongful life," 142n68. *See also* tort

Žižek, Slavoj, 102
Zong, 70